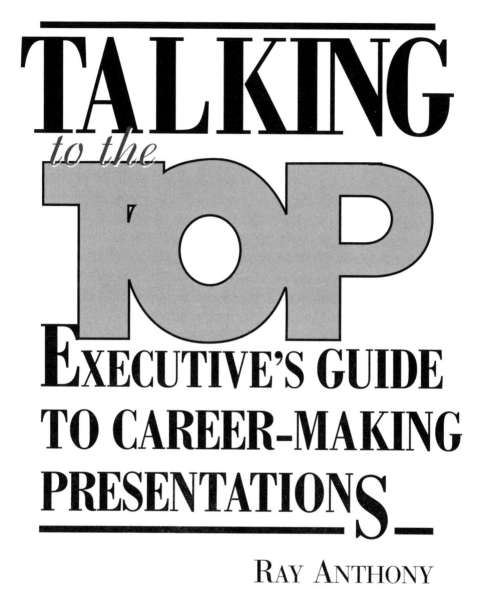

TALKING

to the

TOP

EXECUTIVE'S GUIDE TO CAREER-MAKING PRESENTATIONS

RAY ANTHONY

PRENTICE HALL
Englewood Cliffs, New Jersey 07632

Prentice-Hall International (UK) Limited, *London*
Prentice-Hall of Australia Pty. Limited, *Sydney*
Prentice-Hall Canada, Inc., *Toronto*
Prentice-Hall Hispanoamericana, S.A., *Mexico*
Prentice-Hall of India Private Limited, *New Delhi*
Prentice-Hall of Japan, Inc., *Tokyo*
Simon & Schuster Asia Pte. Ltd., *Singapore*
Editora Prentice-Hall do Brasil, Ltda., *Rio de Janeiro*

©1995 by
PRENTICE HALL, Inc.
Englewood Cliffs, NJ

10 9 8 7 6 5 4 3 2 1

Library of Congress Cataloging-in-Publication Data

Anthony, Ray E.
  Talking to the top:executive's guide to career–making
presentations/Ray Anthony
      p.   cm.
  Includes bibliographical references and index.
  ISBN 0-13-124470-1
  1. Business presentations. 2. Public speaking. I. Title.
HF5718.22A56   1995
658.4'52– –dc20

                                                    94–43440
                                                       CIP

ISBN 0-13-124470-1

PRENTICE HALL
Career and Personal Development
Englewood Cliffs, NJ 07632
Simon & Schuster, A Paramount Communications Company

Printed in the United States of America

DEDICATION

To my wonderful parents who have always encouraged and supported me to reach the top.

ABOUT THE AUTHOR

Ray Anthony is the author of many articles and several business books including *Power Presentations* (R&R Newkirk) and *Skyrocket Your Sales* (Pelican Publishing). He is a management consultant, keynote speaker, and workshop leader who designs and facilitates programs for major corporations and other organizations on sales, creativity, advanced presentation skills, and leadership and management topics. He has a B.S. and an M.A. degree in Economics (with expertise on national productivity increase) from the City University of New York. He was formerly a senior salesperson and senior sales trainer for Digital Equipment Corporation. He is president of Genesis Training Solutions located in The Woodlands, Texas. He can be reached at 23 Skyland Place, The Woodlands, Texas 77381. Phone (713) 364-7739.

FOREWORD

by Warren Bennis

Creative communication is at the heart of persuasion, and persuasion is the essence of effective leadership. Leaders who communicate their visions well will enliven their organizations and fill their supporters with passion.

History is filled with examples of persuasive talkers, both ethical and amoral, altruistic and political. Over time they have become either great leaders or great disappointments—some even became both at the same time, or have showed their true character by changing from one to the other.

The future will no doubt be filled with even more persuasive speakers, using advanced multimedia technology to convey their messages on many conscious and subconscious levels and in many different forums.

Ray Anthony leaves the ultimate use of the persuasive skills to us. He describes what the key skills are and we can creatively use the latest advances in communication to enhance our messages—adding flavor and variety to our presentations. He includes insights into how to polish our communication style and improve our presentations as we seek to achieve the results we desire.

According to Ray Anthony, true knowledge of the audience and its beliefs, attitudes, desires, and experiences, coupled with honesty and well-prepared, concise, and insightful messages will lead to successful executive presentations. Executives who offer their followers an important message and do so with an impressive style will emerge as effective leaders in the twenty-first century.

Leadership has become increasingly important as we continue to struggle with the potential applications of the vast technological breakthroughs and libraries of scientific research generated in this century. Insightful thinkers are not necessarily good communicators, and good communicators are not always persuasive speakers (in that they speak their mind so clearly that they offend). What's more, persuasive speakers do not always have an important message, or have the best interests of the audience at heart.

Those who sincerely care about their audiences will not be seduced by long, standing ovations. Nor will they pride themselves in short-term actions generated by their motivating speeches, or even in the implementation of their ideas that achieve impressive short-term productivity or financial results. Rather, they will authentically feel for their followers, leading them to believe in (and it is hoped to reach) the long-term benefits of what they endorse.

Polish alone is not enough. In our society's quest for the very best things, many of us are drawn in by good salespeople—those who somehow know us and their products or services so well that they seem to lead us as good friends toward "good deals." But whenever those "deals" fail to meet what we were led to expect, those same salespeople become in our minds the essence of fraud. We become more skeptical and cautious as we realize just how vulnerable we are in the face of sneaky "used-car salesmen."

Still, we are captivated by appearances and flattery. No doubt the greatest presenters the world has ever known currently have positions in show business, public relations, advertising, journalism, and politics. Their success comes from knowing how to establish just the right mix of creativity and familiarity, and adroitly applying the latest technology. Their impact is felt in the entertainment value of their work and seen in the amounts of money poured into the seemingly endless push for greater name recognition. But without any added value, the polish only seems to add to our growing disgust and distrust of experts in these fields.

Raw knowledge is not enough, either. Anyone who has sifted through a pile of raw data understands this well. Without some sense of meaning or direction, we can draw virtually nothing from the hours of research spent by knowledgeable gatherers.

Many have also noted what some savvy communicators call the Ph.D. syndrome: when talented but unpolished writers present their messages using deliberately clouded sentences, combined with heavy doses of undefined jargon. Many of these writers seem to want to convey the impression that they have somehow become omniscient. The legal profession pioneered this practice hundreds of years ago (apparently to create an intellectual barrier to enter the profession) and now has its own word for the technique: legalese.

A biblical writer of proverbs smartly described the best use of knowledge and style:

> *The tongue of the wise useth knowledge aright;*
> *But the mouth of fools poureth out foolishness*

— PROVERBS 15:2

Well-presented data, coupled with clear and polished language, will allow many more talented people in organizations to participate in important decision-making processes. Such efforts empower more individuals and creatively generate more appealing and diverse options. This is where authentic leadership steps in.

Authentic leaders do more. What is needed are leaders, rooted in strong ethical values, who harness the best of both kinds of talent, and who back up their words with real value. These leaders not only *have something meaningful to say and say it with impressive style, but we can believe their words because they will bind themselves by them*. Such leaders are not threatened by increased empowerment. Instead these leaders creatively assemble the knowledge and passionately articulate the visions that greatly inspire those around them, harnessing their talents—and leading them lovingly into the next century.

When we look at a piece of well-crafted woodwork, which has been carefully polished, we would likely comment, "what a beautiful piece of artwork," and we would probably not say, "the polish is beautiful on that piece of wood." So too with powerful leadership: Listeners, after trusting and following a leader for many years, should feel moved to say, "what beautiful things we have done," rather than "that leader communicates persuasively and dresses well."

In summary, Ray Anthony gives us tools that every true leader needs (remember, persuasion is the essence of leadership). But to be effective with these tools, as with any tools, artisans must first understand the medium. Wise artisans will rarely craft things that are useless, and wise leadership artisans know that:

- raw knowledge is useless unless it is patiently and carefully packaged to reach a wide audience,

- such packaging is also useless without a meaningful message (it will waste our time), and

- even with an important message and a persuasive style, long-term leadership is impossible without trust, generated by adding real value and honoring commitments.

What you do with the tools Ray Anthony offers will determine whether or not you have what it takes to be a true leader.

Warren Bennis is a professor and founding chairman of the Leadership Institute at USC and is the author of two recent books: *An Invented Life: Reflections on Leadership and Change,* and *Learning to Lead: A Workbook on Becoming a Leader* (Addison-Wesley, 1993 and '94, respectively).

WHAT THIS BOOK
CAN DO FOR YOU

This unique book will work wonders for you if you want to give an impressive presentation to executives or other important and influential audiences. It will help you achieve stunningly successful results whether you're proposing an innovative new project, pushing a visionary idea, selling a high-ticket product or service, highlighting your plan or strategy, or otherwise trying to convince decision makers to support (with unflinching commitment) a program or course of action you're advocating. "Talking to the Top," which is the phrase I use for executive-style speaking, gives you the ammunition to blast away their resistance, apathy, or doubt. It's more than getting them to agree with you or even motivating them. It's about getting them to enthusiastically follow you! And follow you they will if you apply the concepts, formulas, ideas, and techniques that pack this book. While Talking to the Top focuses on giving executive-style presentations to high-level groups such as executive committees, or boards of directors, the model, concepts, techniques, and tips included are superb for any presentation to any group.

I've titled my book, *Talking to the Top*, and use the term, "toptalk" because it's a special way of talking to high top-level people in any organization (hence the word "top"). Also, when I began writing the book, my goal was to describe ways to reach "peak" (or top) levels of communicating with any audience. My book will show you how to power-pack your messages in a tight, concise way, how to flavor your main points with powerful psychological ingredients, how to use creativity, passion, and new technology to give your presentation a unique professional flair that will skyrocket your credibility and professional image to new (top) heights. Talking to the Top is about getting to the top of your speaking abilities.

What really sets *Talking to the Top* apart from all other books about presentations is its treatment of the leadership factor in rousing audiences to action. As we approach the changing, turbulent, fiercely-competitive world of the twenty-first century, we'll need to do much more than simply inform, persuade, or even motivate audiences because of the uncertainty, rapid flux, and unpredictability of events that experts say will characterize the next millennium. Your leadership, powerfully showcased at the podium, will be needed to give your audience the confidence and drive to move forward with supporting your proposal. *Talking to the Top* shows you dynamic ways to elevate your status and image with them. Combined with the power of creativity (which is described in the book), your audience will see you as much more than a polished speaker or presenter. They'll view you as a strategist, problem solver, visionary, innovator, opportunity seeker, and person of action. If you follow the recommendations of *Talking to the Top*, they'll quickly see you as a strong, insightful leader and a twenty-first-century communicator! And that transformation will do wonders for achieving your objectives with that audience, not to mention your career.

GREAT IDEAS AND VISIONS REQUIRE A GREAT WAY TO COMMUNICATE THEM

Senior executives are pushing to continuously reinvent, reengineer, and self-renew their organizations in an effort to make their companies more productive, effective, efficient, quality-focused, and innovative. As a result, they hope to be more competitive, profitable, growth-oriented, flexible, and responsive in the lightning-quick, integrated world economy of the twenty-first century. Radically new breakthrough ideas from forward-thinking people can enable organizations to leapfrog their competitors in a quantum leap way. But the more creative, divergent, and unusual the idea is, the more people (including smart executives) will misunderstand it, doubt it, and even resist it.

Throughout my career with two major corporations and as a management consultant, I've seen potentially earth-shaking ideas mercilessly squashed or relegated to a corporate limbo because they were not properly presented to their audiences. What a waste! People with great ideas and visions all too often naively feel that others will automatically embrace their perceived strokes of brilliance with an open mind and eager heart. They're often shocked to discover otherwise. It's sad to say and hard to accept, but their downfall was usually an inadequate presentation, not an inadequate idea.

Great ideas require great ways to communicate them!

Ideas do not gain acceptance by themselves. The famous psychiatrist and psychologist Carl Jung said, "New ideas are not only the enemies of old ones; they also appear often in an extremely unacceptable form." That's why the manner, style, and image in which you communicate change is critical to the success of people's willingness to embrace it. *Talking to the Top* is an ideal communication vehicle to help bring about change because its techniques help to creatively "package" a bold and daring idea or plan in such a way that it comes across as sensible, appealing, realistic, and valuable to the audience.

WHY I WROTE *TALKING TO THE TOP*

I wrote *Talking to the Top* for two reasons. The first is that I've always been intrigued with giving important boardroom-type presentations. As a former computer salesperson, selling to senior executives in several major New York City banks, I've found that giving an executive-style presentation requires a much more sophisticated and disciplined set of skills than that associated with typical business presentation to peers, for example. Several years ago, I decided to study (via dozens of interviews and a comprehensive written survey that covered 25 detailed questions) what executives need, want, and like about presentations given to them. The written survey involved approximately 90 senior executives from seven companies such as a major computer company, an electronics leader, an insurance company, a chemical manufacturing firm, and several other smaller manufacturing and service firms. I wrote numerous magazine articles highlighting those research findings. The next natural step was a book that included those findings (included throughout the chapters of the book).

The other reason I wrote *Talking to the Top* is because I felt that other presentation books sorely neglected advanced presentation topics desperately needed in today's short-attention-span, "sound-bite" world to add dramatic punch to the spoken word. Creativity, leadership projection, computerized multimedia, and advanced strategizing are those topics that I believe make my book unique. While other books zero in on improving a speaker's verbal and nonverbal speaking techniques, *Talking to the Top* focuses on improving the substance and efficiency of the message and how to dramatically impact an audience with a sense of personal passion, conviction, and commitment— all characteristics executives have prioritized in importance.

TALKING TO THE TOP IS DESIGNED AND ORGANIZED TO COVER NEW, IMPORTANT, AND ADVANCED TOPICS

Talking to the Top has ten chapters solely devoted to making you a more polished, charismatic, and consummately effective communicator. And communication is more than speaking—it's getting through to your audience, connecting with them, and transmitting messages and feelings in an accurate, complete, and convincing way. In Chapter One, I describe the ten characteristics of an ideal toptalk that is rich in communication value. You learn exactly what it takes to give a superb performance that leads you straight to your intended objectives. A critical part of the communication process is learning how to customize your talk to the top to each audience. Chapter Two explains how to effectively analyze your audience and the situation that you're facing to enable you to precisely focus your talk to the top based around those two factors. In Chapter Three, you learn some very important and fascinating things about your primary top audience—executives or others in positions of eminent power. You'll discover who they are, what they do, what their priorities and concerns are, what their composite profiles look like. And you'll get to know the 14 traits that are common to successful decision makers. These valuable insights will enable you to best tailor and target your messages to these power brokers.

Executive presentations require meticulous planning. In Chapter Four, you'll find out how to carefully plot your Talking to the Top objectives and strategize on ways to reach them using a six-step planning process. There are also many examples of how to create an extraordinary executive summary that will set a great tone for the start of your presentation. High-level presentations are very stressful because of the important audience people are facing. Chapter Five discusses in detail some powerful and proven ways of beating the terror monster of stagefright that can counter all the preparation you've done and the confidence you've tried to build up.

In Chapter Six, I discuss how to create an overall winning image that gets your audience to like, respect, and trust you quickly. You learn about boosting your charisma and sharpening your stage presence. And you'll discover what executives describe as "deadly" actions, behaviors, and traits exhibited by presenters that will cause them to tune out immediately. Chapter Seven adds yet more rock-solid substance to your image by showing you how to project a leadership "command presence" at the podium. The audience will know that you're in charge, and this will inspire their confidence, loyalty, and trust.

Chapter Eight describes how to "strategically" use visual aids for maximum creative effect. I give you tips and techniques on how to design and use them to better help reach your Talking to the Top objectives, while avoiding pitfalls of visual aids. Computerized multimedia will be the hottest visual aid over the next ten years. It can add enormous punch to your ideas and proposal in a way that was never available before. In Chapter Nine, I cover this exciting new technology that can help you sell tough concepts, abstract ideas, and creative approaches like nothing else ever before. I cover how to begin using the awesome creative and persuasive power of it in a way that will appeal to both the right- and the left-brained members of your audience.

Creativity, which is covered in Chapter Ten, has been sorely neglected as a vital tasty ingredient in presentations, especially executive-level ones. In this chapter, I tell you how further to tap into the power of your imagination to develop a sparkling presentation that captures the interest and ignites the fervor of your audience. You'll receive dozens of creative ideas on how to make your toptalk stand out brilliantly from the crowd.

Whether you consider yourself an innovator, changemaster, or visionary out to capture the world with your imagination and plans, or simply someone looking to give the ultimate bottom-line briefing, I think you'll find *Talking to the Top* to be of great help in your quest to be a supreme communicator. I wish you the very best of success!

Ray Anthony
The Woodlands, Texas

CONTENTS

The Keys to a Successful Toptalk

When a thing is thoroughly well done it often has the air of being a miracle.

—ARNOLD BENNETT

AN EXECUTIVE PRESENTATION IS DIFFERENT

It's time to give that "big presentation." Maybe you're a manager who has been invited to the executive meeting room or boardroom for the first time to discuss your innovative program. Or perhaps you're a seasoned executive who has been honored with presenting your ideas to a respected association of the country's leading business people. It's a great opportunity for you to strut your stuff and impress them with your ideas and proposal. You want to succeed and you definitely don't want to blow the chance to advance your career, enhance your prestige, and make a *real* difference.

When you're given a unique golden opportunity to get in front of a powerful or influential group to propose change, you've got to seize that moment and rise to the occasion by giving a superb winning presentation, one that illuminates you with a brilliant shine and gets the audience to follow you. What does it take, though, to stand out—to make an indelible mark in a powerful and meaningful way? *It takes Toptalk!*

1

Giving an executive presentation is clearly different from other types of lower-level presentations. It's the "Big Kahuna," Major League, or "Bolshoi" (Russian word for grand) performance. It requires a different set of skills and mindset to win over senior decision makers. First of all, *higher stakes are involved.* Executive presentations involve discussions of projects, proposals, and ideas that are usually large in scope and can impact the long-term success of an organization. A lot can be riding on a new product or service or major research and development project that is being advocated. It's one thing to make a presentation that advocates a department-based project that involves 12 people and a budget of $37,000. It's another to give a boardroom presentation that affects the careers of hundreds, if not thousands of employees and involves funding in the tens to hundreds of millions of dollars or more.

Second, you only have a *limited time.* Giving an executive presentation is one of the most difficult presentations to design and deliver because of the limited time executives allow a presenter. You have to be able to deliver a complete and persuasive message in an extremely concise way. The acid test of a great talking to the top presentation is brevity . . . brevity . . . brevity. Executive presentations typically last only 15 to 30 minutes. Third, it can be *career lifting or diving.* Give a great presentation and you find yourself suddenly the fast-track runner in the marathon of competitors. Screw up and you're out of the race until you redeem yourself.

HOW YOUR TOPTALK WILL MAKE YOU SHINE

I've always been intrigued with high-level presentations of the boardroom and executive conference-room type. Maybe it's the atmosphere of power and deal making and the beckoning challenge of getting smart, influential people to back a new big-bucks project or smaller innovative venture I'm proposing. As a former senior salesperson selling computers to major banks in New York City, I've given my share of presentations to senior executives. Some were wildly successful and some were duds that never went off . . . or that fizzled out quickly.

I had one demanding account in the Wall Street area that was responsible for stock transaction processing for the New York City exchanges. Their executives were brilliant, but extremely temperamental and mercurial. It was an adventure . . . sometimes a rigorously capricious one to present one of my technically complex computer solutions to them. I used to call it having a "Close Encounter of the Third Kind" after the movie, starring Richard Dreyfuss, about alien contact with earthlings. Some of the questions, comments, and exchanges among the eccentric personalities in the group during my presentation were definitely out of this world! I've had some interesting experiences presenting to senior executives.

HOW TO MEET THE DEMANDS OF THE BOARDROOM

Presenting in the executive meeting room is much more than the art of making deep sounds from the chest sound like important messages from the brain. I've found that executive-style presentations are probably the most demanding types of presentations to give because they require a greater degree of communication excellence than all others. After all, you've typically got 30 minutes or less to sell them on an idea, concept, product, or venture. Creative communication leadership is definitely called for. Presenters often have to "measure seconds and make every word, gesture, and visual aid count" one CEO of a small Connecticut chemical company and member of several boards told me. And you're generally dealing with some very smart people who demand organized and precise information that gives solid answers and well-thought-out, on-the-mark solutions to issues they're facing.

Executive presentations are a critical rite of passage for those chugging upward on the rungs of the ladder of success. The brief time that we spend on our feet formally presenting our latest project or proposal to corporate chieftains is oftentimes one of the most important periods in our career. What a difference between nearly right and exactly right. So, it's got to be done *just* right!

Most people get anxious anticipating being ushered in and standing up before the organization's decision makers for their first "Big Presentation." They're eager to inform, impress, and please. Yet for all the preparation they go through to get it right, many presenters unfortunately still get it wrong.

A number of years ago, as my fascination began to rise with the topic, I decided to find out exactly what it took to give a great presentation to high-level decision makers in the corporate arena or other organizations. So I conducted the comprehensive research study (that was described in the Introduction) regarding what high-level managers liked, disliked, needed and wanted when it came to someone giving a presentation to them. One of my goals was to determine what the common denominators of success were and what primary factors created *consistent* communication excellence for a speaker. I wanted to form a *big picture* that identified these critical success factors that all but guaranteed top achievement during a high-level executive (or for that matter *any* type of) presentation.

This chapter covers the characteristics of a great executive-style presentation, gives the summary findings from my research survey to executives, and provides a model of toptalk success.

Give a Sincere and Natural Performance

The world recognizes nothing short of performance,
because performance is what it needs, and promises are
of no use to it.

—PHILIP G. HAMERTON

Worthwhile metaphors are great symbolic tools to quickly enable people to understand concepts in a crystal clear and memorable fashion. That's why I was looking for one for the topic of giving a great presentation. What could I use to galvanize my findings into a valid and simple model to help you, the reader, see how everything fits together in a way that would define a "winning" presentation—one that consistently produces exceptional results? I chose to compare a great toptalk to that of a *sincere and natural performance* as in some arts or entertainment event. While the concept of a speaker engaging in a performance is not new, the full value and true nature of it has not been explored and developed.

A *performance* typically invokes the image of an actor, singer, comedian, dancer, musician, poet, magician—someone who "performs" in front of an audience for the purpose of entertaining them and leaving them with some messages or newfound or reawakened opinions and feelings. However, "performing" implies a kind of *nom de guerre* of a transitory type of showmanship by a person who takes on a stage "persona." The performer is assuming a role outside of his or her normal character and personality; the performance is usually *an act* by one who assumes a different identity. In Chapter Five, Overcoming Boardroom Speaking Fear, we learn that when people envision their presentation as a life-or-death performance to be judged by "critics" (their executive audience), their anxiety level shoots up. So a contrived performance of golden-throated oratorical or theatrical techniques is definitely not what I'm suggesting.

Be Yourself and Be Your Best

A *sincere and natural performance* is, indeed, a different and more valid concept to look at ways of making a good impression. It means that a business presenter is *naturally* (using his or her real self) to communicate in an interesting, thought-provoking, attention-grabbing, entertaining, and emotionally exciting way. Being a sincere *performing artist* means that a toptalker is using every professional presentation technique and planning system to communicate in a way that *sharply impacts* people in a positive intellectual and emotionally stimulating fashion.

Here, a performance means that someone is having a *comfortable* and *natural conversation* (Those are the three key words!) with the audience in a way that creates and builds a positive impression of the speaker and develops rapport with the group. A sincere performance doesn't accelerate anxiety—it *reduces* it because the requirements for this type of peak performance means the presenter is well-prepared, organized, and optimistic and therefore is confident, relaxed, and ready to go.

Ask any executive, though, if he or she wants to "see a performance" or be "entertained" during a business presentation and you'll probably get a raised eyebrow or even a gruff response like, "Are you kidding? The boardroom is not a stage!" But, if one approaches the concept of performance and "infotainment" (giving important information in a entertaining way) from a different perspective, we could ask executives if they want: (1) information delivered in a poignantly interesting and thought-provoking way; (2) a speaker to be articulate, polished, and know her topic better than anyone else;

(3) the presenter to use a creative approach to help focus and settle the issues when the board seems to be lost or deadlocked; (4) the speaker to show enthusiasm, passion, and conviction while speaking and be well-prepared and organized.

If you put it in that fashion, my research tells me that executives would reply in this kind of way: "Sure I want to be stimulated, maybe even entertained by a good presentation performance . . . as long as it is interesting, but not frivolous, doesn't detract from the main points, but instead, helps to focus my attention, and, most important, assists me to make a decision about the proposal being spoken about. That's the type of performance I need and want!"

"Academy Award" for a Toptalk?

Imagine someone like actress Meryl Streep and General Electric's CEO, Jack Welch, tearing open and reading the contents of the envelope and announcing, "Academy Award for the best presentation performance in the executive meeting room goes to. . . ." Farfetched? Perhaps. But some of the greatest business coups and leaps-of-innovation projects of the century were the result of non-publicized but dramatic creative communication leadership in the boardroom. It was communication *artistry* at its finest, all because someone did something extraordinarily well involving every area of presentation planning, organization, and execution.

A great idea or plan deserves *to be communicated in a commensurably great way!*

To better understand and appreciate the metaphor of giving a sincere and natural performance, let's examine the similarities between a complex business presentation and some performance in the arts or entertainment field. Do you remember a special movie or a theater play that you've loved, one that's cemented in your mind and heart after all these years? Do you recall how you felt inside—that special "something" that touched you, impressed you, or perhaps amazed you about that performance? There were things about it that made you feel hopeful, happy, energized, strong, optimistic, giddy, or "alive all over." Maybe it was a motivational speech that left you feeling that you could conquer the world. A dramatic movie might have brought on surprise, fright, melancholy, sadness, or righteous anger. Your mood was transformed. You became part of the experience. It was an unforgettable event. While it might have been intellectually simulating, what stood out was the emotional impact. You were dramatically *moved* by it!

A *great* toptalk or public speech is like an entertainment performance designed to grab your mind while prying open the emotional floodgates in your heart. Let's explore the "secrets of success" shared by both entertainment events and peak toptalks. Take a great movie, for example, that garnered several Academy Awards. It had a top-notch script supported by great casting and outstanding acting performances. Add in breathtaking scenery, creative props, staging, and "awesome" special effects. Finish the recipe off with the ingredient of excellent cinematography and a stirring musical score, and, chances are, you've got a potential blockbuster in the making.

But suppose you have a great screenplay offset by mediocre acting. Or, imagine a movie with fine acting, a solid plot, but below par special effects. The same analogy applies to giving an executive presentation, motivational speech, or even a training workshop: you need a number of well-designed and smartly executed elements to make it a winner. It's getting all those key components *just right*. To make it a "piece of cake," you need a Performance P.I.E. to give Academy Award quality in a business presentation.

THREE CRITICAL STEPS TO TOPTALK SUCCESS

Famous stage actor Alfred Lunt advised thespian hopefuls, "Say the words so they can be heard and don't bump into the stage furniture." Many business presenters feel that 50 percent of success is what you deliver and 50 percent is *how* you deliver it. Sex researchers Masters and Johnson probably feel the same way, but it's a bit more inclusive than just that or the advice of Lunt. "The model of a winning toptalk has three important components to it that comprise what I call the Performance P.I.E., which consists of: (1) Preparation, (2) Impression, (3) Execution. As Illustration 1-1 shows, each of these consist of elements that form the common denominators of success and excellence. If any of them are omitted or performed in a haphazard way, your presentation will lose much of its impact. The more your Performance P.I.E. is mastered, the better your performance will be. *The following chapters in the book will describe in more detail each of the components that make up the Performance P.I.E.*

Illustration 1-1
P.I.E. Chart

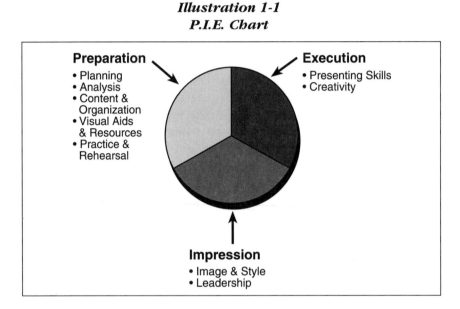

How Do You Know If Your Toptalk Has Been Successful?

Many presenters have varying concepts of what is successful when it comes to giving a presentation. Just *getting through it* without any major problems is for some an achievement. Others aim much higher. However, I believe there is only one real measure of "success" in giving a toptalk. I define it as:

> *Success is* ... setting challenging objectives that you intend to reach as a result of your presentation, and then by using the elements of P.I.E., you reach ALL your objectives as quickly and easily as planned.

When a person focuses on developing Performance P.I.E., he or she becomes a Creative Communications Leader. As a result, what the presenter ultimately communicates to the audience are these following important overall impressions shown in the following illustration:

Illustration 1-2
A Presenter Using the Elements of P.I.E. Communicates Much More than Words . . .

- I'm a trustworthy professional in every respect.
- My ideas are valuable and they can help you.
- I'm very knowledgeable about my topic and have good expertise in my area.
- I'm a strong leader who can take charge of the project I'm proposing and bring it to a successful completion.
- I'm an excellent communicator who can deal with myriad people-related situations.
- I can handle any challenges that come up with my proposed project.
- I'm an effective problem solver and I'm a forward-thinking innovator.

Will your audience crackle with eager anticipation or wrench with dread at the mention of your upcoming presentation? Will your executive-style presentations have the impact of an electrifying experience or that of a burned-out short circuit? Will you reach all your objectives or just some (or none) of them? Afterwards, will you get rousing approval from your audience or veiled apathy? It depends upon your mastering each of the components of the Performance P.I.E. If you work at it, you'll be elevated from a "presenter" into an influential *toptalker* who commands respect from even the most demanding decision makers. Following is an overview of individual P.I.E. components:

Preparation: Planning

A good plan is a great roadmap to success.

A toptalker knows that success is all but guaranteed if he or she carefully plans *every part* of his or her presentation down to the smallest detail. After all, how can an executive audience expect a person to be in charge of a significant new project, for example, if he or she can't plan, organize, and deliver a "simple" presentation? Time and time again, I have sat through boardroom presentations and have been amazed at how often the speaker was not as prepared as he or she should have been, especially when it came to answering "tough" questions. The result was often a delay or a refusal to get the audience's approval of the project or plan.

Planning includes determining what your specific toptalk objectives are, how you intend to reach them (your strategy), what resources you'll need, and how to handle any (people, equipment, logistics, etc.) problems that might crop up. While it was being shot, I was invited by the executive producer to sit in on the set to watch the filming of actor/martial artist Chuck Norris' film *Sidekicks* for a particular restaurant scene. I couldn't believe the incredible amount of prefilming work that preceded the very short segment shown in the movie: the precise positioning of all the numerous lights, seemingly endless measuring of camera distances and angle determination, prop setup, sound adjustments, and numerous actors, rehearsals. The same applies to a great toptalk: A lot of careful planning and preparation beforehand will make it look easy.

Preparation: Analysis

A great performer knows what his audience needs and expects.

A great plan for anything begins with "intelligence gathering" and effective analysis of all the data received. Great toptalkers are like investigative reporters and good trial lawyers. They have a story to tell and a "case to win," and they do their homework beforehand in a *very* thorough, *very* accurate way. I've had lawyers tell me that a case is almost always won *outside* the courtroom (prior to the trial) by meticulous investigation and superb preparation. If that's done, their trial *performance* in the courtroom will go smoothly and predictably and will often appear "brilliant."

Our research found that a major predictor of communication success in the boardroom was directly correlated with the quantity and quality of the often tedious work of analysis of the audience and their organization beforehand. Everything starts with gathering information and analyzing what you've found and then precisely focusing the right information on your audience. You need to find out what the audience already knows about your presentation topic, what their needs and desires are, and what their priorities, attitudes, and motivations are as it relates to your proposal points. Doing your analysis helps to create rapport and credibility with your group and enables you to better persuade them with a focused strategy.

When presenting to executives in an organization you're not familiar with, you also need to find out more about its short- and long-term goals, strategic thrusts, priority problems facing it, and its mission and vision of the future. You also need to about how the organization's *culture*—how it operates and what its values, principles, and beliefs are.

Preparation: Content and Organization

A great "script" should accompany a great performer.

After determining what an audience needs and wants to know, the toptalker selects just the right types of information (content) and organizes it in such a fashion as to enable the presentation to hit the mark perfectly. The boardroom performer tightly focuses on only several major points that comprise the essence of his proposal or idea. He makes use of only those critical facts, statistics, examples, or illustrations that are necessary to support those main points.

You'll find consummate communicators being very selective about their presentation content by asking themselves questions such as, "What must I say to convince the audience to go along with me?" and "What information is critical to reaching my presentation objectives?" As such, he always concentrates sharply on only those most relevant audience points, leaving no doubt in the audience's mind what his solution, idea, or proposal is all about. The audience *never* has to ask or wonder, "What's the point?" The most successful toptalkers also have "information in reserve" to use in greater detail if anticipated questions or resistance comes up. As part of superb organization, the performing boardroom artist always begins with a strong impacting introduction to grab audience interest and ends on a high note with a brief (but again powerful) conclusion.

Preparation: Visual Aids and Resources

Performers use lots of resources such as staging, lighting, props, sound, and special effects.

Like other performers, toptalkers use resources too. Selection and use of presentation materials such as visual aids, handouts, props, models, office supplies, equipment to demonstrate, lighting, and other meeting aids/equipment are instrumental in meeting the presenter's objectives. Well-designed visual aids and attractive handouts that supplement the content will give added "punch" to a presentation. Our survey results conclusively prove that executives not only expect visual aids to be used, but they definitely feel that they greatly contribute to a more effective presentation to them.

The successful presenter always strives to create a conducive environment for audience concentration and participation. An effective meeting room (with properly arranged seating configuration to stimulate discussion and facilitate viewing of the projection screen), and a well-controlled environment (with good lighting, temperature, ventilation) will provide for overall audience comfort and convenience to enable them to better focus on the speaker. A toptalker may also use "people resources" such as co-presenters, or he may make use of subject matter experts or technical advisors (e.g., audio-visual specialists) to assist in the planning and delivery of the presentation. The right resources can make a big difference.

Preparation: Practice and Rehearsal

Movie actors will sacrifice money and time to do regional theater to stretch and polish their acting skills to a fine luster. Presenters who aspire to excellence will also work at improving their overall public speaking skills by using every opportunity to participate as a speaker, presenter, event emcee, or any other speaking role in front of a group. Some people join organizations such as Toastmasters International[1] or National Speakers Association[2] to learn from others and to have a forum where they can safely try out their techniques or new topics on a regular basis in front of a supportive audience that makes recommendations for improvement.

Linnet Deily, chairman of First Interstate Bank of Texas, N.A., oversees a $5.3 billion institution. She told me, "Experience in doing presentations will make you better. Before I became chairman, I did a fair amount of public speaking. But in my role now, I'm called upon to do a lot more speaking to internal and external groups. I'd have to say that I'm infinitely more comfortable and better at it today than I was four or five years ago because I just do it a lot."[3]

Rehearsal is different from the practice of general speaking skills. It means working toward making that *new* presentation material come across smooth and polished. Performers rehearse *new* acts numerous times until they become instinctively ingrained in them. And speakers need to do the same before each new important presentation. It means going over the material in a dry-run fashion several times with at least one time being done preferably in front of an audience of peers or subject matter experts who can critique speaking abilities and content. By rehearsing, a presenter can know the content so well that, instead of being nervous with the material, he can devote all his energy and concentration to delivering it in a natural, more relaxed and dynamic fashion. Both practicing and rehearsing are needed for toptalk excellence.

Execution: Presenting Skills

A performer will use his or her voice and body for effect.

One thing becomes evident if you've had the opportunity to listen to a highly skilled toptalker—you can listen to him or her for hours. He or she uses formal speech techniques adapted to business presentations in a supremely competent way. That person is a "robber" of sorts, just like other performers such as actors or singers. They'll steal your mind and heart and total attention without your ever realizing it. They do it with their finely honed and powerful verbal and nonverbal (body-language) speaking skills. These presentation skills enable a speaker to inform, fascinate, charm, amuse, motivate, beguile, inspire, cajole, and stir the audience to immediate action. You won't find people fidgeting, yawning, daydreaming, or clock-watching with these speakers of dynamism and finesse. An effective toptalker adds layers of excitement to any topic he or she delivers to the audience with this kind of "special delivery."

Great presenters are easy and enjoyable to listen to. They pull out all stops to deliver information in an interesting, caring, sincere and electrifying way. The human voice is an incredibly powerful, yet delicate instrument. It is much more flexible and adaptable than any musical instrument available. Presenters who vary their voice volume, pitch, tone, and rate will add rich variety to their style. They use pauses for impact. They vocally highlight and emphasize key points and use their voice variation to "force" the audience to listen to them. They are masters of body language, using eye contact, gestures, facial expressions, posture, and body movement that enables them to "personally engage" each member of the audience. And they use their body language to support their spoken words. Developing your verbal and nonverbal speaking skills will give you more charisma and presence.

Execution: Creativity

Creative performances brilliantly shine.

Creativity can add a rich dimension to any toptalk and help a presenter to better sell ideas, concepts, products, services, or other proposals to groups that might be resistant or apathetic. A creatively persuasive approach can ignite the fires in the minds and hearts of your audience. Unfortunately, too few people use their imagination to create memorable messages that stir people up, visual aids that slam points home, and handouts that beg to be read. Those who add innovation to their presentation will skyrocket the quality and impact of their briefing to a much higher plateau of audience interest and acceptance. Creativity has always been a staple of the finest movies, plays, and music videos, and it is a requisite of great toptalk performances as well.

Consummate toptalkers use relevant props, cartoons, clever visual aids, fascinating stories, colorful language, and they organize the presentation in such imaginative ways that their ideas stand out in a blazingly attractive light beckoning the audience nearer and nearer to them. Creative ideas and approaches combined with exciting technology such as computerized multimedia (covered in Chapter 9) are needed today to help speed decisions on projects and critical issues facing an organization's leaders. Oftentimes, a presenter can use creativity in the form of powerful metaphors, for example, to give a unique perspective on a proposal. And by using a dramatically novel approach, the toptalker can shift the perspective to get the audience to view and feel an idea or concept in a totally different way. Communication "artists" use creativity in their presentations for magical effect.

Impression: Image and Style

*Projecting charisma, presence, and professionalism
assures winning.*

Do you know how you come across to a new audience? Did you ever study a videotape of yourself giving a presentation and wonder what overall first (and continuing) impression you made? Did you ever have the nerve to ask a colleague or friend to list the pros and cons of your personal and professional image? It might prove extremely enlightening and beneficial to find out the exact impression you make. Chances are you're probably doing a lot better than you expected, but you might also be surprised at some perceptions people have formed about you that you need to correct.

Everything you say and do and the manner in which you do them and the way you're groomed and dressed can make a world of difference to your executive audience as to whether they accept your proposal or pass on it. Superb toptalkers always aim to put their best foot forward. They know that "who you are speaks as loudly as what you say." Presenters must sell themselves by establishing commanding credibility with the audience of higher-ups before they can sell their ideas, proposals, or projects. Just like skilled entertainers, consummate presenters use their personality, appearance, and "performance skills" to create a favorable image of themselves before their group. Projecting even one negative trait (e.g., opinionated, awkward, defensive, rigid, self-serving, or crude) will hurt rapport and credibility with the audience and endanger the hoped-for outcome of the presentation. Great performers project a polished and profession overall image.

Impression: Leadership

O the orator's joys!

*To inflate the chest, to roll the thunder of the voice out
from the ribs and throat,*

To make the people rage, weep, hate, desire with yourself,

To lead America—to quell America with a great tongue.

—WALT WHITMAN

Executives have stressed to me that if a person is to be successful in convincing a high-level audience to approve a big-ticket project or a new strategic plan he or she is advocating, that person must show solid leadership and moral character in front of that group. Presenters need to learn ways to strengthen and polish their platform "leadership persona" by showing conviction, dynamics, charisma, confidence, passion, and vision. As a solid performer, a toptalker must give the audience a rock-solid sense of impressive *command* of himself or herself, the topic, and the audience and situation.

The real task of a leader is to communicate a great sense of excitement and importance about a project or proposal to the audience. A leader paints a vivid positive *vision* of what is to come as a result of it. In many respects a leader communicates dreams and hopes and desires, and he or she reaches deep into the depths of people's hearts, minds, and souls to touch them in ways that inspire and motivate them to march steadfastly on the path the leader advocates. In word and deed—directly or indirectly—with bombastic power or with a quiet reverence and self-assuredness, you'll see a toptalker with leadership qualities broadcast to the audience, "I know the way . . . Follow me now!" And they will. Shakespeare said, "Action is eloquence," and a toptalker comes across as a decisive person of action. Leadership is the essence of performance.

TEN CHARACTERISTICS OF THE "IDEAL" TOPTALK

In my personal interviews with senior decision makers, I asked them two questions: (1) "How would you describe the characteristics of the ideal executive presentation? and (2) Could you describe for me the most impressive and memorable presentation you've attended?" When I carefully analyzed the answers and pieced them together, I found the ideal presentation included the following ten characteristics:

1. Concise and to the Point
2. Simple and Clear
3. Interesting
4. Relevant
5. Friendly and Relaxed
6. Interactive
7. Effective and Efficient
8. Strategically Focused
9. Persuasive
10. Motivating, Energizing, Entertaining

1. Concise and to the Point. This was a point executives stressed and repeated over and over to me to pass along as strong advice to presenters: BE BRIEF! Busy executives cannot afford to waste time. One senior vice president of a major West Coast bank related to me that he got sick and tired of lengthy harangues from windbag presenters and told one manager, "Thank you for that comprehensive little talk. In one presentation, you went from trespassing on our time to encroaching on eternity."

Executives don't want a lot of detail about your proposal; they don't want to hear the whole history of a problem; they don't need the speaker to demonstrate his or her entire mastery of the topic at hand. Just give them the highlights, the major points, the "bottom line" of your oral proposal. The key thing to remember is to give the executives a "detailed summary," rather than a lot of detail with a summary. They want a *strategic* overview of your topic with all the critical success factors. They want to hear the big picture first. "Get to the point *quickly*" were the oft repeated pleas, demands, and requests they made. Walter Elisha, CEO of Spring Industries and Harvard Business School classmate of IBM's new CEO, Louis Gerstner, Jr., said this about him, "All of us predicted Lou would be among the most successful. When he spoke in the classroom, it was with a minimum number of words, but maximum insight."[4] David Miller, a World War Two U.S. Navy pilot got right to the sharp point on February 26, 1942, with his radio message: "Sighted sub. Sank same."

Executives don't want the speaker wasting precious time "bouncing" around or embellishing the topic with nonessential chatter. A vice-president of sales for a West Coast software company told me, "A good presenter is like an accomplished archer—he smoothly, quickly, and accurately shoots his arrow directly to the bullseye with little strained effort and motion."

Seymour Cray, acknowledged maverick computer genius who

founded the company and supercomputers (he is the father of supercomputers) bearing his name, was legendary for his disdain of bureaucratic communication and epitomized brevity, sometimes to the annoyance of his bosses or board of directors. As a brilliant young engineer at Control Data Corp., he was asked to produce a lengthy document detailing his five-year and one-year development plans. Choosing to spend his time on doing, rather than on talking, he fired back two sentences: "Five year goal: Build the biggest computer in the world. One year goal: Achieve one fifth of the above." He was certainly different from Texas state senator, Mike McKool (known as "Little Hercules"), who spoke for 42 hours and 33 minutes practically nonstop on June 26-28, 1972, in a filibuster for inclusion of $17 million for mental health services. Experts on anatomy tell us that the jaw muscle can work the longest of all the body's muscles without getting tired.

Some Thoughts on Brevity . . .

Be sincere; be brief; be seated.

> —Franklin D. Roosevelt's advice to son James on speechmaking

In all men of real intelligence we find the tendency to express themselves briefly, to say speedily what is to be said.

> —George C. Lichtenberg

Always be shorter than anyone dared to hope.

> —Lord Reading

Let thy speech be short, comprehending much in few words.

> —Ecclesiastes

He can compress the most words into the smallest idea of any man I ever met.

> —Lincoln regarding an opponent

It is nothing short of genius that one uses one word when twenty will say the same thing.

> —David Grayson

The secret of being a bore is to tell everything.

—Voltaire

Here comes the orator with his flood of words and his drop of reason.

—Benjamin Franklin

No sinner is ever saved after the first twenty minutes of a sermon.

—Mark Twain

Part of being a *prodigy behind the podium* is letting the words of George Bernard Shaw sink in, "Whatever reputation I have is due to the fact that I never open my mouth unless I have something to say."

2. Simple, Clear, and Organized. Simply put, executives are paid to think, make decisions, and then act upon them. Their responsibilities for overall planning, creating organization-wide strategies, solving complex problems, deciding the outcome of critical issues, and identifying and weighing major opportunities means that executives have to make *lots* of decisions every day. Some are routine and easy; some are complex and difficult. And some profound decisions will affect the future direction and health of the corporation.

Executives want presenters to make their points with *extreme clarity, simplicity,* and *organization* to help them make responsive and "correct" decisions about the proposed ideas or plans being presented. Instead, I've discovered that many presenters make the deadly mistake of providing too much data or covering too many topics during an executive presentation, either in an attempt to impress them with their preparation or command of the subject or because they don't want to leave anything out, lest the audience, in the opinion of the presenter, not get the full panorama of the proposal.

They think executives are passive collection boxes where every fact is as salient as any other. Executives are quick studies, but they're drowning in data pollution from all sides and they are highly impressed by speakers who can take a weighty, complex topic and weave it into one of *elegant simplicity.* Great toptalkers organize their presentations in a way that swiftly and effortlessly moves their points directly, clearly, and logically to their final destination—the inevitable and undeniable conclusion. Former President Ronald Reagan's presentation advisers (or "handlers" as they're called) gave him this advice to make sure his messages got through to the public: "Keep it simple and repeat it over and over and over." When General Motor's new CEO, John F. Smith, Jr., had an unprecedented meeting with several hundred United Auto Workers union leaders, they emerged singing his praises, "He didn't use $600 words and he was frank."

Some thoughts on Clarity and Simplicity . . .

Eloquence is vehement simplicity

—RICHARD CECIL

Seeing then that we have such great hope, we use great plainness of speech.

—CORINTHIANS 3:12

Eloquence is the power to translate a truth into language perfectly intelligible to the person to whom you speak.

—RALPH WALDO EMERSON

It's critical to recognize that we're in the midst of an information explosion and it's creating anxiety for executives and others. According to Richard Saul Wurman, author of *Information Anxiety*, more facts were discovered in the past 30 years than in the entire previous 5,000. For example, Americans are writing close to 60,000 books a year. We publish over 9,500 periodicals, with about 800 new magazines being launched every year. Approximately 40,000 scientific journals are published each year. There are over 3,000 computer public databases available.[5]

Lots of loose data called "stray factoids" can make life miserable for executives who have to expend large amounts of energy piecing together the puzzle in order to make a decision. Consummate toptalkers can endear themselves to their important audience by assembling the needed and timely data into clear, neat, highly understandable modules of *useful information*—knowledge—to make them quick, easy, and simple for the executives to digest and act upon. Back in 1597 Francis Bacon observed that "knowledge is power." A supremely organized presenter will shift the power of knowledge over to the audience to facilitate their decision making.

The winning toptalker, then, is a great "translator, simplifier, and organizer" who distills reams of data into the pure essence of the salient points he or she is making in such a highly organized fashion that it leads to an undeniable conclusion—that it's obvious to the executive group what the decision should be. Albert Einstein believed that "everything should be made as simple as possible, but not simpler." If information is power, then the sharp ability to effectively communicate the *right information* can make YOU very powerful!

Finally, executives have also told me that the best presenters they have seen and heard brilliantly use metaphors, parables, examples, comparisons, and analogies to take abstract, intangible, or conceptual topics and provide a solid reality—tangible and concrete understanding to complex issues or ideas. Executives give *much more weight* to examples presented concretely than to assemblages of facts abstractly pitched.

3. Interesting. Executives sit through a lot of meetings and committees. It's been estimated that they generally spend anywhere from 50-70 percent of their time in some type of meeting. In our survey, we found out that almost 20 percent of executives sit through 11-15 formal group presentations per month, while 33 percent sit through 6-10 per month and 13 percent sit through 16 or more formal presentations. Many of these are typically all-day affairs with several presentations given. They hear speaker after speaker drone on. It can get quite tiring and boring. Some find it excruciating to concentrate in the afternoon after lunch listening to a monotone speaker. Several executives have admitted to me that they've even semi-dozed off with their eyes open. English journalist and critic Gilbert Chesterton has noted that, "a yawn is a silent shout"—most often a shout for relief from a presenter's mediocre and boring presentation. An engineering vice-president from a London firm told me of his colleague, "There never is a dull moment when you're listening to Clive's presentation . . . . It lasts the whole time he's up there!"

I have repeatedly had executives and lower level managers tell me how much they have appreciated speakers who add some appropriate zest and spice to their presentation (after all, communication should be hellfire and sparks as well as sweetness and light). Enthusiasm, speeding up the pace of the presentation, adding humor that makes a point, getting the audience involved more, using colorful language, themes, making use of eye-opening examples, vivid illustrations, comparisons, quotations, anecdotes, and great visual aids were just some suggestions to take a freeze-dried topic and prepare it into a savory meal.

Executives expect an effective speaker to get their attention *right away* and *keep it.* One engineering executive from an Alabama aerospace firm jokingly told me of a conference where at the end of a particularly boring slide presentation (with the room fully darkened), the speaker ended with what sounded like mild applause. He was surprised at this response until he realized it was several people slapping themselves in the face to wake up! Keep it interesting—no one likes to preside as Chairman of the Bored.

4. Relevant. It's frustrating to listen to a topic that has nothing to do with your area of responsibility or interests. Executives want speakers to make their presentation meaningful to and purposeful for them; it should be appropriate to their specific needs and wants and timely in terms of focusing on their priorities and problems. Information, examples, illustrations, and language should be tailored just for that group. In selling, it's long been preached to salespeople to "sell benefits, not features," and that advice is applicable to senior- level groups. Audience members are *always* wondering, "What's in it for me—what will I get out of this presentation? How will I benefit?" While it may be difficult to try to satisfy everyone in the group, the toptalker needs to try to satisfy some area of need for each of the executives hearing his or her talk.

5. Friendly and Relaxed. When a presenter is nervous, hyper, or otherwise acts hurried, worried, defensive, or pompous, it quickly rubs off on the audience; it puts them ill at ease—on edge. And, if there's one thing executives don't need more of it's stress. Besides, if they're uncomfortable with the presenter in any way it takes their concentration away from the information that is being doled out. Any presenter who can deliver a briefing in a relaxed, natural, friendly, and cordial fashion will be appreciated and respected by the executive audience.

The best toptalkers create a conducive environment for safe, open communication among the group. Executives are very impressed by a poised and calm presenter who can take a challenging or even a volatile situation within the group or between the group and speaker and resolve it in a tranquil, diplomatic, and an oh-so-effective way. Some have that subtle art of quickly defusing negative group dynamics in order to help build beneficial consensus and teamwork among the individuals. Executives generally agree with the English writer William McFee, who said, "The world belongs to the enthusiast who keeps cool."

Executives like to feel that the speaker is developing solid rapport with them. Smiling, lack of nervous mannerisms, good listening skills, soliciting feedback, and the sterling ability not to take oneself too seriously are all things that make executives feel comfortable about a speaker. In our study, we were curious as to what "style" of speaking was preferred by executives. Do they want ballet or flashdance? Is hardball or softball their preferred game? Are granite-tongued conservatives or evangelistic motivators desired? We asked them to choose among four choices that describe speaking style. A large majority (76 percent) agreed with the statement, "I enjoy listening to speakers who are organized, but nevertheless informal, relaxed, and conversational in their presentation delivery."

Conservative, formal speakers belong in the British Parliament. Motivational speakers—who bounce off the walls—belong at sales conventions, not in the boardroom. But speakers who are inspirational in less excitable and obvious ways are valued, as one anonymous executive in our survey nicely summed it up: "Sincere, low-key enthusiasm and a soft-sell approach always works."

And there are those presenters who make the mistake of talking fast in a veiled effort to get through lots of their content within the short period of time allotted to them. It can be done. Fran Capo from New York (where else, of course!) made the *Guinness Book of World Records* by talking at 585 words per minute (the range for most of us is 115-140 words per minute). That's almost 10 words per second and even faster than the 450 words per minute that John Moschitta, Jr. (another New Yorker) used to buzz through as he blitzed his way to fame on those amusing Federal Express commercials several years ago. Fast talking can make any audience uncomfortable and on edge. Don't be tempted to speed things up to a feverish pitch to get through all your details. Good selection of *relevant priority* information and effective organization of your presentation is the answer to time management, not being a motor mouth at full throttle.

6. Interactive. An effective toptalk is one who provides sufficient interaction between audience members and between the group and speaker. In order for them to reach consensus and a decision regarding a project being proposed, for example, the audience usually must discuss the various aspects of it. Executives laud the observation of nineteenth-century English statesman Thomas Babington Macaulay, "Men are never so likely to settle a question rightly as when they discuss it freely."

That means that a presentation should definitely not be a *monologue*, but a free-flowing *dialogue* between speaker and group. As such, a 30-minute presentation does not mean 30 minutes of nonstop talking. A presenter needs to build in flexible time for questions, and comments and must be fully prepared to deal with possible points of resistance, confusion, or indifference that will prevent the speaker from reaching his or her objectives. At times, a presenter will need to shift roles from being a "speaker" to that of being a "facilitator" who asks questions, elicits feedback, and gains group consensus. This means dynamically restructuring his or her presentation on the spot as a result of audience discussion needs. One chief financial officer from an Atlanta bank pointed out, "Because of limited time in front of executives, some speakers become very selfish about using every minute of *their* time to sell *their* proposal to us. If a speaker doesn't allocate adequate time and display a sincere positive attitude toward full discussion of his points for *our* sake, I'm hesitant to back it."

Executives repeatedly stressed to me that being an *effective listener* was rated as a critical trait for a presenter to have. That means being receptive, open-minded, and empathic to all forms of feedback including constructive criticism. It takes someone with a healthy ego to deal with resistance, but the leaders I interviewed told me how much they respected someone who could positively take criticism or other feedback and turn it to their advantage.

7. Effective and Efficient. Well-known management guru and author Peter Drucker consistently told managers to focus on the importance of doing the "right things"—performing those priority activities that best impacted an organization. That's being *effective.* Now when someone does "things right" (e.g., uses resources in an optimum way, getting the most for ones money), that's being *efficient.* The analogy I use is that the horsepower of a car's engine is effectiveness and gasoline mileage you get is efficiency. The goal in giving a great toptalk is to be able to be *both* effective *and* efficient. One New York City advertising executive who described himself to me as a *laconic personified,* related that "the best presentation is one that says all that *should* be, but not all that *could* be."

Effectiveness means covering the relevant critical points of a proposal and providing just the right supporting information to enable the audience members to make a good decision about the proposal or plan. Effectiveness means that presenters have a strategy and solid topic content with a high probability of reaching their objectives. That is, they do all the right things to dramatically boost their chances for meeting his toptalk objectives.

Efficiency means that presenters are extremely good at time management and design their presentations to reach their objectives with as little wasted energy and words as possible—moving the audience to consensus as quickly and easily as possible. Efficiency means having a lot of "lean muscle" in the information content and very little "fat." Everything is laid out logically and organized in such a fashion that the points flow smoothly and directly to an obvious conclusion. No time is wasted. *Efficiency, then, is the concept of communicating a lot in as little time and with as few words as possible.*

Efficiency is the ultimate acid test of a presenter because it requires that a person be able to be both concise and sufficiently thorough at the same time, which is a very challenging balance to accomplish. The right words organized in a very precise and logical way (forming complete and clear messages), use of appropriate body gestures and tone of voice (that broadcast meanings), and technologically advanced audiovisuals, such as multimedia (explained in a later chapter) can significantly raise the efficiency quotient of your presentation.

8. "Bottom Line" Strategically Focused. Toptalkers who concentrate on the critical issues and major success factors of their proposal will have the undivided attention of their audience. Consummate high-level communicators are persons who can transmit their messages like a laser beam—an intense concentrated, narrow beam of high-energy coherent light that focuses all its power on a small area (as opposed to a diffused spotlight)—that brilliantly illuminates for the audience the key decision points to focus on.

A strategic focus means that a presenter concentrates not on the details of the proposal (the "tactical points"), but on the projected overall positive outcomes, intended results, and anticipated impact on the organization—the "bottom line" financial and operational results to be gotten from the proposal. Executives want to understand how plans, projects, and new ventures, for example, will directly tie in to their company's mission, priority problems, objectives, and strategic opportunity plans. The benefits of the proposal being discussed need to be clearly connected to what the organization is focusing on in the short and long term. In addition, the presenter often needs to show how the project leads toward fulfillment of the organization's vision. A presenter needs to get to the "bottom line" in a direct and quick fashion.

9. Persuasive. Almost all toptalks contain elements of persuasion. Few presentations are just sterile, dry "data dumps." We're usually trying to get our audience to like (or dislike) something, to move toward (or away from) a goal or plan of action, to get approval or funding from them, or perhaps to set the stage by getting them to think about the value of what we are talking about before we go to the next step of a more specific proposal. Executives certainly don't come out and say, "Please be persuasive during your presentation. I'm a little soft in the head and I need a good jump start in thinking!" But they appreciate a form of well-prepared and well-executed persuasion that appeals to both their sense of intuition and logic and to their deep-seated family of values, beliefs, principles, and overall mind-sets about business and life.

To some executives, the concept of a speaker "being persuasive" might still impart to them a lingering taste of psychological manipulation, coercion, the "hard sell," blindly opinionated position, or a self-serving form of behavior. After all, who wants to be persuaded or sold something? Yet, executives want an effective communicator to do his homework and give accurate, "untainted" data and crisp facts presented in a highly logical, organized, and believable fashion. Executives want a presenter to highlight all sides of the story or options to consider, to show personal conviction and commitment (to their idea), and to give *compelling, convincing* reasons to support his or her points. While doing all this, at the same time, the toptalker needs to show respect for their judgment and ability to make an informed decision. This translates into professional *ethical* persuasion. High-level decision makers have consistently told me that they prefer a subtle type of sophisticated, low-key persuasion compared to that which is blatant or otherwise heavy-handed.

10. Motivating, Energizing, and Entertaining. When an executive presentation has a positive, forward-looking, "CAN DO!" aura surrounding it, the group is more inclined to link together to support the toptalker's goals. In these difficult and challenging times when corporations are going through wrenching changes such as major reorganizations and downsizing, when urgency is the order of the day, when competition is fierce, and when innovative projects have to be sold to decision makers bent on maintaining an entrenched status quo, the toptalker needs to infuse a level of passion into the briefing to inspire the group forward. Executives see a spirited and energetic toptalk as a desirable thing. Motivating an audience to act upon your proposed plans or ideas is needed beyond presenting persuasive information. It means showing personal conviction and a sense of dynamic energy.

Finally, great presentations are entertaining, even in the boardroom. Who says that business can't be fun? Who says appropriate (tasteful, relevant) humor, amusing anecdotes, or creativity in communicating a point should not fit within the confines of the traditionally staid executive briefing room? If a presenter makes a presentation interesting and thought-provoking, or uses humor in an ever-so-effective way to add punch to an idea, he or she is much more likely to get the audience to sit up, pay close attention, and be deeply receptive to the points being made. Entertainment for its own sake is unwarranted, but woven into the fabric of the presentation to give it substance and meaning can bring wondrous results.

EXECUTIVE RESEARCH SURVEY FINDINGS

Understanding the Rules of the Game

In the introduction of this book, I've explained the reason and nature of my survey and research regarding giving presentations to executives. In the following chapters throughout this book, I've included the detailed facts with accompanying statistics regarding answers to the survey questions and interviews with organizational decision makers. However, the following table condenses the major research findings in a simple summary fashion to enable you to quickly see what executives say about speakers and their presentations to them.

Table 1-1
Summary Research Findings

- Executives typically attend 10 or fewer formal presentations per month.

- They believe the overall quality of presentations given to them is just acceptable to mediocre.

- The ideal length of time for an executive-level presentation to last is 30 minutes or less.

- Executives very much want presenters to use visual aids; their favorite ones are overhead transparencies; their least favorite are films and flip charts.

- Executives feel that the overall quality of visual aids used by people presenting to them should be much better.

- They believe a strong and clear presentation introduction and conclusion are absolutely critical.

- The biggest problem with handouts is that they are distracting (e.g., given out at inappropriate times) and too lengthy or detailed in nature.

- Most executives will not think less of a presenter if that person is slightly nervous during his or her presentation.

- Good eye contact, dress and grooming, enthusiasm and energy, rapport with audience, use of creativity, effective use of visual aids, and the ability to quickly adapt or change a presentation ranked high among executives.

- Knowledge of topic, ability to be very concise (yet thorough) and to focus on strategic issues, and being fluent in a highly organized fashion were seen as the most positive important traits for a presenter to exhibit.

- Executives prefer speakers who are informal, relaxed, and conversational in their presenting style as opposed to either formal and conservative or consistently high-energy/lively/enthusiastic styles.

- Most executives admit to frequently using intuition as the main technique for decision making during a presentation.

- The *worst* "deadly sins" a presenter could commit, according to executives, would be to display any lack of integrity such as to lie, fake an answer, knowingly misrepresent facts, unreasonably exaggerate something, or be indiscreet; second on the list was any presentation activity that was perceived as time wasting (time management is critical).

- Other common things that bother executives about a presenter are: being pompous, arrogant, argumentative, or dogmatic; grandstanding or having self-serving intentions; being ill-prepared or unsure of subject knowledge; not listening to audience feedback; having contradictions or inconsistencies; using a monotone or dull speech delivery

- When it comes to *their* speaking skills, most executives rate themselves as being good to very good and most of them experience mild to moderate stage fright before giving their presentations. Most give from 1 to 5 presentations per month.

- When it comes to improving their presentations, most executives would like to be more dynamic, polished, and articulate. Being able to use more appropriate humor was also on their list of improvements.

Knowing Your Audience

By failing to grasp the critical issues, too many senior managers today impose great anxiety on themselves and their subordinates, whose efforts end in failure and frustration."

—KENICHI OHMAE

Knowing about the individuals in your audience and knowing about the organization you're pitching your proposal to is a very important key to your toptalk success. First, you need to carefully cater your ideas and messages to the exact *needs* and *wants* of your audience. Then, you need to show how your proposal neatly fits within the situation and operating environment of the organization: its vision, mission, objectives, culture, strategies, priorities, problems, and directions. When you do this, you're in a state of what I term "receptive alignment" with your group. You're on the same *wavelength* as the individuals in your audience and on the same road as the collective organization. There's a fit . . . a commonality . . . a parallelism . . . and a marching in step toward shared realities. If your ideas or solution does not completely fit in with the prevailing thinking of people in your audience, then knowing *who* and *what* you are facing becomes even more paramount as you attempt to change their thinking and feelings.

This chapter covers what you need to know about your group and what you need to find out about the organization your presen-

31

tation is geared to. The following chapter will show how analyzing your audience and situation will fit together when creating a toptalk plan.

GETTING TO KNOW YOUR ORGANIZATION AND ITS PEOPLE

Pat Shinn, a successful sales leader in one of Houston's Mercedes Benz dealerships, makes a lot of money selling expensive luxury cars to corporate chieftains, doctors, high-powered lawyers, entrepreneurs, sports stars, and entertainers. He's polished and professional, but he doesn't come across as one of those velvety-glib, high-powered, "charm-them-and-disarm them" types of salesman. I asked him his success secret with important buyers:

> I try to quickly and accurately get to know the person who is looking to purchase one of our fine automobiles. That greatly helps me to build rapport and trust with him or her. Then I can offer just the right —relevant—information in a low-key and natural persuasive strategy designed exclusively for that person's personality, motivations, and needs. My precisely focused sales presentation is always personally suited to my important buyer. I don't waste their time![1]

He practices two key elements of presentation success: **Know your audience and don't waste their time!** It certainly pays off for him, and it will certainly do the same for you. Throughout my motivational speaking and business presentation experiences, I've found that all audiences are unique—some differ in small, almost imperceptible ways while others are radically distinct in their attitudes, temperament, and reaction to you and your topic material. For example, some might laugh uproariously at one of your humorous lines, while the next group might sit stone-faced. One group might see your proposal as visionary and brilliant; while another would view it as marginally useful.

HOW TO WIN OVER YOUR AUDIENCE

While I don't have any statistics on it, my experience tells me that most presenters spend about 85-90 percent of their time developing their presentation content and only 5-10 percent of their time carefully analyzing their audience and creating an effective strategy to reach their objectives. As a result, they may have an otherwise impressive presentation that, unfortunately, misses the mark with that group because it wasn't focused and specially designed for their unique needs and wants. As one executive responded to our survey: "Just last week, a data-processing manager made the mistake of trying to give our operating committee 'off-the-rack' solutions when we needed a custom, tailored fit. He didn't do his homework with us. He should have known better." How many presenters fail to do what I call *presenter's market research* with their audiences with the result that much was wasted and the credibility of the presenter was tarnished? They mistakenly concentrated on *what* to say and not enough about *whom* they were saying it to and *how* it should be communicated.

You need to accurately find out as *much as possible* about your audience. When you do, you'll be able to reach your presentation objectives *faster* and *easier* because you're creating and targeting your messages to that particular group. When you know the characteristics of that group, you can also develop better rapport, trust, and an open communication forum and cooperative relationship with them. By tailoring your proposal to their unique *personal* needs and desires (not just business needs), your presentation will have high-octane performance, punch, and lasting appeal. You'll be well on your way to riveting their interest and gaining their respect.

Buck Rogers, famed IBM worldwide marketing senior vice president (now retired), was idolized by many in his company for his extraordinarily dynamic and effective presentations, according to Peter Blakeney, IBM's manager, U.S. Operations Multimedia.[2] His stirring, motivational presentations made him a hero to his vast army of marketing troops, while his crisp, well-prepared boardroom presentations impressed his peers and bosses. Blakeney told me that at large IBM marketing and sales meetings, Buck would build rapport with his audience members by moving to the very edge of the elevated stage to get physically close to them and he would talk to them in a very informal and friendly way that communicated, "I care for you. I'm here to help in any way I can."

When I spoke to Buck, he told me that a secret of his success was doing extensive homework regarding his audience. "Before I presented to the IBM board, I not only did research about every person there, but I'd review information about their company in case I needed to reference what they're doing in relation to what I was proposing."[3] Buck realized how important it was that even though he had presented to that group before, situations change or a person's attitude might have shifted over the last couple of months, or priorities might have flip-flopped in relation to one another. Nothing remains static, so a new audience and situation analysis was called for.

GUIDELINES TO CONDUCTING AN AUDIENCE ANALYSIS

When you know your audience, you can anticipate potential problems from them. As the saying goes, "To be forewarned is to be forearmed." If you know what you're facing, you can develop several optional strategies and approaches to deal with resistance or other impediments to your toptalk objectives. When analyzing your audience, find out about their:

- Knowledge and experience with topic.
- Attitudes and opinions toward it.
- Needs, desires, and expectations regarding your toptalk.
- Priorities and "pain points" facing them.
- Mood and condition.
- Size of group.
- Positions and professions.
- Personal backgrounds.
- Decision-making process.
- Problems they might create.

What Do They Know About Your Topic?

How much does each person in the audience know about your topic and what has been his or her experience with it? The answers to these two questions will determine the categories of information and level of detail you'll use with your audience. If they are reasonably knowledgeable, you can cover much information in a summary way while speaking about more advanced material without having to lay much foundation.

If your ideas or proposal concepts are new to them, you will have to spend more time building up to and around your main points. If you dwell on areas they are totally familiar with, you can waste precious time, annoy them, and lose credibility. If you don't spend enough time on introducing new material to them, they might not understand the big picture and finer points of your ideas and you'll quickly lose them. Oftentimes there's a fine line: Talk over their heads and they won't understand you; talk down to them and you'll offend them. You may have an audience mixed with people who are at two ends of the spectrum when it comes to what they know. It's tough, but in that case, you'll have to balance the needs of both groups. Here are some questions to consider getting answers to:

- What exactly does my audience already know about my topic?
- What has been the extent of their experience with it? What topic areas are they most familiar with? Least familiar?
- Has anyone covered this topic with them before? To what extent? What were the audience reactions and results?
- How much can they adequately digest during this one presentation?

What Are Their Attitudes and Opinions?

You need to find out the audience's "temperature" regarding your presentation topic. Are they favorably inclined—"warm to hot"—toward your overall topic? Or are they basically negative—"cool to cold"—toward your ideas or proposal? Perhaps the group is at odds with one another on how they stand. Is your audience at least interested in hearing you out? Perhaps their feelings are ambiguous or apathetic.

Knowing where they stand *emotionally* and *intellectually* is critical for you, to enable you to successfully design the content of your talk, your persuasive strategy, and determine *how* you'll deliver it.

The attitudes and feelings of your audience can be mixed or homogeneous. How would you generally describe most of the group?

- open-minded
- eager
- curious
- cynical
- condescending
- supportive
- very positive
- prejudiced

- sympathetic
- committed
- neutral
- believing
- jaded
- resistant
- negative
- mixed

- favorable
- concerned
- skeptical
- hostile
- challenging
- bitter
- friendly
- confused

The more positively inclined the audience is toward your topic, the more direct you can be; the more hostile, the more indirect and careful you must be, and the more you must overcome negative inertia. With "tough audiences," you need to develop rapport quickly, defuse negativism, and quickly set the stage for beginning to turn around their beliefs and attitudes. Skeptical groups tend to absorb and accept information and ideas you "suggest" rather than push or force upon them even with a preponderance of evidence. "Talk softly and carry a big smile," a vice-president of a large New York City bank put it to me. Consider getting answers to these types of questions:

- Why is this audience assembled here—is it a "captive" audience or are the members there because they want to be there?
- How can they benefit (or be harmed) by what I'm proposing?
- What is their personal and professional stake in my presentation?
- What is their present attitude toward my topic and why?
- Who might be strong supporters of my topic and will speak out on my behalf in front of the group?
- Under what circumstances might they change their attitudes and positions?

What Are Their Needs, Desires, and Expectations?

As a presenter, you expect certain things from you're audience. You have certain needs you want fulfilled from them. Usually it's getting approval and funding for something you're advocating or presently doing. Likewise, the audience has needs and requirements from you. They're listening to your presentation to get something out of it, even if it's just getting updated information about your on going project.

If you're asking them for a decision about funding a new marketing program, for example, they'll *need* specific financial and market-related information to assist them in making a decision to go ahead with it. They may *need* to see a new prototype machine in operation before they agree to begin its full-scale development. And they may have certain *expectations* as it relates to your presentation. For example, suppose you're the manager of Plant #17, which has been experiencing a lot of production problems recently. The audience may be *expecting* you not just to give a full explanation of the situation at the monthly executive's meeting, but a proposed (short and long-term) solution to fix the problem.

Desires (versus needs) of the audience usually have more to do with emotions than anything else. "Wants" are very different from "needs" and are oftentimes difficult to rationalize. The audience may need to hold down costs in the organization, but may really want to build that new long-overdo showcase research and development building. Pride, accomplishment, satisfaction, self-worth, the excitement of doing something worthwhile and innovative or a longing hope to reduce anxiety by solving a nagging problem draining everyone's energy may be some of the many feelings the audience may have. Through your presentation, they may *want* to get involved in your challenging project; they may *want* the exposure and success they perceive it may bring to them. They may *want* to learn something new. They may *want* to change the course of current events via your idea. These questions can help you find out more about their needs, wants, and expectations:

- What does the audience absolutely have to know in order to make a decision about my idea or proposal being discussed?
- What are their needs in priority order?
- What communicated and "silent" expectations does the audience have regarding my presentation?
- What have they been told about it and by whom?
- What exact outcome do they want from my presentation?
- How did they arrive at their expectations?

- Are the audience expectations in line with my presentation objectives?

- How can I set audience expectations before the presentation (e.g., sending out a written description, list of objectives, or summary)? Can someone else be used to set a positive expectant tone?

- What does the audience know about me, my experience and credibility?

- What would motivate this audience to act on my proposal?

- What do they really *want*, not just need?

What Are Their Priorities and "Pain Points?"

Every department, division, or entire company/organization has short-and long-term priorities that they focus on, and this means they become job priorities for people. Priorities always change, though, in a changing world, and sometimes they change quickly. This year, the focus might be on restructuring the company. The next two to three years' priority might be innovation and quality improvement. After that, it might be overseas expansion. Unexpected events such as new competitive threats can flip-flop priorities.

Many strategic focuses are planned in an effort to improve the organization's overall fiscal health and financial objectives (i.e., market share, revenues, return on investment, profits, equity ratios) in some direct or indirect way. They may go by many names: plans, programs, hot points, focus areas, or strategic priorities. Successfully dealing with these priorities means that involved managers get rewarded accordingly. So if your presentation points can help them meet their priority goals, you can become a hero.

In addition to the priorities that executives and other managers are focusing on, they also typically have what many call "pain points"—those things that tend to keep them awake at night. Maybe it's personnel problems, or cash flow, or fierce competition, or outdated products. Whatever it is, it causes excessive worry, confusion, anxiety, aggravation, or even mild depression. Pain points often occur because a manager finds it difficult meeting his or her planned goals and objectives. For a successful manager, the prospect of not fulfilling a commitment is very distressing.

If a presenter can (1) focus on the priorities and (2) reduce the level of pain, the audience will listen with rapt attention. For example, company executives in the midst of a dramatic across-the-board cost-cutting program would most likely be loath to hear a presentation about a new expensive venture even though it appears very attractive and has the potential to be lucrative in the future. Right now their minds and hearts are locked and zeroed in on cost cutting . . . cost cutting . . . cost-cutting. Receptivity is all about perceived priorities, timing, and inertia. In this case, if you want to reduce *their* "pain points," you must focus on a project that is designed to slash costs. Or, if you can, *refocus* your present proposal in a way that shows true cost cutting. You have to home in on their bullseye, once you find out what the circles look like. Questions to consider are:

- What are the primary interests and concerns of my audience that my presentation should address? Why are they important? What are the next lower levels of priorities?

- What are the emotional "pain points" of the group that my presentation can help to alleviate?

- What are the personal motivations of the people in the audience that my presentation can be shown to satisfy?

- How do people in my audience measure their success on their jobs and how can my presentation help them achieve better results with their jobs?

- What "sensitive issues" should I avoid or deal with in a special way?

- How can I use the presentation of my proposal to show that I can address in some way one or more of the organization's top strategic priorities?

What Are Their Mood and Condition?

The emotional, mental, and physical state of your audience can dramatically affect their receptivity, decision making, and participation.

If your presentation is scheduled for 4 P.M. on Friday after the group has sat through five other presentations the entire day, you may be in trouble as compared to speaking with them on Tuesday morning at nine o'clock when they are more relaxed and fresh. Or, they may be coming into your presentation in a "bad mood." Perhaps the day before your presentation, most of your group was involved in cutting 30 percent of their staff and they're still feeling the biting remorse, pain, and hurt while they're sitting in on your presentation.

If they're tired, for example, you may have to add more enthusiasm to your talk or give them an extra break (or ask them to stand up and take a stretch break). Based upon the anticipated or suddenly discovered negative mood of your audience, you may decide to change your strategy (e.g., reschedule your briefing if that's an option). It's a good idea to find out:

- What is the present mood and condition of my group and, if needed, how might I help to change it to a more positive one?
- Is there any way I can capitalize on a positive, upbeat mood to keep it going to better help reach my objectives?
- What plan do I have if the group is distracted, tired, aggravated, impatient, anxious, restless, or feeling pressured?

How Many Will Be There?

Find out the size of your audience to enable you to plan for how you will handle interaction such as comments, discussion, and questions from the group. The larger the group, the more difficult it will be to have everyone adequately join in on a discussion. Audience size will dictate the visuals aids you decide to use and the number of handouts needed.

Studies have shown that people in larger groups tend to "abdicate" their individuality by blending with the crowd and developing what's popularly called "groupthink" (but it's really more of a "groupfeel"). When this happens, each member bonds to the group whole and tends to exchange his or her personal feelings for the collective emotionalism of the group. In this case, emotionalism increases and individual intellectual contribution decreases.

A smaller audience tends to make people more independent, free thinking, and prone to asking more questions, challenging points made, or outright disagreeing. The smaller group has greater opportunity to be more personal, informal, and interactive with the presenter and between members.

What Are Their Positions and Professions?

Determine the functional specialties of the people in your group. Will they be mostly financial, engineering, marketing, sales, research and development, operations, general administration, or other areas of expertise? Or is there a representative mix of professional people from several of those areas? If you're talking before a board of directors, what companies and industries are they from? This makeup of your group will be a factor in how you present your content and deliver your presentation. As a generalization, engineering, financial, scientific, and other numbers-oriented groups tend to need more detailed explanations of how you arrived at your claims or conclusions. Formulas, measurement data, statistics may have to be detailed. They also tend to favor more comprehensive handouts for later study or review. While they appreciate a polished presentation style, this group generally is more concerned with the nitty-gritty nuts-and-bolts substance presented.

Marketing, sales, public relations, and general administrative people, on the other hand, tend to prefer seeing a *big picture* of the situation with a focus on the implications, benefits, and projected results of a proposal rather than getting into a detailed analysis of each point. As a generalization, they tend to favor a more spirited, high-energy style of presenting with brief summary handouts.

Next, you need to determine the levels of your audience members. Are they professional individual contributors, middle managers, general managers, vice-presidents, senior or executive vice presidents, or higher? The higher the level, the more concise, strategic, and global your presentation must be. Based upon all these characteristics of your audience, tailor your examples, quotations, level of content detail, and appropriate jargon to them.

What Are Their Personal Backgrounds?

In order to adequately communicate to and persuade people, you need to know about them as "living, breathing human beings" who have strengths and weaknesses, likes and dislikes, and who are shaped by their unique life experiences, accomplishments, beliefs, values, and attitudes. All these affect their decision making and how they will relate to a presenter's style and personality and, therefore, his or her proposal. For a small boardroom group, for example, it's valuable if you can do some "detective work" to find out each individual's "personal profile"—his or her age, sex, geographic and cultural background, personality type, education level, military background, political affiliation, socioeconomic level, hobbies and interests, and whatever else will give you clues about the "person." It's often difficult to do, but the more you know about each person, the more you'll be able to intuitively get a feel for how that person might think and feel about your proposal. That will help when you are creating your persuasive strategy.

For example, the interests, needs, attitudes, values, and motivations of people will vary with age. More mature people usually hold on to their beliefs and habits more tightly and don't respond as quickly to new ideas or approaches as younger audiences do. They're open-minded to the extent that they'll look at the pros and cons of your idea while demanding strong, concrete evidence of your statements and claims. Older, more conservative groups are not receptive to high-charged, boosted-energy speakers. A younger audience is more swayed by its emotions, the sparked enthusiasm of the presentation, and the intellectual and emotional stimulation brought about by novelty, variety, and interesting information.

Highly educated listeners (particularly those in science, academia, engineering, and the legal profession) are more prone to carefully analyze (some say totally scrutinize) *what* you say, rather than the possible charming and dynamically friendly *way* you say it; they're more suspect of your presentation and less likely to accept it readily. Highly educated audiences generally favor a more formal, sophisticated style of speaking with ample use of examples, illustrations, definitions, and proof sources. Less educated listeners, such as some self-made entrepreneurs, for example, will most likely pooh-pooh theories, concepts and "intellectual speculation" and, instead, will pride themselves on common-sense "school-of-hard-knocks" experience, and their "street wisdom." This group favors a direct, straightforward, no-nonsense approach. A presentation that appeals to emotions, makes use of inspiring, relevant human interest stories, humor, and a very informal, conversational style of speaking is typically preferred.

By finding out about their personal backgrounds and analyzing them, you're ultimately trying to find out what their values, beliefs, attitudes, and principles are. Try getting answers to some of these questions:

- What types of people generally impress the audience? Who are their "heroes or heroines"?
- What achievements were audience members particularly proud of?
- Are they formal or informal types of people? Conservative or liberal?
- What degree of risk takers are they? None? Very cautious? Prudent? High? How do they view innovation and creativity?
- What is their leadership style?
- What do they fear or worry about?
- What drives them and turns them on?
- How might your audience members describe themselves?
- What clubs, associations, or groups do they belong to that would give you a clue as to who they are?

How Do They Make Decisions?

If you're going to face the power brokers to get their approval and funding for your project, you need to understand completely how they will evaluate your project and how they will arrive at a consensus decision. First of all, is your audience able and willing to make a decision on the spot regarding your proposal? Or do they need to study it in more detail or meet with you individually afterwards and set aside time for a follow-up toptalk to reach a decision? How does the group normally make decisions on proposals or projects such as yours? Here are some questions to consider:

- Who are the most influential people in the group who sway decisions?

- What elements of a proposal such as yours would they absolutely need to get information about prior to making a decision?

- What decision-making criteria (e.g., financial payback, technological superiority, market experience, attractive long-term benefits) has the most weight and why? The least and why? What are the other criteria in descending priority they will use to evaluate your proposal?

- Besides getting your audience to base their decision upon a solid foundation of data you present, what emotional appeals and ways to sway their intuition might you use for maximum persuasive impact?

- What would they perceive as the level of risk inherent in your proposal and how would that affect their decision?

WINNING OVER DOUBTERS, SKEPTICS, RESISTORS, AND OTHER UNSUPPORTIVE AUDIENCE MEMBERS

It would be wonderful if all your audiences would gleefully find your presentations acceptable in every regard. But, of course, that's the stuff of Alice in Wonderland! You may have people in your audience who genuinely have doubts or skepticism about your ideas or plans and may voice concerns or show outright resistance to them. Perhaps they are simply apathetic and are not motivated to support you. Satisfy them and you've won them over. You may also have stronger detractors and even "saboteurs" who are not about to cooperate with your well-meaning (even generous) efforts to assuage them. Whatever their agenda, they're out for some bloodletting and they want your vein as the offering.

Identifying and dealing with people who pose an obstacle to reaching your presentation objectives is critical because you will either need their support or you'll need to neutralize their behavioral venom with an antidote strategy before they poison the attitudes of others and quickly get your presentation off to a mourning death knell. If unanticipated, they can upset you and knock you off kilter and possibly change your planned course of events during your presentation. Here are some questions that will help you prepare for even the worst:

- What "tough" questions (hitting on your proposal "weak spots") can they bring up?
- Why might individuals in your audience want to see your presentation proposal fail? What damaging hidden agenda items might surface? How might their "attacks" on you and your ideas come about? Who might be threatened by you or your presentation?
- What claims, facts, conclusions, data, examples, etc., might they dispute?
- What incorrect perceptions, past misunderstandings, rumors, or falsehoods regarding your proposal or ideas need to be addressed?
- Is there anything in your topic or your planned way of presenting it that might antagonize your audience that you need to be sensitive to, handle in a special way, or avoid?
- What are the possible negative political implications of your proposal as seen through the eyes of others?
- What audience members would be your supporters, and how can they be called upon to counter the detractors?
- What are the worst possible things your audience can do for which you need to create an "emergency disaster plan"?

Performing Your Audience Analysis

Getting to know your audience means you have to take on the roles of researcher, detective, and possibly psychologist. But, don't worry—it's not very difficult or even time consuming if you do it smart and do it right. The idea is to use several avenues to find out about your audience as the following guidelines explain:

- Time and opportunity permitting, get together with several of your planned audience members *beforehand.* A prepresentation meeting with a representative sample (or even all of them if it's a small group) of those attending will help you find out the audience analysis factors we covered in previous material and help to build rapport with them. If your presentation is important, it's always advisable to give an *informal minipresentation* to key decision makers to gauge reactions to your proposal's main points and to get suggestions for improvement. Tell them you'd like to get their insights and advice about the general ideas you'll be presenting in detail at the formal presentation. By doing this, you're trying to sell your ideas *before* the main event so that it will be much easier to get group consensus (commonly referred to as "rubber stamping") at the formal presentation. And the feedback they give you will enable you to modify your proposal to their satisfaction.

- Talk to people who've given presentations to that group. They can give you great insights into personalities, priority, sensitive issues, politics, meeting dynamics, and much more. Also talk to people who know and have had individual dealings with the people who will be at your presentation.

- Ask the executive's administrative assistant to give you a biography of his or her boss (most executives have one). It may be a long shot, but you might want to ask the executive assistant's opinion about the boss's possible reaction to your proposal. Besides being complimented that you value his or her input, that person might give you some inside scoop on how to "position" your ideas. But, you have to carefully explain why you're asking this and how it would benefit the boss because his or her protective loyalty might discourage giving away what may initially be perceived as confidences or inside information.

Consider something like the following request: "I'm giving a presentation to the executive group in two weeks. And I'm planning for it now by doing my homework. It's important that Ms. Leytan gets the right information during the presentation to make a decision on my project. I'd like to know a bit more about her and how I can best present to her. Can you give me some insights about . . . ?"

- If you're suddenly asked to address a group (especially a large audience) with your "usual speech or presentation," you may have to do an on-the-spot audience analysis if you've not had an opportunity to do a more detailed one. In this case, you ask the audience a series of short questions in the beginning of your presentation to enable you to quickly adapt your presentation (as best as you can) to their needs. Here are some example questions: "Raise your hands if you believe in the concept of planned product obsolescence. How many of you here today have had experience with product export licenses?

Situation Analysis: Alignment and Congruency

Every successful proposal that was ever developed was based upon audience needs *and* the situation encompassing the organization the proposal was aimed at. Your presentation has got to be "congruent" with the overall situation the organization is facing and its operating environment. When your presentation points are congruent, they "fit in"—they're superimposed upon the way the organization feels, thinks, and works. When your ideas, concepts, plans, and professional style are in *alignment* with the organization you're proposing to, you're pushing in the same direction they're going—you're not in misalignment with their goals, strategies, directions, or operating characteristics. The visions, mission, goals, strategies, thrusts, and other characteristics of your proposed project, for example, become subsets of and neatly fit within the larger ones of the organization (as shown in illustration 2-1).

Certainly there are times when you need to go against conventional wisdom of the organization and propose changes that conflict with alignment and congruency. Paradigm shifts, innovation, and creativity go against the grain of status quo. Proposing these things are risky and takes courage, but with the right toptalk strategy, you can get the audience to slowly come about and eventually accept your ideas.

Illustration 2-1
Alignment and Congruency

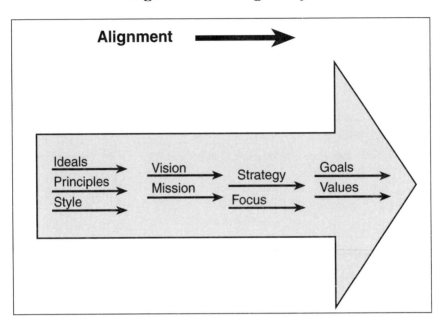

TUNING IN TO THE
ORGANIZATION'S CULTURE AND
GOALS

There are two overall key areas that high-level presenters need to be aware of when it comes to being aligned and congruent with the organization: (1) *culture* of the organization and (2) *direction*—vision, mission, and plans of the organization.

1. Organization's Culture. The culture of an organization can dictate how a proposal is "packaged and opened" during a toptalk. For those who have worked in an organization for a number of years, their awareness of its social system (based on a central set of values and beliefs) is mostly intuitive, and they naturally behave according to the well-known accepted norms of that culture. But an "outsider" (someone new to the organization or from another company, for example) presenting to executives needs to be very sensitive to the various aspects of the organization's culture. He or she needs to present ideas and concepts that are in tune—again, congruent—with that culture. Values and principles are the heart of an organization's culture and guide its short- and long-term planning, operations, and decision making.

Social scientists describe "culture" as a whole way of life— intertwined ways of perceiving, thinking, feeling, and acting. Corporate culture is typically defined as the *shared patterns* that appear across an organization based upon shared beliefs, values, ethics, assertions, and norms (which themselves arise from the history and tradition of the organization as modified by contemporary events). Simply put, an organization's culture revolves around the spoken and unspoken assumptions and written and unwritten rules about "how people do things around here."

An organization's culture reflects assumptions about relationships with clients, stockholders, employees, suppliers, competitors, and the community at large. Culture affects the vision, mission, products, and general activities of that organization. An organization's values are often organized and codified into a philosophy of operations that outlines how an organization approaches its work, how its internal affairs are handled, and how it relates to customers and employees. Texaco Corporation's culture, for example, has published their ten "Guiding Principles" that they stand for: (1) Quality, (2) Customer Service. (3) Shareholder Return, (4) Inspired Leadership, (5) Corporate Responsibility, (6) Respect for the Individual, (7) Highest Ethical Standards, (8) Teamwork, (9) Communication, (10) Technological Leadership.[4] Knowing these can help you better align your presentation to them.

Highly innovative and profitable Intel Corporation, the world's leading multibillion dollar producer of microcomputer chips (used in IBM compatible computers) and other semiconductors, has a distinct people-oriented atypical culture that has been largely responsible for its incredible success. In Intel's case, day-to-day activities are guided by "Intel Values"—a statement that is printed on the back of each employee's identification badge. Regarding risk taking, for example, the Intel statement notes, "We embrace change, challenge the status quo, listen to all ideas and viewpoints, encourage and reward informed risk-taking."[5] The reality is that the stated values are *believed and practiced*. Instead of being penalized for taking calculated risks on their own, employees are judged more favorably for trying and failing than for not doing anything.

Intel employees work in a culture that promotes setting challenging goals, executing "flawlessly," focusing on output, and assuming responsibility to confront and solve problems. Employees often are aggressive, outspoken, self-starter-type personalities who are expected to still be caring and "human." Expertise is valued over rank or title, and people (even senior executives) work in very unpretentious open-door cubicle environments. Casual atmosphere reigns with few neckties seen (Friday is blue jeans day). Information-sharing is extensive and people at even low levels will make decisions worth millions of dollars. Intel's culture is often captured in one-liners and images such as the terms "disagree, but commit" or "constructive confrontation." Teamwork, openness, and even creative fun are part of the culture.

As a result of analyzing the culture of Intel, for example, a toptalker can determine that they: (1) look at long-term opportunities; (2) are not risk-averse; (3) focus on innovation; (4) engage in spirited open discussions during presentations given to them; (5) value crisp plans leading to superb execution; and (6) look for strong team-oriented project leadership.

What to Find Out About an Organization's Culture

Here are some things you might want to find out to help make your proposal more congruent and in alignment with the organization's values, principles, philosophy, and operating policies:

- What types of achievements has the company been especially proud of over the last ten years?

- What does the company primarily focus its time and energy on?

- Is it a formal or informal company? Conservative or progressive?

- What consistent values (those things that are considered "important") are held to by its employees? What might be considered "noble" ideals?

- What types of investments are most valued?

- Is teamwork the norm or is it an organization of "lone rangers"?
- Do they expect change and deal with it optimistically or tenaciously cling to the status quo?
- What has been their history regarding risk taking and innovation?
- What types of people get rewarded and for what reasons?
- What motivates people to achieve in the organization?
- Is cooperation or competition the norm among employees?
- What are the stated (and real) principles that guide the organization?
- Who are the past and present heroes and heroines?
- What popular myths about the organization are a staple of the culture?
- What are the taboos regarding the way a person might think, feel, or act?
- What symbols or metaphors permeate the organization?
- How readily are decisions made and what is the process?
- How is well-intentioned internal opposition handled?
- How does top management interact with the lower echelons?
- What groups (engineering, finance, marketing) wield the most power?
- What behaviors are reinforced, and which ones are squelched?

2. Direction, Mission, Focus, and Goals. Finding out *where* an organization wants to go and *why* and *how* and *when* it intends to get there will give you a big picture of their overall plan. That entails understanding their vision, mission, goals, objectives, and strategies. If you're an "outsider" to their organization, you can find that much of this information can be taken from public sources such as their annual reports, magazine interviews with their senior executives, and other publications and research reports that detail the strategies and cultures of organizations.

Today, leaders place much emphasis on creating shared visions and crafting defined missions for their organizations, whether that organization is their entire corporation or a single department. Visions are like pictures of what an organization sees itself doing in the future—its aiming point or destiny. It's an optimistic, forward-looking idealized image of itself—what the "promised land" looks like ("visioning" is described in more detail in Chapter 7, Developing Your Leadership Aura).

A clear and inspirational vision gives members of the organization a sense of pride, purpose, and motivation to function at a higher level than was previously thought possible. It provides direction and a focus for all activities. Texaco Inc.'s vision, for example, is "to be one of the most admired, profitable, and competitive companies, and to make Texaco the leader in the industry."[6] If your toptalk points give a clearer focus or add more vibrant colors to . . . or somehow make the organization's vision seem closer and more achievable, you stand a greater chance of its being accepted. The project you are proposing can have a vision of its own—one that is congruent and in alignment with the bigger vision of the organization you are presenting to.

An organization's (region, division, etc.) *mission* gives its members a clarity of focus—an understanding of how what they do is tied into the greater purpose of the mission of the entire company, for example. Every organization of every size from small departments within the company to the entire company itself should have a clearly defined *mission statement* that typically describes many if not all of the following components: (1) customers; (2) geographic markets; (3) primary products and services; (4) major technologies; (5) dedication to growth, and profitability; (6) key areas of corporate self-concept and philosophy; and (7) intended public image. You can find out the mission statement from the manager of the organization, or if it's a mission statement of the company, from the public relations or communications department.

A mission statement acts as a constant reminder to people of the role of the organization and the scope and direction of its activities, and it can help the presenter to better understand what that organization stands for and its primary roles and responsibilities. You might have a mission statement for your project or plan that ties into the mission statement of the organization you're presenting to. Whether the thrust of your presentation is to advocate building a new plant, development of new products, services, or programs, or creation of a new competitive long-range strategy, your toptalk points should attempt to fit neatly within the mission of that organization.

Almost all organizations have strategic plans (often called "Grand Strategies") designed to have them gain a competitive edge. Knowing about those plans in a detailed way will significantly help a toptalker at a senior executive presentation. Briefly, some of these strategies typically include: (1) becoming the industry leader... making a massive investment of time and resources to get into a new market or launch a new product or service; (2) maintaining status quo with minor adjustments—keeping to the present situation that is deemed desirable; (3) concentrating power at narrow points—focusing on niche markets (that competitors are neglecting) to gain an edge quickly; (4) taking a strong offensive—to aggressively battle one or more major competitors in an established market in an effort to wear them down rather than react on the defensive; (5) looking for weak points— finding and exploiting a competitor's product, service, or distribution weakness, for example.

Doing a Situation Analysis

Here are some things to analyze about the situation of the organization prior to designing the strategy and content of your toptalk:

- Does the organization have a vision and mission statement for you to see?

- What general direction will the organization be taking over the next five years?

- What are the short- and long-term financial and operational goals and objectives of the organization?

- What are their critical strategic thrusts that will better accomplish their mission (e.g., opening new markets, technological breakthroughs, alliances/joint ventures, expansion, vertical/ horizontal integration, diversification, cost reduction)?

- What critical success factors (e.g., sales, sales per employee, return on equity/assets/investments, inventory turnover, customer satisfaction, market share increase) do they evaluate for short-and long-term progress?

- How do they see their overall business operation changing in the near and distant future?

- Can the organization identify some of the distinctive competencies it has over others like it (internal groups, competitors, etc.)?

- What are the forces that tend to drive the organization's strategic vision (such as technology, new product or service development, productivity and efficiency, low-cost production capability, distribution or sales methods)?

- What changes or trends are occurring in the organization's industry that will likely have significant impact upon them?

- What is the nature of the rivalry between the organization and its major competitors?

- What threats of new (competitor) entrants might be on the horizon?

- What general "external" economic, social, or political situations are affecting the performance of the organization? What future threats or opportunities are likely as a result of "macro" conditions and factors?

Learning What Makes Executives Tick

Really great men have a curious feeling that the greatness
is not in them but through them.

—JOHN RUSKIN

Most of us probably typecast successful, highly paid senior executives as being direct, decisive, impeccably dressed, powerful, charming, articulate, and supremely self-confident. Straight from central casting, movies and television portray them as cocksure commanding icons of sharp instincts who have a magnificent grasp of the big picture and who exude an awe-filled presence to lead and inspire people. Voila—the typical big shot. Or is it? We'll see . . .

If you're giving a presentation to influential decision makers, you need to be familiar with how they work, what their responsibilities and priorities are, and, generally, what makes them tick if you're to strike an impressive chord with them. Emulating them in style and attitude and focusing on what they like and admire in a person will help you "connect" with them during your presentation. You can't afford to waste a golden opportunity in front of them.

This chapter will help you to better target your toptalk to that special breed—the executive—by giving you some insights about the roles, challenges, values, mindsets, and background profiles of senior executives.

BIG, SMALL, SKINNY, ROUND: UNDERSTANDING THE MANY TYPES OF EXECUTIVES

They come in all sizes, ages, and shapes. They run the personality and psychological gamut just like the rest of the population. Some are the I-love-to-step-on-toes types. They're seen as aggressive, tough human pit bulls who earn the reputation of men or women who are clearly willing to set heads rolling if necessary. Others are folksy, benign, low-key, and soft-spoken. A few are monklike recluse kings or queens who sequester themselves away in glass-enshrined, mahogany-encased corner offices on the exclusive top floor. Others easily and frequently mingle with their hoi poeloi and occupy a disarmingly simple cubicle office while shunning the usual trappings and traditional perks of power and prestige.

There are those who are incredibly charismatic, forceful, and dynamic with a flair for creativity and publicity. For example, years ago, new CEO of Campbell Soup Company, David Johnson, marched into Campbell's with a brass band playing the corporate jingle music, "M'm! . . . . M'm Good!" and "Mr. Showmanship" himself, Lee Iacocca (former CEO of Chrysler), also couldn't resist the beckoning tantalizing spotlight of publicity and controversy that enlarged and energized him. While there are those who exude the untouchable arrogance of the gods, others are Supermen as Clark Kent—publicity-shy, humble, low-key, and unassuming who lead quietly and competently with only subdued notes of fanfare.

Some even defy the image of a conservative and stodgy bureaucrat. Digital Equipment Corporation's CEO, Robert Palmer, is known as "GQ Bob" (as in *Gentlemen's Quarterly*) for his stylish and impeccably dressed style and grooming. C. Michael Armstrong, CEO of Hughes Aircraft company really shatters stereotypes when he dons his leathers and mounts his powerful iron steed Harley Davidson motorcycle for romps around town. Even Peter Middleton, chief executive of Lloyd's of London, takes on the role of motorcycle easy rider.

Getting a First Glance at "Them"

There is a great diversity about high-level decision makers. Business authorities and social scientists generally agree that there is no such thing as a *stereotypical* executive. However, the successful ones share certain characteristics, values, and strengths (such as their demonstrated judgment, decisiveness, self-confidence, insight, and ability to lead and inspire their employees) that have brought them to the pinnacles of their careers.

One of the country's leading executive recruiters from New York City, James Cornehlsen, told me that the successful executives he's worked with: (1) are well-focused in their career goals; (2) have a deep sense of responsibility to themselves and their organizations; (3) are very competitive; (4) are decisive; and (5) are time-driven. He believes they are motivated by the social and business impact they make and are driven by their sense of accomplishment and contribution.[1]

Walter Kitchel, assistant managing editor of *Fortune* magazine has met and interviewed lots of executives in his career. He's related to me that they ask a lot of questions, have a capacity to be good listeners, have a "kind of calm about them," can genuinely engage you in a conversation, and are very clear about what their business is about and where the organization ought to be going.[2] What do they fear? "Losing power and embarrassment," former Houston mayor Kathy Whitmire told me.[3]

Prominent executive recruiter Lynn Bignell from New York City adds, "They don't know how to fail. They don't look upon a roadblock as stopping them. They see it as a challenge—a way to create a new and innovative solution. They see adversity as their mountain for the day to climb, as opposed to a barrier."[4]

While each top-level leader has a distinct individuality about him or her, we'll later sketch a more complete composite of successful executives and CEOs from which we can draw further insight.

HOW TO PUSH THE "HOT BUTTONS" OF HIGH-LEVEL EXECUTIVES

The Job and Responsibilities of the Executive

Before we get into the personal characteristics and background profiles of successful executives, we need to understand their jobs and overall responsibilities. There are several metaphorical examples we can use to put high-level executives and their roles in a clearer focus. In a traditional analogy, you can view the organization's top person and his or her executive-level minions as the generals in the military. The CEO or president is the four-star general and his or her executive vice-presidents, senior vice-presidents, and vice-presidents are lower ranking generals. The middle-level managers and professionals are the colonels, majors, and captains. The supervisors and foremen are the lieutenants and sergeants. Finally, the lower-echelon workers (the "troops") report to them. In this example, the executives, like those in the military, are the top leaders responsible for the vision, mission, role, and future of their organization. They are the commanders, planners, big-picture thinkers, strategists, visionaries, and inspiring leaders. They don't get involved in the mundane details of the day-to-day battle and operations, but with a stroke of a pen or the uttering of a command, resources are allocated and movement is heralded.

Another analogy is that of the high-level executive as the architect of an organization (e.g., his division, area, or entire company) with his employees as the engineers and builders. As an "architect," he or she is the imaginative visionary and leading force who designs the look, feel, atmosphere, purpose, and day-to-day operating environment of the organization and leaves the actual construction and operation of the "building" to others. With the tremendous change facing us over the next ten years and beyond, organizations need to continuously reinvent and reengineer themselves. They need to be flexible, adaptable, and continuously change to meet technological, economic, political, and other challenges. As such, the "architect" executive analogy is always redesigning and enhancing the organization for optimal use.

Another way of viewing a senior executive's job is that of a skilled maestro—conductor of the "orchestra"—guiding everyone to play his or her best "music." Because of all the lightning-quick change we mentioned, the CEO and other senior executives along with their staffs have to take on the role of composers writing new music (i.e., new missions, goals, strategies) to conduct as change or opportunities dictate.

A senior-level executive is rewarded with a hefty salary and bonuses because of his or her difficult job. They're paid to foresee trends, quickly spot emerging opportunities (before other competitors do), solve complex problems, and to create effective short- and long-range strategies to keep the organization fiscally healthy and moving innovatively forward in a turbulent and quickly transforming world. Organization leaders have the tough job of planning and coordinating how all the capital and human resources of their company should operate in a highly synchronized and optimized fashion.

CEOs are, indeed, paid well in terms of high salaries, with bonuses and stock options. Many consider their salaries to be disproportionately high compared to what they do and how others in their organization are paid. In 1992, for example, Thomas F. Frist, Jr., CEO of Hospital Corporation of America, made a little over over $127 million (mostly by cashing in stock options) and Charles Lazarus, CEO of Toys 'R' Us, made $7.025 million on just salary and bonus (with an additional $57+ million in stock options).[5] Perhaps General Electric's fiery chief executive, Jack Welch, might have indirectly justified high earnings when he described the effective corporate executive in today's complex and mercurial business environment as "someone who can change the tires while the car's still running." For that money, I'll change all four tires!

Everyone Has His or Her Role in the Organization

Recent "management-speak" has conceptually focused on the possibilities of corporations changing their organizational structure from the rigid traditional pyramid to configurations like process structures, webs, matrices, or other informal and fluid arrangements (with a focus on interdisciplinary and project teams). The goal of experimenting with different configurations is to make cooperation and resource use faster and better and to create a more efficient, agile, and response-operating environment. However, experts in organization development believe that the conventional hierarchal pyramid will be in effect for a decade or even longer in most organizations. The pyramid, however, is losing height and becoming flatter as excess management levels are being stripped away in the process of evolving into a more "lean" organization.

One CEO of a medium-size New Hampshire manufacturing company explained to me his organization's breakdown of responsibilities: "People at various levels in my company perform three basic activities: (1) mission and strategy; (2) tactics, and (3) logistics.

Mission defines the job. Strategy and tactics determine how the job is done, and logistics provides the resources to get the job done—not only material and capital resources, but also manpower, funds, and data." The following Illustration 3-1 highlights the fundamental responsibilities of people at various levels in the organization as it relates to the conventional pyramid structure.

Illustration 3-1
Management Responsibility Structure

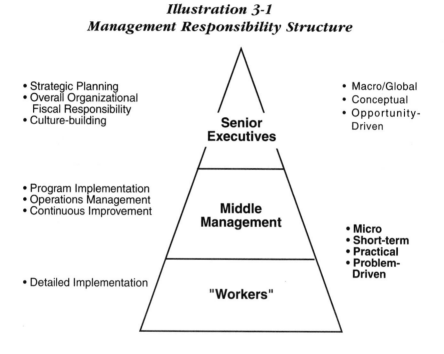

The top of the organization starts with senior executives (few in numbers) who are concerned about the big issues—internal and external—facing the organization. These are the *macro* (from the Greek meaning "large,"or "great") or *global* and all-encompassing issues. The higher up the management echelons, the broader and more critical are the range of situations and priorities that they deal with and the bigger the chunk of the "machinery" of the corporation they have to manage. Senior executives are informed generalists who know a lot and about a lot, and most importantly, how it all connects together and works. Effective executives know their organization well and the extent of their power over it, the industry they're operating in, and, the overall economic environment they are facing. Successful CEOs plan and coordinate the *mix* and *flow* of resources and activities within the organization to focus on strategic objectives. Their decisions, actions, and role modeling become the signals, cues, and symbols that nudge and guide the organization in the desired direction.

Many of these decision makers are "groomed" early in their career by taking a wide variety of "rotational jobs" for perhaps two to three years each in various functional areas of the company (e.g., sales, manufacturing, distribution, operations) and some in various foreign markets (which is becoming increasingly important as the global economy weaves tighter together). The goal is to make future leaders well-rounded and knowledgeable about how the organization functions in an integrated way in today's quick-paced, complex economy.

Senior executives have a daily agenda that can span many different and far-reaching challenges; they have to make decisions on wide-ranging fronts. For example, during a brief time period, a CEO might oversee a major stock offering, make a decision (together with the board) on a $40 million new plant development, discuss plans for a sizable corporate restructuring, investigate the attractiveness of the acquisition of one company and a major alliance with another, and handle a sticky public relations setback. The higher up the pyramid of command, the more strategic and long-range the planning is and the more one devotes time seeking out opportunities and fine-tuning visions and plans to keep the organization humming ahead at full speed.

Middle managers (in the midsection of the pyramid) are more narrowly focused on their own defined (divisional, departmental, regional, etc.) operations. Their expertise is focused on more shorter-term, day-to-day operations, and they devote a lot of time to solving problems and implementing the plans from the top (to which they've given inputs). The numbers and percentages of middle managers is decreasing as organizations worldwide push to become more competitive and cut costs by "delayering" the organization (laying off middle management). These people are increasingly being replaced by self-managing teams.

At the lower levels of the pyramid, the worker's jobs are highly specific and totally devoted to fulfilling the goals of their department or other functional area. Their concerns are generally, "How do I do my job better (faster, with enhanced quality, fewer errors, higher productivity, etc.)." While empowerment, team building, and participative management is encouraging more planning and participation in decision making even at these lower levels, it is still minimal compared to the other higher levels going upward in the pyramid.

A Toptalker's Focus Points for Executives and Managers

Since the focus and priorities for middle management versus senior management are different, you need to customize your presentation to that particular group. Illustration 3-2 following gives a more detailed listing of the major focuses of the two management levels to help you better strategize and target your presentation content to them.

Illustration 3-2
Comparison of Management Focuses

Senior Management	*Middle Management*
Focuses on:	Focuses on:
• Stockholder satisfaction	• Improved efficiency and productivity
• Increased marketshare	• Employee morale and satisfaction
• Increased revenues and profits	• Project management
• Asset management	• Reduced personnel problems
• Return on investment	• Increased production
• Strategic planning	• Better customer service
• Research and development	• Quality improvement

- Organizational innovation
- Long-term growth
- Capital improvements
- Executive development and succession
- Crisis management
- Community relations
- Company vision and mission
- New management techniques
- Organizational restructuring
- Overall competitive strategies and risk management
- Balance short and long-term goals

- Cost control, budgeting, forecasting
- Enhancing department status
- Effective resource allocation
- Reduced waste and administrative errors; purchasing
- New programs implementation
- Systems, policies, and procedures
- Information management
- Worker training
- Continuous improvement
- Team building/worker empowerment
- Goal-setting/detailed planning
- Incentive plans

Strategic • Financial
Long-term • Wide Focus

Tactical • Operational
Short-term • Narrow Focus

THE MOST COMMON STRATEGIC QUESTIONS EXECUTIVES GRAPPLE WITH

To give you yet another perspective of what an executive thinks about in today's world, look at the following "big picture" questions that tend to monopolize their thoughts—ones they seek answers to and solutions for. The more your toptalk proposal, plan, or idea can address these, the greater impact it will have on them:

- How do I keep our organization moving ahead now and in the future with *steady* progress?

- How can I restructure our organization to reduce needless management layers to speed up communications and decision making and make our organization more responsive to each other and customers?

- How should we strategically plan and prepare for major changes in the world economy, political situation, demographics, and other areas that might dramatically affect us?

- Where will we find the best global opportunities for us to expand?

- How can we optimize the company's use of resources?

- How can we improve our overall competitive situation? What niches should we be concentrating on?

- What will be the most impacting changes, threats, and problems facing us short- and long-term? What might be a worst-case scenario for each?

- What should our organization be like in three, five, and ten years and longer?

- What short- and long-term trends might have the most dramatic effect on us in terms of both problems and opportunities?

- What competitive advantage of ours can we leverage even further?

- What technologies should we be carefully watching to take advantage of to either develop new products or services or to improve our operations?

- What mix of projects should we be concentrating our research and development budget on?

- What types of strategic alliances should we be considering with other organizations?

- What broad opportunities and new markets should we be looking at in the future?

- How can we keep our stockholders and employees satisfied?

- How should we be evolving our culture and organization structure to meet future conditions and needs?

- How can we slash costs and improve overall operations for efficiency and productivity?
- How do we ensure a steady flow of creativity, innovation, and quality throughout our organization?
- What types of prudent risks should we be taking to grow?

An Executive's Legacy of Success

Senior executives want to feel that they've left their organizations in much better shape than when they came into the job. They want to leave a legacy of accomplishment . . . achievement . . . betterment. They want to feel that they have indeed made a *real difference* and will be appreciated and remembered for it. When asked, "When you leave your job as CEO, how will you judge whether you've been successful?" Numerous studies and my interviews with executives point to focus on these factors in *priority order.*

- Ensuring their company's financial growth and profitability.
- Creating a high-quality and innovative organization with vision and values transcending "mere wealth."
- Building depth and continuity of management.
- Enhancing the company's market position.
- Improving employee skills, morale, and loyalty.

The Intrigue of the Executive Persona

About 20 years ago when I was a relatively new salesperson selling computers to major New York City banks, I described to my parents an upcoming important sales presentation to a group of executive and senior vice-presidents. It was my most important account, a large Wall Street area bank that was interested in computers and sophisticated check-processing equipment that my company sold. I was clearly nervous since this one deal was worth over $1 million and perhaps intimidated by these successful movers and shakers. My father tried to reassure me with the old standby, "Son, don't be anxious—those big shots put their pants on the same way you do." To which I remember replying, "Yeah, but their pants probably cost over $400!"

F. Scott Fitzgerald observed that "the very rich are different than you and me" while Ernest Hemingway, who preferred the company of bartenders, fishermen, and smiling contessas to industrialists and other power-lunchers, rebuked Fitzgerald's romantic view by responding witheringly, "Yes, they have more money." Whether it's the rich or prestigious who have megabucks, success, social standing, fame, or "juice" (as street slang for power is called), there's a mystique we impart to those we see as "special"—influential—people in business, politics, science, academics, the military, and the arts and entertainment.

We bathe some of them in our awe, are held spellbound by a few, and are perhaps intimidated by others. Many of us wish we could be but a part of what is publicized as a lifestyle of exciting deals, influence, and respect. But, don't elevate them on a pedestal and enclose them in a glass-cased shrine just yet. While they have intelligence and many are richly endowed with "style and grace," they're not perfect or superhuman. Many dynamic CEOs, such as Jack Welch in his youth, never even pictured themselves heading a major corporation. And many executives admit to just being lucky in their careers—"being in the right place at the right time."

They're Really Like Us, but Different

Many executives are not the picturesque regal crown princes or princesses of their corporate kingdoms. Most are "regular folks" who have the same needs, tastes, weaknesses, foibles, insecurities, and neuroses that afflict us all to various degrees. They wear scruffy jeans, take their kids or grandkids to McDonalds, putter around the house, and generally do other normal "down-to-earth stuff." But, unlike the rest of the population, they were born with certain strengths and developed a set of skills and behaviors that have enabled them to move to the head of the pack. To successfully deal with them, to impress them, and to persuade senior executives to go along with that "brilliant" proposal of yours, you need to understand the psyche and profile of the power broker.

According to the stereotype, successful executives are supposed to be cool, dispassionate, rational, totally fixated with success, professional, conservative, and narrowly (and obsessively) focused on profits. Clearly, some are, but this oversimplified stereotype is based more on fiction than on fact. They're a diverse mix of swashbucklers, nerds, idealists, risk takers, geniuses, hard-core bottom liners, delegators, hands-on managers, intimidating autocrats, sweet pussycats, blatant copycats, visionaries, illusionaries, introverts, and flamboyant egotists. They're like us.

However, there are certain shared experiences, traits, and attitudes needed to leap to the top. I asked many of the country's top executive recruiters that I've spoken to what their high-level clients are like. They've told me that, while they are unique in a lot of ways, many of the executives they know tend to have somewhat common interests, they see each other socially, and they have the same traditional values. And, in a lot of respects, when it comes to business issues, they think alike.

THE KORN/FERRY EXECUTIVE PROFILE STUDY

Korn/Ferry International, a respected and well-known major executive recruiting firm, did a comprehensive study of the executive profile in 1979 and a follow-up study 10 years later. The 1989 sample comprised the Fortune 500 industrial corporations and service firms. There were 698 responses from vice-presidents and corporate specialists (the group from which future CEOs and presidents would be selected). Here are some of their findings[6]:

Composite Profile of the Typical Senior Executive

A-52-year old Caucasian, college-educated male who is married with three children—Protestant, Republican, and conservative, and works an average of 56 hours a week and takes an average of 16 vacation days over the year. He prefers to spend his leisure time (in priority order) with spouse, recreational pursuits, and his children. He is most likely from the Midwest or Northeast.

1. Success Factors. When asked to name a single factor most significant to their success, these were the top five with percent listing them: (1) hard work (19.5%); (2) effective execution (15.2%); (3) interpersonal skills (9.9%); (4) perseverance/family (9.6%); and (5) integrity (6.9%). The executives had a major breakthrough at the average age of 35 putting them on the path to success. The six top factors in that career turning point were given as: (1) different functional responsibility (42.7%); (2) luck (40.7%); (3) improving performance of a division (34.5%); (4) switching companies (33.5%); (5) taking on a high-risk project (33.4%); and (6) aligning with the right people (19.1%).

2. Definition of Success. When asked to define success, most executives (59.3%) said the ability to affect change was key. Enjoying your work (56.9%) came in second, contribution to company profits (30.7%) came in third, position was listed fourth (28.1%), and power was fifth, with 24.2 percent responding. Sixth was control over environment (21.8%), and money came in seventh with 18.3 percent responding.

3. Education. Of the executives surveyed, 96.9 percent were college graduates, with most (32.7%) obtaining a business/accounting degree: 62.6 percent had graduate degrees; 41.7 percent of that group had an MBA; 35.3 percent received an LLB/JD degree; and 9.9 percent earned a Ph.D. The schools most named were in this order: Harvard, Michigan, NYU, Columbia, Northwestern, Wharton, Stanford, Wisconsin, Cornell, UCLA, MIT, Chicago, Illinois, Georgetown, and Dartmouth.

4. Board and Other Organization Members. About 17 percent sit on their company's board of directors and almost 35 percent sit on other company boards: 42.4 percent sit on at least one other board of directors, 34.7 percent sit on two, and 11.4 percent sit on three, with the small remainder sitting in on more than three boards. Of the groups, 72.6 percent belong to professional organizations, about 54.4 percent belong to a country club and the same number belong to a charitable board, and almost 35.6 percent belong to a health club.

5. Gender, Race, Religion, Political and Marital Status. The group included 95.1 percent males and 2.9 percent females, with the remainder not responding; 96.9 percent were white, 1.3 percent were either black, hispanic, or asian, with the remainder not giving a response; 57.5 percent were Protestant, 27.5 percent were Catholic, 5.9 percent were Jewish; 91.4 percent were married, 2.9 percent were divorced, 1.6 percent never married, and 1 percent were widowed. A little over 71.4 percent were Republican, about 73.8 percent said they were conservative on fiscal issues, and 45.5 said they were politically conservative on social issues versus liberal or moderate.

6. Resume. They averaged 17 years with their current employer and averaged 3 relocations. When asked what would motivate them to go to another company, the major reason listed by 27.9 percent of them was increased responsibility, with the next being increased challenge (22.5%), and the third being better compensation (17.6%). They worked for an average of about 3 companies during their career. They reported that 69.9 percent are satisfied with their current level of responsibility/attainment in their job. Only 12.8 percent has ever been transferred overseas during their career. When asked what functional area will be the fastest route to the top within the next 10 years, most (23.6%) said marketing/sales, with general management being given second (21.5%), international given third (18.2), and finance/accounting fourth with 14.3 percent listing it.

Previous data was used with the permission of Korn/Ferry International.

Successful Executives are Hard Workers—Not Chronic Workaholics

Many of us might have the impression that successful executives are totally married to their job—no family life, no fun, no leisure or rest for the weary—just constant exhausting schedules that never seem to be able to accommodate all the plans fermenting in their ever bubbling minds. Captains of industry and those directly under them are, indeed, committed to their position, companies, and community responsibilities because these are people who take their responsibilities *very* seriously. But they are not classic "workaholics"—at least not in the stereotypical sense.

Successful executives and CEOs believe that off-hours recreation, leisure, and relaxation refreshes and recharges a person to be more effective after the needed brief hiatus. Many believe that getting away after periods of intense work promotes subsequent creativity and overall enhanced job productivity and quality. While achievement-oriented executives are extremely hard workers, they are not the fanatical stay-in-the office-seven days-a-week-till-midnight stereotypes many make them out to be; they play or relax with the same fervor as they chase success. Most lead a healthy balanced life with family and friends and indulge in pleasurable avocations. John Neulinger, a professor emeritus of psychology from my alma mater, The City College of New York, and author of *The Psychology of Leisure* states, "Those not interested in doing anything but work are not likely to be CEOs."[7] Successful executives are generally described as hard workers, who maintain a full, healthy, balanced life.

In her book, *Workaholics: The Respectable Addicts*, author and clinical psychologist Barbara Killinger sees workaholics as extremely competitive and so driven they can't stop even for a moment. According to her, workaholics always have a rushed feeling making them prone to headaches, chronic fatigue, and also failed relationships with spouse, family, and friends. It's nearly impossible for workaholics to relax on weekends or vacations because they feel they should always be doing something "productive" or because they fear thinking themselves "lazy" for relaxing.[8]

Leisure activity is boring to them, and workaholics are usually intense perfectionists who thrive on being "control and power addicts." They've developed a hostile, critical, and judgmental attitude. This often causes them to be uncompassionate and unempathic to others they work with who, they feel, are not as devoted and committed to the company's goals as they are. The "healthy" executives are hard workers and they share many traits of the workaholic *but* minus the dysfunctional aspects of it. Hard workers passionately love what they do, get self-satisfaction and self-esteem from their jobs. And they put in long, hard hours in their jobs, to which they are deeply dedicated, but the well-balanced executives judge themselves on their accomplishments and how "efficient" they are at work, not how many hours they put in. And they feel that relaxation is a reward for jobs well done—they don't feel guilty about getting away. Author Barbara Killinger stresses that work, as important and rewarding as it is to hard workers, does not prevent them from enjoying their family, friends, and other nonbusiness interests. These people enjoy a warm positive outlook on people and life in general and they don't neglect personal relationships to the exclusion of work.

Playtime Activities That Relax and Re-energize Executives

Successful executives do relax. According to authors Louis E. Boone, David L. Kurtz, and C. Patrick Fleenor, who interviewed more than 100 Fortune 500 CEOs for their book, *CEO: Who Gets to the Top in America*, reading is their number one hobby. They're voracious readers of news and business magazines. They are twice as likely to read fiction (mystery and detective stories) as nonfiction. Golf was their favorite sport, with tennis second. The authors found that CEOs prefer enjoying classical and easy-listening music.[9] When executives take off for the weekend, they're *off*—spending time on hobbies or activities that run the gamut; restoring old cars, gym workouts, wine collecting, snorkeling, hunting, speed boating, photography, fishing, building model planes, amateur carpentry, running, model trains, collecting art, riding horses, piloting jets, swimming, home handiwork, rowing, playing musical instruments, magic, raising thoroughbred horses and dogs, ham radio, triathlon participation, hockey.

THE 14 TRAITS
OF SUCCESSFUL EXECUTIVES

As we've said before, while executives vary greatly in their personalities and styles, the successful ones appear to share certain common qualities and traits that are generally associated with them as a group. Most authorities who have studied successful business and organization leaders will agree that they possess many of the following:

1. **Driven and Responsible.** While many successful executives lead a balanced life and are not fanatical workaholics, they'd rather burn out than rust out. *They want to achieve!* Many are obsessive and determined to leave a legacy of solid accomplishments behind. They echo the Irish proverb, "The work praises the man." These are people with extremely high energy levels needed to fuel unrestrained ambition. They strive to press their way to the top and are totally committed to their professional growth.

Successful executives show an extraordinary sense of responsibility to complete what they start. Tenneco Chief Executive Michael Walsh gave a courageous example of this deep sense of commitment and responsibility to the job. After being diagnosed with a brain tumor, he was back at work as soon as possible carrying out his former full range of responsibilities. His comment was, "I intend to finish the job I started at Tenneco. This kind of work is my life. It is me."[10] Executives like to feel a high degree of responsibility and commitment from a toptalker, knowing that he or she will bring their project to a successful conclusion regardless of the effort or obstacles.

2. **Quick Studies.** Executives are quick studies and they're very good at piecing things together to understand a big picture of a problem or opportunity. But many newcomers to the executive meeting room are troubled during their presentation because they wonder if the high-level audience "got the point" and is aware "of the importance of it all." Many senior executives I know rarely feel the need to react directly to points or arguments being presented, as their staff might. You probably won't see a lot of nodding, facial expressions, or verbal comments from them. They might not give feedback to something they like. This often causes less experienced presenters to repeat and emphasize their points, in hope of getting an affirmative response. This might bore or irritate the executives. Don't belabor the obvious. Automatically assume they got your point and move onto the next one.

3. **Good "People Skills."** Effective executives genuinely like people and they've developed polished interpersonal skills that have enabled them to deal with all types of personalities in all types of situations. They realize that everything must be done with and through the efforts of others and so they use good conversational skills and listening to build rapport and trust. They are more subtle than direct and usually expect others to pick up on their "suggestions." They appreciate diplomacy and tact from a toptalker and other displays of consideration, openness, sincerity, and "approachability."

4. **Focused.** Successful executives can focus on something just as a high-powered laser beam pinpointed at a specific target can.

When it comes to getting the job done, they focus a combination of their mental, emotional, and physical energies to ensure that success happens. During a toptalk, they respect that same degree of tight focus on the key issues. They tend to become impatient with a presenter who bounces around and goes off onto tangents.

5. **Effective Decision Makers.** Top achievers pride themselves on being decisive. For them, making good decisions is based on a combination of analytic and intuitive ability. Solid "gut" feelings backed by research data is very important in their decision-making scheme. They can separate the important issues from those that are tangential. Successful executives do not have to have exceptional intelligence, but they do have excellent overall judgment and insight, being able to sort through reams of information (much of which may be contradictory) to reach very good decisions.

In dealing with high-level types, be careful about discussing topics that you have not given a sufficient amount of thought to. The senior executive will usually give you a definitive answer to it rather than just a passing reaction.

6. **They Love What They're Doing.** It was Sigmund Freud who listed "work" as one of the two necessities of mankind ("love" was the other). Executives synthesize the two—they *love* their *work*. They talk about it in the same way that people describe their most cherished hobbies or proud activities. Work for them is "life sustaining" and incredibly stimulating. They have a passion about the particular business they're in. The result of getting so much satisfaction from their work is that they spend the effort to excel. Thomas Kempis, a fifteenth century German monk noted that "it's much safer to be in a subordinate position than in one of authority." It may be safer, but successful executives love being in charge. Typical heads of corporations don't seek power as an end unto itself, but they do feel comfortable in high leadership positions. It was Goethe who said, "We are shaped and fashioned by what we love." What executives love is achievement, challenges, and progress. They appreciate that same type of passion that a toptalker exhibits about his or her proposal or program being discussed.

7. **Confident and "Cool."** Preeminent executives exude a high level of confidence in themselves that facilitates following from their employees. A significant part of accomplishing great goals in life is deeply believing that you can do it—that you can climb to the top of the mountain or even move it by sheer determination and ability. Their sense of self is almost epic. That genuine mega-confidence (not arrogance or cockiness) helps them weather trial and error and even major setbacks knowing that tomorrow is "a new day dawning with promise."

Most of the successful executives I've known have shown consistent and oftentimes remarkable composure, poise, and "grace under pressure." They have a certain peace about them and are generally unflappable when problems or even emergencies develop. They usually appear to be in complete control of a situation, and this gives them powerful credibility with their followers. To impress them, demonstrate your confidence and refuse to get ruffled when they ask tough questions or bite back with stinging rebuttals. Composure under fire wins you *lots* of points with them.

8. **Seize Opportunities and Take Risks.** Successful executives are trend spotters who are always on the lookout for creative opportunities that others might not see. Many are also innovative trailblazers who won't wait for someone else to make a path. They're not afraid to make some mistakes and create their own road to achievement. Executives are "doers" by nature, and they usually prefer risking blunders to losing opportunities. The executive mind also carefully analyzes anomalies rather than screening them out. Executives constantly ask themselves: Is the anomaly an opportunity or a threat or a harbinger of a new period of change? They're *very* competitive and feel that there's nothing more fun and euphoric than winning in the marketplace. They respect a toptalker who thinks boldly, is innovative, takes *well-thought-out* risks, and seeks progressive change.

9. **Value and Manage Time Superbly.** These are people who try to squeeze every second into every day to get maximum output from their schedule, whether it's working with people, traveling, or handling correspondence and paperwork. Punctuality is also a hallmark of theirs. Successful executives are excellent

time managers who guard their time jealously and treat it as a delicately perishable resource. They devise little strategies to best optimize time, and they regularly record and analyze their use of time. For example, many catch up on general reading on the plane or use their laptop computer for work, and they delegate duties very effectively. They expect others who work with them to deeply respect and use their time with them wisely. Toptalkers need to have a tight, crisp, very concise presentation that gets right to the point and stays on time. Everything about your presentation should communicate precision, accuracy, and efficiency. *Start on time, stay on it, and end on time.*

10. **Results-oriented and Priority-driven.** "Output" is very important to executives, but their definition of work revolves around the quality of results and worthwhile accomplishments. They are not concerned with sterile activities (e.g., how many tasks they've completed or how efficiently they cleared their "in box"). Successful executives have learned the fine art of concentrating on areas of opportunity where outstanding performance on their part will yield big payoffs for the organization (and themselves). Spending time on priorities that will give the greatest (tangible and intangible) returns on investment is what they're good at identifying. The best of them appear to operate intuitively in this regard. This is often true because the higher up an executive goes in the organization, the more he or she is at the center of the organization's network and the more information he or she has than anyone else, which enables him or her to decide which situations deserve priority.

Management guru Peter Drucker tells us that topnotch executives concentrate on being *effective* (doing the right things) rather than just being efficient (doing things right) although executives try to do both. Another strength of their personality is their ability to be consistent in both behavior, moods, and accomplishments. The executives I know do not have abrupt starts and stops or an ongoing cyclical habit of spectacular successes mixed with dismal failures, although they do have periodic setbacks. They are consistent in their work habits, communications, relationships, problem solving, and other areas of work. As a result, they are viewed as reliable, dependable, predictable, and, therefore, trustworthy. Their accomplishments tend to be solid and steady. A toptalker who has a well-thought-out plan for his or her proposal that focuses on results and priorities will keep the attention of the executive audience.

11. **Voracious Readers.** They don't read—they devour, consume, absorb information, trivia, concepts, ideas, philosophies, and theories. Exceptional achievers are well-rounded readers and learners who don't just peruse *The Wall Street Journal* or the latest business book. They think deeply about how they could use diverse information and ideas to their advantage. They read about wide-ranging topics such as philosophy, art, biography, fashion, history, religion, politics, sociology, military campaigns, economics, architecture, technology, science, and numerous other topics knowing that it will enrich them not only as human beings but will provide ideas and inspiration for company-related activities. During your toptalk, it's advisable to tastefully (in a non showoff way) sprinkle your content with *meaningful* information (quotes, concepts from antiquity, tidbits, etc.) that indicates you are a lifelong student, ardent reader, and thinker.

12. **Patient and Persistent.** A strong trait of executives is their persistence in getting things done. Once they lock onto a vision or pet project, they weather setbacks, resistance, and obstacles with incredible patience knowing that the strong not only survive, they thrive. They feel that while competency is part of the chemistry of success, tenacity and an undaunted attitude are the long-acting catalysts. The consummate professional believes in paying dues and doesn't believe in overnight success. They subscribe to the adage of J. G. Holland, "There is no royal road to anything. One thing at a time, and all things in succession. That which grows slowly endures."

    Peter Drucker notes that the typical ineffectual executive tries to hurry, and that only puts him or her further behind. The successful executives I know don't race; instead, they set a sure and moderate pace, but keep going steadily and surely upward. A toptalker needs to show patience, whether it's answering stacks of questions or dealing with problematic audience members.

13. **Integrity.** Integrity and high moral standards are the hallmark of a successful executive. Executives believe that being ethical

in business is not just the right thing to do—it's also the smart way to be. Character counts! As our research showed (see Chapter 7, Developing Your Leadership Aura), the worst thing a toptalker can do when presenting to executives is to be devious, deceptive, or otherwise to display even the slightest lack of integrity.

14. **Total Dedication and Responsibility for Their Lives.** In general, you'll see a vast majority of successful executives being totally dedicated to being in charge of their organization and their lives. They take their job as boss *very* seriously. They crave and focus on controlling situations and molding their future. They believe that they can create the path in life they want with a combination of smarts, planning, strong drive, and ambition. While many of them admit to luck sometimes playing a major role in their success, you'll find most of them agreeing with the saying, "The harder and smarter I work, the 'luckier' I become." As such, executives are turned off by a toptalker who makes excuses or evades responsibility. An optimistic appraisal of solving a problem or dealing with challenging situations is what they want to hear.

Designing a Flawless Plan

Hope nothing from luck, and the probability is that you will be so prepared, forewarned, and forearmed, that all shallow observers will call you lucky.

—EDWARD GEORGE BULWER-LYTTON

It was 2,500 years ago that the Greek fabulist Aesop said so simply, "Think before you act." Yet, in my experience as a speech coach and executive presentation workshop leader, I've found that not enough people spend the necessary time to effectively think through the design and execution of their important presentation. And executives that I've interviewed concurred with me that with better planning, presentations would be eminently more successful. Seventeenth-century English clergyman and historian Thomas Fuller said, "A small leak will sink a great ship." Surely even small things omitted as a result of incomplete planning can scuttle an otherwise great toptalk. I believe that successful people either intuitively or explicitly have a plan for every objective they've set in their professional or personal lives. *They have a plan. They understand it. They communicate it to others. They fully work it.*

"I've given this type of presentation before and I know my material. I really don't have to plan" or "I don't have time to go into that. I'm great at extemporaneous speaking" are just some of the typical excuses I hear. In the movie, *Raiders of the Lost Ark*, hero Indiana Jones said in response to a problem, "I don't know. I'm mak-

79

ing it up as I go along." There are some adventurous presenters who pride themselves on "winging it" - making it up as they go along—until they get their wings clipped. Sure, planning never beat dumb luck, but I've seen people who were dumb enough not to plan their important presentation, but to gamble on success. The odds are in your favor when you painstakingly prepare everything down to the smallest detail and then rehearse. One vice-president of sales for a major computer company facetiously summed it up for me, "You can never be too thin or too rich. And you can never be too prepared for that big presentation."

The rest of this chapter covers the overall planning process that includes setting objectives, creating strategies, and selecting and organizing the content of your toptalk. The focus is on showing you how to think as a "strategist" and how to develop an effective planning system to give you consistently superior toptalks.

How Great Planning Gives You That Winning Edge

Effective planning greatly reduces risks by reducing unknowns that you might encounter. It dramatically helps you to think through the entire process and anticipate possible barriers to reaching your objectives. Comprehensive planning dramatically raises a toptalker's level of confidence and plugs up potential presentation gaps that might damage credibility. *Time spent on thorough planning will give you an excellent return on your investment.* It's the rock-solid foundation upon which rests creative communication leadership. When it comes to preparation for that big toptalk, "good enough" isn't.

Great leaders are great strategists. Alexander the Great of Macedonia, in the Battle of Issues in 333 B.C. changed the course of history. His flawless logistical planning, his brilliant battlefield strategy, and his innovation of weapons enabled his military to fight and win when vastly outnumbered six to one by the Persian army! His belief was always that a commander who was a consummate strategist and who courageously and vigorously implemented that strategy was truly invincible. Alexander, like many other greats throughout history, believed that with superb planning, battles are won *before* they are ever fought. *Victory is encoded within the plan.* General George S. Patton noted that "a pint of sweat will save a gallon of blood." Sweating the details of planning and coming up with a winning strategy will make you victorious in the battles of persuasion even in the most blood-thirsty of boardrooms.

When Planning and Preparation Are Paramount

When do you dedicate a lot of attention to planning your toptalk? Here are some guidelines:

1. The more important your presentation is (in terms of influential audience, proposed project size, and its dollar value)

2. The more complex, abstract, or controversial your topic and ideas are

3. The more your audience is opposed to your ideas or proposal

4. The less aware they are of your information and concepts

5. The greater the impact your proposal has on the organization in terms of change and risk

6. The less time you are given to communicate your proposal

7. The more interaction and consensus building is required with the audience

8. The more aggressive your presentation goals are

Granted, *all* presentations should be well-planned. But executive and boardroom presentations should be the *best* prepared ones you give. The success of your major proposal and your career simply depends upon it.

THE SIX-STEP TOPTALK PLANNING PROCESS

Effective planning consists of the six-step process—a systematic approach—that is shown in the following illustration:

Illustration 4-1
Toptalk Planning Process

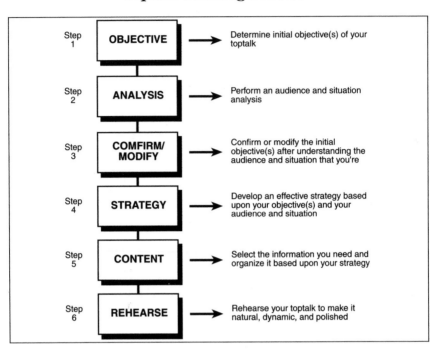

One: Determine Your Initial Toptalk Objectives

I've found that when people have to give any type of presentation, they typically start by asking themselves, "What should I *talk* about?" While that's certainly important, they need to start by asking what they'd really *like to accomplish* with the audience they'll be facing. Determining proper objectives means getting answers to these types of important questions:

"Why am I giving this presentation?"

"What is the purpose of my toptalk and what results am I trying to achieve?"

"What do I *want* from and *expect* to accomplish with this audience?

"What changes (in actions, thinking, feeling) do I want to bring about in the audience?"

Setting specific and clearly defined objectives and then concentrating on them forces you to focus all your energy toward reaching those objectives. Once an objective is firmly set, then everything and everybody on the presentation team is directed toward fulfilling it. And during your toptalk, you should be constantly monitoring how you're doing on the path toward the intended destination (objective) and making necessary changes to get back on track.

Almost all general toptalk objectives are variations of those that are designed to: (1) inform; (2) persuade; (3) educate; (4) entertain; (5) motivate/inspire; (6) sell; (7) gain consensus; (8) obtain audience interaction/feedback; (9) get approval and/or funding; and (10) stimulate action. Your toptalk objectives will typically have several of these woven together and containing a mix of informing, persuading, interacting, and gaining consensus, for example. And most toptalk objectives involve asking the audience members to make a decision (either right after the presentation or some time in the near future) to take action concerning the information or proposal presented. Even a presentation that introduces initial concepts, ideas, and preliminary data, for example, such as a presentation reporting on a feasibility study (e.g. to boost research and development to apply a groundbreaking technology to new products) is intended to stimulate board action—typically approval to go the *next steps* (whatever they are).

Objectives Should Be Specific, Clear, Measurable, Attainable, and Challenging

Setting *initial* objectives means you are determining the results you *wish and believe are possible* to happen. Until you perform your audience-and-situation analysis (and confirm the likelihood of successfully reaching your hoped for objectives) these objectives are tentative. Your audience-and-situation analysis will help you to modify or fine tune your initial planned objectives.

Effective toptalk objectives are specific, clear, measurable, attainable, and challenging. Here's a good example of one that defines those criteria:

> I want the (boardroom) directors to approve the eight elements of my expansion plan for the Merrimack, New Hampshire manufacturing facility and to authorize funding of $15 million within two weeks to begin the project by March 17th.

This objective is also measurable because at the end of your toptalk, you'll know what parts of your eight-step plan they've approved and how much funding they'll grant you. In determining what you want to accomplish with your audience, remember that you're essentially trying to get them to *change something*—their feelings, attitudes, beliefs, opinions, decisions, habits, or behaviors. So, in carefully wording your objective, you might want to spell out these changes. Here are some other examples and variations of effectively designed toptalk objectives:

1. My objectives are: (1) to present the results of Q2's disappointing revenue and profit figures and explain the reasons; (2) to make the audience feel optimistic that my plan to boost revenues and profits will work; and (3) to get their approval to proceed with it and (4) obtain their recommendations for possible changes to it.

2. I want the board to give me authorization to immediately begin to create (and to complete by Q3) a new corporate strategic marketing plan designed to counter serious major new competitive threats."

3. I want the executive operating committee to understand and agree with the five major operating problems (I've identified) that we are experiencing as a result of our rapid growth rate. I will seek their approval for my team to begin a detailed study to determine the precise impact of these problems and to come up with potential solutions for each of them. I will get their agreement to present the results of our study at the next quarter's meeting.

4. My goals are to get immediate board approval for my research and development division to dramatically slow work on two medium priority projects (advanced engine metallurgy and active suspensions) and, instead, divert funds and researchers to developing an advanced electric storage and propulsion car to meet future substantial sales opportunities for these new vehicles.

5. My objective is to get the executive committee (my customers) to approve my company's contract to buy our $17.5 million supercomputer multimedia network solution for their organization.

When you *precisely* define what you want from your audience (as the previous examples have shown) and you communicate that to them, then your toptalk takes on a high degree of clarity, meaning, and direction.

Two: Do an Audience-and-Situation Analysis

Once you've determined your initial presentation objectives—what you *would like* to accomplish—you do an audience and situation analysis to find out if your objectives stand a good chance of being achieved. This was covered in detail in the Chapter 2, Know Your Audience. Through your analysis, you're finding out what your audience knows about your topic and their probable attitudes toward it, and what their desires, motivations, priorities, and concerns would likely be as it relates to your proposal. Also, by examining the situation facing the organization—its current policies, values, strategic directions, short- and long-term priorities—you'll be better able to judge the appropriateness of your toptalk objectives.

Three: Confirm or Modify Your Initial Objectives

Step three in the planned process is to evaluate the initial presentation objectives you've set in view of the findings from your audience and situation analysis. You might verify that you were right on target from the beginning and stick with those initial objectives. Or, your analysis might tell you that your objectives were too ambitious and you need to aim for more moderate results. Or perhaps you were too conservative when you first came up with your toptalk objective and you could aim higher to get a greater level of commitment from your audience.

For example, one vice-president of research for a semiconductor manufacturing company in California was to give a presentation to a smaller, but highly innovative and respected software company. His *desired* goal was to convince them to form a long-term comprehensive strategic alliance with his company to jointly develop advanced video communications products (since his research indicated this was an ideal situation for both companies). Prior to his toptalk, he had lengthy conversations with several key executives from that software company. He discovered that they feared becoming committed "over their heads" and wanted instead to start on a smaller scale to gain experience before making a broader strategic commitment. As a result of his audience-and-situation analysis, the vice-president "downgraded" his original toptalk objective and sought their contractual commitment to form a less extensive alliance based on a shorter-term and smaller scale.

Four: Develop a Strategy to Meet Your Objectives

You can leave your strategy to chance or come up with one in the shower the morning of your presentation or you can carefully craft one as much in advance of your presentation as you can. Consummate toptalkers are masters of strategy before, during, and after their presentation. People who are strategists think ahead of *all* the ways that they can reach their objectives and then they devise the best one that they feel has the most chance of getting results. They're like chess masters who think of move/countermove and "what if." As such, smart strategies avoid hasty reactions, reflexes, and knee-jerk responses.

Toptalk strategy is about changing the audience's attitudes, thinking, and feeling and is designed to get them to act upon your proposal or ideas. German philosopher Friedrich Nietzsche said, "There are no facts, only interpretations." That's where part of your strategy involves taking your ideas and concepts and then interpreting them (with facts and other supporting information) in such ethical ways that are believable and convincing to your audience. Strategy is a set of actions, guidelines, behaviors, and preparation steps that, when linked together, move you toward your planned objectives. It's the rudder on the ship of words. It's an overall course of action—a road map—to get to your destination. If you treat your toptalk objective as the bullseye you're aiming for, then your strategy is your firing technique and trajectory.

> A toptalk strategy tells you *what* to do, *when* you need to do it, *how* to do it, *where* it should be done, and *who* needs to do it.

Strategy is Contingent Upon Two Important Things

Your strategy is built upon and linked with two key things: (1) your objectives and (2). the audience and situation you're facing. If you neglect to consider one of these, your strategy might be useless. The tougher the challenge you face in getting the audience to meet your goals, the more energy and thought must be put into your persuasive strategy. Or, if you are delivering "bad news" such as poor financial or operational performance, outbreak of problems, or losses to competitors, for example, you've got to strategize on how to position that information with your audience and how to propose a solution or plan. However, if you're just giving a "rubber stamp" presentation, where the audience already knows of your proposal and they endorse its merit, and where it is just a quick formality for them to vote on giving you authority and funding to proceed, strategy development is minimal, easy, and quick.

Illustration 4-2
The Connections

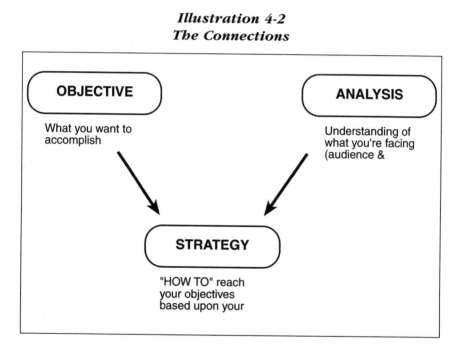

A brilliant strategy that marries effective analysis to creativity is necessary—*and will work*—to outfox your adversaries, defend yourself against attack, or otherwise shift the tides of opposition away from you during your toptalk. The underlying principles of a good toptalk strategy are simple. An effective strategy is designed to: (1) sell your ideas; (2) eliminate doubt, resistance, apathy, cynicism, or other barriers to reaching your objectives; and (3)

get your audience to quickly decide to support your plan or project. While your strategy needs to get the audience to focus on assessing the relative strengths of your proposal, a big part of it has to deal with overcoming resistance to your ideas. For example, suppose you're a senior plant manager and your toptalk objective is to get the board of directors' approval and funding of $11.4 million for implementing a new project within six months—an innovative flexible manufacturing system that would provide substantial improvements in productivity and waste reduction while boosting the quality of the large aircraft components your company's plant is a subcontractor for.

You do your *audience analysis* and confirm that the board consists of 14 members, of which 10 are outside directors. Most come from a financial background and only 1 has manufacturing experience. They are not aware of this new manufacturing process. Their concerns and priorities lately have been on improving the financial picture as operating costs are escalating relative to revenues with resulting loss of profits. They are also aware of increasing competition in the industry, both domestic and with several newcomers from Asian nations.

Your situation *analysis* tells you that the CEO, with the backing of the board, has approved of a new cost-cutting program just last week to improve the profitability picture for stockholders and to legitimately reduce excess costs. It's believed that the board would be reluctant to fund your project *now* in spite of the fact that it would provide numerous impressive benefits and boost profitability at a later date. You have found out that your company's competitors are talking with the same manufacturing vendors you are and that they could gain a competitive advantage soon. As part of your pre-toptalk strategy, you've given presentations (over the last two months) about this process and have lobbied and gained the strong support of your peer managers and several upper-level executives in engineering and marketing. Your cautious boss, the vice-president of manufacturing, believes in your concepts, but refuses to support you at the board meeting until he sees how the CEO and others react to your ideas. What's your strategy to convince the board to give you the go-ahead in spite of their policy and determination to keep company costs down? Here's one possible strategy:

First, you'll try to talk with several executives in your organization to understand the details and implications of the cost-cutting program. Then you will contact several board members before the presentation (either in person or by telephone). You want to give them a concise overview of just the key aspects of your proposal and explain why you feel it would be vital in spite of the cost-cutting efforts. You will ask for their advice on how you might make a strong case in the boardroom. If they have indicated that that they like your approach, you'll ask them to outwardly support you during your toptalk assuming they feel comfortable with the details you will give.

Another part of your strategy is to provide two handouts. The first one is a two-page executive summary that covers all the critical reasons to go ahead with this project. The second is a detailed handout consisting of approximately 30 pages that covers all the operational and financial benefits (payback, return on investment, profitability contributions, etc.) of the new manufacturing process. Emphasis is on the attractive short- and long-term financial returns. This handout is designed to give them persuasive specifics on the priority financial reasons to implement the new system.

Your strategy during the presentation is to indicate that you clearly understand the importance of the cost-cutting program, but that your project should be viewed as a unique exception because of the tremendous opportunity it affords in terms of productivity improvement, waste reduction, and boosted quality. You'll be stressing that the conservative estimates of the return on investment is higher than any capital improvement project over the last four years and that cumulative savings over five years will amount to between $26 and 37 million. Another aspect of your strategy is to stress that your competitors are seriously considering upgrading their manufacturing processes, and if that happens, your company might lose business worth between $66 and 94 million over the next three years because your customers will be drawn to higher quality components with reduced delivery time. This part of your strategy is to convince the audience that the cost-cutting program will actually hurt revenues and profits if this new process is not begun within 3 to 6 months.

There are two board members who were instrumental in getting the cost-cutting program approved, and they would be the strongest opponents of making any exceptions. Your strategy to deal with them is to praise the overall objectives of "their" program, to tell them how needed it is, and how strongly you generally agree with it. You want to convincingly show them that your new manufacturing process is perfectly in sync with their program. While it costs money to get started, it will actually be one of the major contributors toward reducing costs after one year with dramatic savings starting in year two.

When Devising Your Strategy, Here Are Some Things to Think About

Any strategy is oftentimes better than no strategy at all. But there are good, better, and best strategies to reach your objectives. Here are some questions to ask yourself that will help you toward constructing the *best* strategy you can:

1. What actions or activities need to be done *before* the presentation to set the stage and build the foundation for meeting my objectives? How, when, and with whom should they be done?

2. What strategy can I employ to deal with "ego issues" at the meeting?

3. What is my overall strategy to motivate the audience to make a decision to support my project?

4. How direct or indirect should I be with my audience? Should I keep things low-key or fever pitched or somewhere in-between?

5. What areas in my toptalk require boldness and aggressiveness in terms of communicating action, urgency, hope, challenge, or distress?

6. Do I focus on logic and data or use emotional appeals to overwhelm the data? Do I use a combination of both, and where in the toptalk should I focus on each type of appeal?

7. Whom in the audience can I call on to support/back-up my major persuasive points? Specifically, how should they support me?

8. How can I use humor to disarm resistance or make an impacting point?

9. During my toptalk, where should I *attack* a certain position or idea? What strategy should I use to *defend* my proposal against

criticism, skepticism, or ridicule? Under what circumstances and how should I go on a *counterattack* if my proposal is attacked? What audience concerns or points of opposition should I *ignore* because my persuasive strategy will kill it before it surfaces?

10. What is the *single biggest* obstacle standing in the way of reaching my objective and what is my countering strategy?

11. What can I say or do that will "shock" the audience into changing their entrenched attitudes, beliefs, or position?

12. What data, evidence, and information has the most explosive power to change their minds?

13. What are the gain/risk factors with this strategy? How can I improve the odds?

14. What can I do diplomatically to get back on track if interruptions continue?

15. What can I do to reduce tension and make the climate more conducive to open discussion and cooperation?

16. What can I do to help those who are strong detractors of my proposal to save face if they would like to reverse their position about it?

17. What strategy can I use if they seem to be hesitant or want to put off making a decision about my proposal?

18. What actions (next steps) do I need to do *after* the formal presentation to ensure the fulfillment of my objectives?

19. What strategy will I use to impress my audience and gain credibility if they do not know me or know about me?

Strategy for Asking for Audience Commitment

For many of us it's a difficult time when we reach the end of our toptalk and the moment of reckoning is near. Some presenters are hesitant or nervous to ask for audience approval, funding, or committed participation in their program or plan. Even if the audience appears to be interested during the presentation, there's always that chance of painful (embarrassing to oneself) rejection. Yet, it's critical to attempt to reach satisfactory closure—to reach your objective.

Toptalkers show leadership. They appear confident, poised,

relaxed, and almost matter-of-fact when asking the audience to go along with them. Their assumptive attitude of *positive expectation* is the extra nudge that gets an audience convinced to act. To help you smoothly and naturally ask for the audience's buy-in, following is an effective three-part strategy. Let's assume you've given a conventional presentation where you've spoken for about 20 minutes, finished with a concise and powerful summary of the major highlights and benefits of your proposal, and now it's time for discussion.

Step One: Gauge Their Reaction (Before You Ask for Their Commitment). Unless you're sure that your audience is delighted with your toptalk, asking for their approval, action, or other support might be considered presumptuous until you first appraise their reaction to your ideas and recommendations and give them full opportunity to discuss it. You might say something like, "Although you've asked some questions, I've been essentially talking for the last 20 minutes. So, before we get to your questions, though, I'd like to now get your full feedback on how you feel about the plan that I presented?" And if you want, you can add, "What do you see as the strengths of it and possible concerns or areas that you feel need revision?"

The faster you find out where you stand, the more time you'll have during the remaining portion of the meeting's agenda to address any concerns, points of resistance, doubts, recommendations, or issues that need to be satisfied before the audience is willing to commit to it. Here are some additional sample questions to "take the temperature" of your audience:

> Overall, how do you ladies and gentlemen feel about implementing this approach?

> Let me ask all of you: Do you generally feel comfortable with the plan as I've highlighted it?

> Before we get to specific questions, I'd like to gauge your feelings and thoughts so far. From your comments and questions during my presentation, I'm reading that the group feels positive about supporting and funding this project. Is that an accurate assessment?

Step Two: Asking for Questions. After they've given you their reaction to your project, actively encourage questions and other comments (requests, thoughts, ideas, recommendations). Make sure you've answered all the questions they have and carefully listen, respond, and check with each questioner to make sure their questions were answered to their satisfaction. During the Q&A session, actively stimulate additional questions with something like, "What other questions can I answer for you?" This is more encouraging and proactive than asking, "Do you have any other questions?"

Step Three: Asking for Commitment. Only when your high-level audience has indicated that they're generally supportive of your plan, that you've satisfied the concerns they've voiced, that you'll follow their recommendations, and that you've satisfactorily answered all their questions, is it appropriate to ask for their commitment. When you do, you have to be *very specific* as to what you want. When asking your audience for commitment, you may want to *ease into it* by making sure there is nothing left to cover prior to your asking for an audience decision or commitment. Here's an example:

> Are there any other last questions you have of me? (If so, you answer them.) Is there anything else I need to go over for any of you before the group makes a decision? (If so, you address it.) We've gone over several of your concerns which you've told me that I've addressed to your satisfaction. At this point if there's nothing else to consider, I'm asking for your full approval to begin this project immediately and to provide total funding of $15 million over the next six months with $7 million being allocated for next month. And to fulfill the objectives of the plan, I'll need the assistance of this committee in three specific ways. First . . . etc.

Make Use of the Powerful Eight Points of Impact

Every toptalk strategy should consider incorporating the Eight Points of Impact. The following "points" directly affect the persuasive quality of a presentation:

Point One: Primacy. Primacy is the state of being first in order. People strongly remember first impressions and can accurately recall the first things said during a presentation. That's why it is vital to construct the *introduction* of your presentation to immediately grab the audience's attention and interest, set their expectations, and establish your authority and credibility. Your first words should be like a tasty appetizer that wets their appetite for the entree—the main portion of your presentation. Make your introduction short, quick, interesting, and, if appropriate, creative. Consider including quotations, thought-provoking questions, a challenge to the audience, reference to a current event, newspaper or magazine article, a vivid short story, comparison, analogy, or illustration. A strong executive summary (such as the following examples in the section on content) can set the stage very effectively.

Point Two: Recency. Just like a tasty dessert that tops off a fine meal and leaves the last pleasurable taste in your mouth, *recency* is the last thing the audience hears, sees, and remembers. It sticks in their minds and hearts more than what they've heard and seen during the middle of your presentation. That's why a powerful *conclusion*—where the toptalker is convinced, confident, and relaxed—can firmly cement your key points with your audience. A concise, clear, positive, and enthusiastic conclusion leaves the audience on a high note. The opposite is a rambling, off-the-cuff, weak, inconclusive ending that leaves the audience wondering what the highlights of the presentation were and what the presenter expects from them. Every conclusion should poignantly summarize the toptalker's critical points and boil everything down to one or two overriding reasons why the audience should follow the plan or proposal.

Point Three: Repetition. Repetition of key points is one of the strongest ways to hammer your points deep into the psyches of your group. Marketing messages such as television or radio commercials and print ads use repetition for dramatic persuasive power. Even a 30-second television commercial might repeat the same point or concept up to a dozen or more times. I recall a speech given by President Reagan, and while I don't recall the context of it, I do remember that he convinced me of his message at the time. He was backing up his claims with statistics and other information. Every two minutes or so he would make a point, back it up with information and data, and then pause and emphatically say, "Facts are stubborn things!" He repeated this about four or five times and its effect was memorable and dramatic. Repeat your main points *throughout* your toptalk, starting in your introduction with your executive summary, in the body of your talk, and in your conclusion. You can repeat your key ideas either by using the same phrases several times or by saying the same thing but using varied terms (substituting words that have the same meaning).

Point Four: Statement of Threes. Authorities in the field of human communication aren't quite sure why, but statements made in threes appear to have an expressive poetic quality to them that makes them memorable and persuasive. For example, "life, liberty, and the pursuit of happiness," "faith, hope, and charity," "red, white, and blue," and "honor, duty, and country." You might consider using a statement of threes as the main points that you begin with, that you repeat several times in the main part of your toptalk, and then that you conclude with. For example, a toptalker might say, "What my plan really boils down to is: "Opportunity, opportunity, and opportunity" or "This new system I'm recommending will give us power, control, and flexibility." Well-known author and speaker on leadership topics, Joe Batten suggests using such alliteration as, "vision, valves, vitality, and voltage" or "compress, repress, depress, and suppress." This is Reverend Jesse Jackson's trademark. But, it shouldn't be overdone!

Point Five: Simplicity. Executives have a lot on their minds. They have a variety of important decisions to make on a wide range of priorities. The more simple you can make your toptalk points, the easier it will be for them to be persuaded and the more impact you'll have. There's a certain genius in taking what appears to be a complex subject and making it suddenly appear crystal clear, "obvious," and evident. William Barrett noted, "It is the familiar that usually eludes us in life. What is before our nose is what we see last." Ask yourself how you use analogies, metaphors, examples, stories, comparisons, anecdotes, and others to bring everything into a single crystal-clear focus. Remember: Simplicity is persuasive power!

Point Six: Involvement. When I used to sell computers to senior executives in major New York City banks, we had a saying, "If they don't share, they don't care!" What that means is that if my customers did not have an active part in the sales presentations I gave, they would be reluctant to make a buying decision with me. When people in your toptalk are involved in asking questions, making comments, and feeling a power to control the direction of the discussion, they are much more receptive to persuasion and to the recommendations of the toptalker. Executives have strongly noted to me that when a presenter discourages interaction because he or she wants to do all the talking, they turn off. Your strategy should always include ways of getting them involved.

Point Seven: Interest. Boring presentations where speakers hide behind wads of overflowing data and packed visuals is not what executives want. Anything that adds interest to perk up the presentation means it will be remembered and will help in the persuasion process. *Meaningful* humor, shocking statistics, dramatic comparisons, eye-opening analogies, insightful quotations, industry gossip, short and poignant human interest stories will help rivet the audience's attention. Computerized multimedia is a superb way of holding the interest of your audience. When designing your content, ask yourself what you can say to add flavor and interest.

Point Eight: Pace. A toptalk that moves along in a lively and brisk way keeps audience interest focused. In my opinion, too many presentations get bogged down in extraneous details where the speaker sometimes belabors points ad infinitum. That's when the delicate attention span of busy executives starts to wander to other pressing items on their mind. To keep their attention span, move your topic along as quickly as you can without suffering confusion or seeming to rush. Remember: Don't belabor points—executives are quick studies.

Strategizing for "What If?" Scenarios

George Herbert, seventeenth-century clergyman and poet noted, "The mouse that hath but one hole is quickly taken." Murphy's law tells us, "If anything can go wrong, it will, and at the most inopportune time." Even eagles—those smart birds, seem to know that law. If they have a chance, they build getaway nests close, but not too close to their originals. Survival for a toptalker also means thinking about "escape routes" and using alternate paths to reach a destination when an obstacle pops up. As well as you can plan, you know things will usually not go exactly as hoped for.

Contingency strategies are needed to anticipate and effectively deal with a range of possible problems, obstacles, and situations that may crop up unexpectedly. You don't want to be jolted off-guard. So envision every aspect of your toptalk and think about situations that might *seriously impair* your ability to meet your objectives, and then plan effective ways to deal with each. William Shakespeare said, "To fear the worst oft cures the worst." Preparing for *what if* scenarios can dramatically raise both your level of confidence and your effectiveness in dealing with problems. Your audience will notice how well you handle it and will be duly impressed. For example, ask yourself questions such as, *"What preparations can I make beforehand or what should I do on the spot if . . .*

- the group is behind schedule, and they ask me if I'm willing to give just a five-minute overview and come back at the next meeting to give the full presentation?
- the computer running my electronic slide show malfunctions or the overhead projector bulb burns out?
- people in the audience I counted on for support take a stand against my proposal or act neutral?
- the audiovisual equipment did not arrive as scheduled or the wrong handouts were sent?
- people ask many more questions than I anticipated and have time allotted for?
- people disagree with what I believe is overwhelmingly convincing evidence?
- someone verbally attacks me seemingly without provocation?
- something "unusual" is going on in the group and they seem to be tense, preoccupied, or unable to listen?
- people are having a problem making a decision about my proposal (e.g. they seem to be undecided; one side loves it, the other hates, it they want to postpone it for yet more analysis)?"
- an emotional exchange occurs between two ego-heavy audience members while I'm presenting?
- the audience wants to deviate greatly from my planned agenda?

The basic rule is if something can seriously jeopardize reaching your objectives, you need to have one or more backup strategies to deal with it.

Five: Design Your Content

Once you've established your toptalk objectives and have created a strategy to get there, you now have to figure out what you're going to talk about and how you're going to organize it. People often agonize over this part because they fret, "I've got only 30 minutes to talk about my proposal. There's so much to cover, how can I do it? What do I really focus on?"

First of all don't think you have to saturate your audience with mounds of information and data to convince them. Gertrude Stein said, "Everybody gets so much information all day that they lose their common sense." It's true! What you want to do is cover the priorities and highlights, make it very simple to digest and remember to make it convincing. Most importantly, make it easy for the audience to make a decision the way you want them to. Toptalkers are more likely to succeed if they understand these few really important variables that eventually swing the audience over to their side.

What information you present and how you do it is determined by the strategy you set. When it comes to designing their toptalks, I tell my clients, "Always have your objectives and strategy in mind when you're thinking about what information you'll be presenting." This helps to keep a person's focus always on the bullseye. For example, let's say a marketing vice-president wants to convince the board that his concept of a new innovative way to use computerized networks (such as the Internet) to sell is worthy of further study and possible implementation within a year. His objective is to get the board to approve of his department performing an interim feasibility study that outlines the details of how a computerized network can benefit the company. The results of the study will be presented at the next quarterly meeting at which time he hopes to get approval and funding for the project.

His strategy has four components, (1) to "shock" the audience by giving them projected figures that show dramatically escalating costs of doing marketing and selling the traditional way over the next five to seven years; (2) impress them with the results that other (competing and noncompeting) organizations have had with their marketing use of computer networks; (3) communicate a sense of urgency that something must be done to stem the rising costs relative to revenues, and this feasibility study is needed; and (4) challenge the audience to begin a process to out-innovate the competitors in this area.

The next step is to determine the types of information (content) that must follow the strategy. He decides to (1) describe and explain how two other similar companies have dramatically benefited from use of computer networks to market; (2) include escalating five-year costs of expanding traditional marketing and selling efforts in six defined areas; (3) explain how an inexpensive pilot program can be easily launched to prove the value of network marketing; (4) describe what the feasibility study will involve and what results it will provide for them to make a decision at the next meeting.

General Information to Cover in Your Toptalk

Executives have told me that when it comes to approving a plan, project, proposal, or program being pitched to them, they typically want these six "universal" questions answered:

1. What is the plan or project?
2. What are its goals and intended benefits?
3. Why is it being proposed and recommended?
4. What are the alternatives?
5. How much will it cost and what's involved in implementing it?
6. Why should we approve it now?

Part of being a toptalker is also to be able to translate two ends of the spectrum of information (as Illustration 4-3 shows) where, for example, you first cover theory and then relate it to real-world facts, discuss general principles, and relate it to specific examples in your company, and so on. Decide where in your toptalk you need to cover the spectrum.

Illustration 4-3
Both Ends of the Spectrum

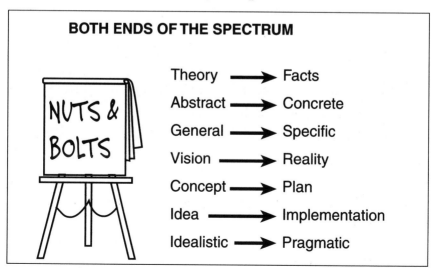

BOTH ENDS OF THE SPECTRUM

Theory ⟶ Facts

Abstract ⟶ Concrete

General ⟶ Specific

Vision ⟶ Reality

Concept ⟶ Plan

Idea ⟶ Implementation

Idealistic ⟶ Pragmatic

To assist you in fleshing out these six important topic areas and to help cover the information spectrum, I'm including the following checklist of additional questions that might require answers during your toptalk. These more detailed questions give you a deeper level of information to get into as dictated by your objectives and strategy. Because of time limitations, you obviously won't be able to cover these all at once. Look through the following checklist and determine which ones you need to give information about. However, to be *fully* prepared to discuss any aspect of your proposal or plan, you should be able to provide answers to these questions in the event that they come up.

Checklist: Ideas on Additional Topic Areas to Discuss

Situation Background and Impact

- What exactly is the problem, opportunity, or situation being addressed by this toptalk?
- How important is it and why?
- What are the critical issues revolving around it and what is the order of priority?
- When did the situation, opportunity, or need first develop and what's been its history?
- Does it require quick (or immediate) attention?
- What evidence proves its existence and degree of importance or widespread nature?
- What has changed recently (better or worse and how much)?
- What areas, operations, and people in the organization are impacted by it now? What will its impact be in the future? Where is its effect most felt and by whom now and later on?
- What will happen if nothing is done?
- What has been done to date with it and what were the results?

Proposal Highlights

- What is the overriding purpose of this proposal and what are its goals?
- What is the real change expected (present situation versus desired outcome)?

- What are all the key features and associated (tangible and intangible) benefits of the proposal, solution, plan, program, or project?

- How does it fit within our organization's mission, goals, direction, strategic focus and other priorities?

- What is the scope of technologies, products, services, markets, or industries being considered by the plan? Is the market ripe for it?

- How long will it be until we see expected results and to what extent?

- What are the possible "cons" to the proposal: drawbacks, problems, disruptions, limitations, special requirements, and risks associated with it and how can we deal with each?

- What issues may impede this plan or solution from achieving its goals?

- Is the solution or idea an original concept or a new adaptation of known elements?

- How well does it fit within our current systems, processes, procedures, and methods? What impact will it have on other areas and operations in the organization?

- Besides this proposal, what other viable options were considered before recommending this course of action? What were the pros and cons of each of those?

- What were the critical factors that made this proposal the best one among other alternatives considered?

- Have all important bases been covered by this plan or proposal?

Implementation and Decision-Making Considerations

- What is the process, time frame, and strategy to implement the proposal or plan?

- What resources and activities are required? What are the next steps?

- How simple or complex will the implementation and on-going operation/execution be?

- What milestone measurements are built in to monitor and evaluate its progress and ultimate success?

- What tradeoffs are involved in solving this problem or implementing this program?

- What progress reports are planned and how often?

- What preventative measures, contingency plans, or other safeguards are built in to deal with unexpected events, changes, setbacks ? How foolproof are they?

- Is there any way we can test this plan out in a fast, small, and inexpensive way before committing to the full-scale project?

- What are the absolute critical factors to make this project implementable?

- How much will it cost to (1) implement; and (2) sustain operations? What is the breakdown of fixed and variable costs for all resources?

- What short- and long-term financial returns can we expect? What are worst-to-best case estimates? What is the most realistic—probable—expected return?

- In terms of value for the money, how does this project compare with others that are vying for precious resources in the organization?

- What concrete proof is there that the plan or project will produce the desired outcomes? What track record do others have in this area?

- How would those affected by this proposal accept it? What consensus building has been done to date?

- Why should we consider supporting and funding this proposal? Is this project warranted in view of the expenses, effort, and risk involved?

- Why should we begin immediately?

Boiling It Down to the Bottom Line

During a 15-30-minute toptalk, there's not a lot of extraneous detail you can afford to get into. Yet you can give your audience a *thorough overview* of your proposal with key pieces of information to enable them to make a decision. I tell people in my workshops to look at any well-written article in *Business Week, Fortune, The Wall*

Street Journal, or *Forbes,* for example, and you'll see how information within a story format can be packaged efficiently and effectively and tell a lot within a relatively short space. Your toptalk content should follow that type of oral magazine story.

Think of your toptalk as shown in Illustration 4-3 where information is given to the audience on three basic levels. Carefully selected detailed information (that goes into the funnel) is needed to adequately explain and describe the important features of your plan or proposal. It consists of the topic areas that were previously covered (in the checklist) and then fleshed out by supporting details such as the following:

- Analogies
- Humor
- Cartoons
- Quotations
- Definitions
- Descriptions
- Short stories
- Research studies
- Test reports

- Facts
- Assumptions
- Metaphors
- Contrasts
- Statistics
- Exercises
- Explanations
- References (to news articles, etc.)

- Anecdotes
- Illustrations
- Comparisons
- Examples
- Themes
- Testimonials
- Demonstrations
- Rhetorical questions

You then want to make sure that you distill these details down to three to five salient points that summarize all the information that has been put in the funnel. The third distillation level is that one overall critical point that represents the ultimate "bottom line" of your toptalk. This distillation process makes it easy for the audience to follow you. For example, suppose you're a top research scientist for a major pharmaceutical company. Your objective is to get the board to fund purchase of a breakthrough (most advanced in the world) computerized microscope that would be used to design exciting new classes of drugs. In front of the board, you describe the applications for the microscope, the new drugs that would be invented as a direct result, projected financial payback calculations, and other topics that support your objective.

The four major points that you distill it down to are (1) radically reduced time to bring new drugs to the market before competitors; (2) significantly reduced research costs via use of the micro-scope; (3) the ability to create customized variations of each drug that would dramatically reduce side effects and increase its pre-scribed usage; (4) innovation of potential breakthrough drugs. You further distill these points down into the bottom line for the audi-ence—*increased market share and (short- and long-term) profitability.*

To keep the audience focused on the real issues, you can repeat your three to five major points throughout the toptalk and also repeat your bottom line point, mentioning it in the introduction, throughout the main part of your presentation, and strongly con-cluding with it as well. In this way, the audience will clearly know the priority points you are making. *And always start out with the most important points first and then the others in descending priori-ty order.*

Illustration 4-4
Distillation Process

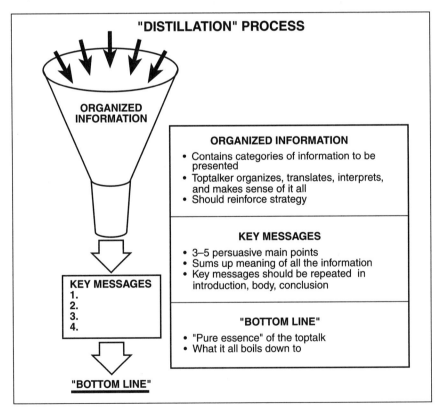

"DISTILLATION" PROCESS

ORGANIZED INFORMATION

ORGANIZED INFORMATION
- Contains categories of information to be presented
- Toptalker organizes, translates, interprets, and makes sense of it all
- Should reinforce strategy

KEY MESSAGES
1.
2.
3.
4.

KEY MESSAGES
- 3–5 persuasive main points
- Sums up meaning of all the information
- Key messages should be repeated in introduction, body, conclusion

"BOTTOM LINE"
- "Pure essence" of the toptalk
- What it all boils down to

"BOTTOM LINE"

An Effective Executive Summary Gives "Punch in the First Round"

One of the most powerful ways to get everyone's attention and set the stage for your overall presentation in the introduction is to give a short and impacting executive summary. It's the epitome of the distillation process and should be used at all toptalks. Some people think of a summary occurring only at the end of a presentation, but the purpose of the executive summary in the beginning of your toptalk is to give the audience a *big-picture snapshot*—right up front—of all of the main points and the "bottom line" you will be stressing. It's an efficient encapsulation of your whole toptalk, on the same vein as a condensed story in a business magazine article.

Many executives have told me that they've sat through too many presentations where it took them a long time to figure out the major highlights of what the presenter was getting at. Done right, an executive summary can almost immediately set the tone and expectations for the information that will follow. A crisp, concise, and interesting executive summary will get you off to an impressive start. Here are a couple of questions to answer for yourself when creating your executive summary:

- How long should my executive summary be (30 seconds, 1 minute, or longer)?

- What feelings, expectations, or overall impression do I want the audience to have after hearing or seeing my executive summary?

- What three to five critical points do I need to include?

- What "bottom line" message should I directly or indirectly mention?

- What summary information (statistics, financials, etc.) should I include?

- How creative should I be in trying to get their attention and interest?

- How can I defuse some potential resistance or challenges to my proposal or information I'll be giving?

- What words with a "special flavor" should I use to precisely paint an upcoming picture of my presentation?

Following are several examples of executive summaries, each with its own purpose and "tone." As you read each, note the intended effect that the toptalker wanted from his or her audience.

Example One: A Concise Summary Highlighting Main Points

The following example is a "no-nonsense," brief, nonemotional, to-the-point executive summary that focuses on the financial priorities that will dictate the audience's decision making:

> Ladies and gentlemen. This morning I'm going to be discussing with you a proposal I'm advocating for a new plant expansion. My engineering and financial team worked with me and we meticulously reviewed every possible detail about present and future business scenarios. We found that a worst-case scenario—an expanded plant operating at only 60 percent capacity—would give us an acceptable return on investment of 17 percent, while best case would give us a staggering 54 percent return on our money within the first year. Very conservatively, we believe that a return of 25 to 30 percent is about 95 percent probable. My proposal will also highlight two other significant financial and operating benefits to expanding our Wilmington plant and the main factors involved in getting it up and running within six months. This is a great opportunity for us to grab. I'm looking to get your approval for funding. Let me begin by covering . . .

Example Two: Executive Summary to Excite and Challenge the Audience

This example is about setting the psychological stage for advocating innovative change with an executive audience (which has been traditionally cautious and sometimes reluctant when others have advocated new strategies and opportunities). This executive summary also gives more detail than the more concise one in the previous example because the presenter feels he needs more "ammunition" to get his opening shot off with a bang.

> I'm here to share with you further details of a major opportunity we shouldn't pass up. Every automobile company in the world is further refining V-8 engines with overhead cams and four values per cylinder. So are we. And we should continue to pursue that path of refined evolution. Within the last four months, my advanced engineering team made an exhaustive study, and they had endless debate among themselves and with noted combustion technology engineers, metallurgical scientists, and well-known marketing analysts. Their strong conclusions have surprised . . . and convinced me that we need to dramatically accelerate our efforts on breakthrough ceramic gas turbine engine technology!
>
>   When my team began to give me details about this breakthrough, I've got to emphasize to each of you that my initial bias was definitely

against it, probably for all the reasons you have brought up in the past. However three significant points totally reversed my prior position when I studied them carefully. I'm here today to share those with you. And if you're as convinced as I am now, I'm going to ask you to give me your support and initial funding to help us out-innovate the Japanese and Europeans in a way that will make their heads spin. We have a rare window of opportunity available to us.

The three points are: One: New ceramics technology has been discovered and we can apply it immediately. We've recently discovered radically new ceramic fabrication procedures from one of our government research labs that has been proven superb for ultra-high-temperature engine operation. We can imbed it within our prototype within three months and fully test it within another six and get it to market in another two years after that. We believe we can leapfrog the Japanese by at least three years and the Germans five years before they field a prototype.

Point number two: We can convert 30 percent of our engine manufacturing facilities within one year at modest cost levels that I'll detail later. And point number three: we strongly believe we can exceed government emission controls for year 2006 by 45 percent and do it 8 years sooner. Estimated overall mileage for the new engine will be a very impressive 85 to 95 miles per gallon. Three of the industry's brightest market consultants have created a conservative financial projection report for me indicating that we can grab an estimated 3 points of market share within four years, giving us $6 billion in additional revenues.

We need to grab this opportunity. Let me give you the details starting with . . . .

Example Three: Paving the Way for "Bad News"

Delivering *bad news* is one of the most difficult aspects of giving an executive presentation. You never want to make excuses or "sugar-coat" the disappointing reality. You'll immediately lose the respect of your audience and possibly incur their wrath. Up front, if you paint a dismal picture without some hope, they may *tune* you out or, worse yet, reflexively launch a verbal assault. The following example assumes the audience already knows about the situation and is waiting to hear the details. After reading it, analyze the tone and intended impact the toptalker wants to make on the audience:

> It's very unpleasant for me to be here today to give you an overview of last quarter's performance figures for my division. The news is dis-

appointing for all of us, but the dark clouds should clear to sunshine when I unveil our aggressive plan to get us back to black quickly and directly. For the next three minutes let me give you a quick summary to enable you to see the big picture of our problem before I get into details. First the financial highlights. Revenues were down by 17 percent, profits decreased by 27 percent, and productivity dipped by 12 percent. We've identified and confirmed that there were three major reasons for these downturns. First, the decrease in consumer disposable income affected our orders; second, as we were shifting over to our new flexible manufacturing system, we underestimated the complexity of getting it into production and our productivity fell; and third, was the major advertising program from our competitor that grabbed market share away from us.

We have a four-part strategic plan to reverse the financial picture of the last quarter. That plan involves: (1) increasing our production capacity within a month; (2) entering new markets that are more recession-proof; (3) countering our competitor with a highly creative marketing program; and (4) coming out with eight new innovative product derivatives that should significantly add to our revenue base in the future. While missing our financial and operational targets is never desirable, in this case, it has painfully forced us to rethink many of the things we do. I believe the positive end result is that we will come back much stronger than ever. Let's get into more details in the area of the financial performance and then let me cover our solution.

"Good Ways" to Communicate "Bad News"

Part of giving a toptalk sometimes involves being the bearer/explainer of bad news. Bearers could be CEOs or executive/senior vice-presidents talking to their boards of director, the chairman presenting at a stockholders meeting, or a manager giving a briefing to an executive committee. It could be you. "Bad news" might be that your organization (company, division, department, area, region, etc.) did not meet its planned goals and objectives for the quarter or year—maybe even missed it by a wide margin. Or it could be reporting about any major problem or undesirable situation that cropped up or one that otherwise proved disappointing and impacted the organization in a negative way (e.g., big law suit, natural disaster that affected your company, loss of a major supplier, a major deal with a customer that went to your competitor, errors that caused extensive damage in a plant or strategically important system).

Communicating bad news is never pleasant for the messenger and it's not looked forward to by the audience either. But there is a "good" (effective) way to communicate bad news that can be done with credibility, ethics, and overall professionalism. In my discussions with senior decision makers, there were several critical areas of consensus about how to do it right.

Don't Delay and Come Clean

First of all, *never* delay bad news. Bryce Lensing, executive vice-president of credit at First Interstate Bank of Texas, N.A., told me, "Don't avoid delivering the message thinking that you can soften the blow by delaying. It only makes it worse. Delaying is *always* a poor tactic! Bad news rarely comes as a surprise—it grows incrementally."[2] People might delay delivering bad news because they talk themselves into believing that they need a lot more information (than they really need) to prepare themselves. Another reason is that people might fear being "shot as the messenger." Finally, it's just not pleasant to face an audience that way.

Bill Teague, CEO and president of the Gulf Coast Regional Blood Center in Houston, immediately notifies the Chairman of his board when an important problem erupts. And he sends out faxes to other designated board members (who need to be informed right away) outlining the situation and what steps are being taken to handle it. This gives them quick information and also an opportunity to give Teague insights and ideas to deal with it. And he continues keeping people in the loop as the situation unfolds. "Absolutely no surprises!" he states.[3]

It's vital to be forthright and give your audience *full and accurate disclosure* of the problem or bad news situation. Allen Brown, executive vice-president of trust and private banking for First Interstate Bank of Texas, N.A., told me, "My audiences would always want to know just how bad a situation is—they want the total picture. There's got to be the utmost integrity behind giving the facts and the numbers. The best way is to just come clean—lay it on the line."[4] The audience deserves to know how bad it is and why, what will happen if certain scenarios are played out, and what's been both the impact of the problem to date and corrective measures to deal with it. Bill Teague, like all the other executives who commented on this topic, agrees, "Tell the absolute truth. Be totally honest. The worst thing to do is to hide information or somehow convey information that is not founded in fact." Bryce Lensing cautions, "It's death trying to cover up, hide material, or not give the straight scoop."

If your toptalk involves several topics of which significant bad news is one, then address it immediately. Otherwise, it might give the impression you're beating around the bush. If it's "minor" bad news, you can decide to discuss it in the middle of your presentation, but never at the end—you don't want to end on a low note. And by covering bad news early on, you give your audience a period of time to rethink it and let them have an opportunity to come up with last minute ideas or comments.

Some people make the mistake of painting the problem a bit more rosy than hard facts and self-honesty would have it. Never tell the audience, "It's going to be okay" when it's not. It's better to be conservative and get all the bad news over with at once. You don't want to go back the next month with more residual bad news . As Allen Brown notes, "Once everybody's conditioned to how bad it could be, then that's when you can start climbing out of the hole." Bill Teague concurs, "Some people try to soften the bad news by putting 'positive puffs' around it. People grab at anything positive and optimistic and focus on the 'puffs' so they don't get the real extent and severity of the problem."

An effective way to position the situation is to inform the audience of two scenarios: (1) worst case and (2) most likely outcome. The worst-case scenario prepares them to deal with the rock-bottom situation; the most likely outcome tells them of a high probability likelihood of what will unfold: "While you've just heard of the worst-possible-case situation, this is probably what will happen based upon the evaluation we've done so far." Executives seldom give a "best case" estimate, since, again, people tend to focus on that. However, if you decide to give a best-case estimate because you believe it stands a reasonable chance of coming about, you can carefully guard your optimism with couched words such as, "I really don't think this will happen. However, if [this happens] and that [happens] then we'll see the likelihood of this coming about."

The "know your audience" recommendation especially applies to communicating bad news. Some audiences prefer a very blunt, direct, no-nonsense approach with "spirited exchanges" encouraged, while others require a more subtle, get-into-it-slower approach. Some ask for lots of detail; others want crisp summaries only. There are those audiences that want to help develop the solution while others look for complete leadership from the toptalker who is dealing with the problem.

The Audience Wants Ownership and Leadership

Make the bad news very simple to understand and don't confuse the audience with a lot of data. Lay out the facts as concisely and simply as possible and boil it down to the essence of the problem or situation. Toptalkers must be careful not to use visual aids as a crutch (or talk to them instead of the audience). The toptalker needs to personally connect with them and maintain a close human interaction. The group needs to know it's YOU who is talking and taking charge of the situation. They need to feel your sincerity and your high degree of concern for the situation. Put as much of yourself into it as you can.

One way to display concern for the problem is to take "ownership" of it. According to Allen Brown, "You want to show that you're on top of what's going on—that you're taking charge to see it through. The audience has to know that you're doing everything that you know to do." Also show them that you're open to their ideas, suggestions, and other comments. Take-charge leadership means communicating a solution to the problem.

Here are some areas to cover: (1) review with the group what has happened since they were last informed of the problem; (2) describe your plan to deal with the situation; (3) explain the options you considered and why you chose a particular one as solution; (4) list the next steps you will take; (5) let people in the group know what their specific responsibilities are in helping to solve the problem; (6) explain the situations that are outside your control that would affect the outcome of the solution (e.g., economic changes); (7) describe the incremental (oral or written) reports you will provide on the progress of the situation; and (8) ask for audience feedback and ideas.

Leadership involves being confident, poised, and secure when delivering bad news. Bill Teague even notes that there are times when appropriate (tasteful and timely) humor can suddenly break the uneasy tension of unpleasant news. A remark from the audience or a witty analogy from the toptalker can explode away unproductive stress. "People always need to take their responsibilities seri-ously, especially when communicating bad news, but they should-n't take themselves too seriously. That adds to dire and uncomfort-able feelings," notes Teague. Humor that makes a point should always be a possible tactic to use.

Smart Strategies for Modular Content Design and Effective Time Allocation

Suppose that you requested to have 30 minutes allocated on the meeting agenda to give your presentation to the executive commit-tee. First of all, *don't* assume: (1) that you'll have the full amount of time available when you show up and that (2) that you'll be talking the entire time. I learned a valuable lesson about 10 years ago. I had to give an important presentation to the marketing vice-president for the computer company I worked for. He told me that I had 30 min-utes to "do my thing" as he put it. A competent and bright, but tem-peramental and mercurial individual, he was renowned for running his "zoo" meetings (as they were called) in a highly chaotic, any-thing-goes fashion. I figured I'd really have 10 minutes to present if he was typically behind schedule, and I was prepared for a tight summary presentation to last that long. However, after he introduced me to his group, he said, "Ray, you've got four minutes. *Go!*" I reached down in my stack of about 10 overhead transparencies and pulled out the last visual and *started*, "In conclusion . . . " and I cov-ered the essence of my main points. The lesson I learned was be prepared to give an ultra-brief summary of your toptalk at all times! You've probably had few experiences like that, but the point is don't plan your presentation based upon how much time you've been told that you have.

A smart strategy of *flexibility* and *adaptability* concerning time and content design will greatly boost your chances of meeting your objectives in spite of any situations that may crop up. Here are the parts of that strategy:

1. Ask for more time than you think you'll need. If you are cov-ering new ground with an audience or anticipate lots of questions or resistance to your toptalk, play it safe by asking for more time (if you can get it) on the agenda than you think you might need. Many presenters *under*estimate how long their toptalk will take or the extent of discussion connected with it. So if you think you'll need 20 minutes to present and handle questions, ask for 30 minutes, for example. That extra time is a safety net to prevent you from rushing and to give you more time to reach your objectives. If you get done sooner, the audience will greatly appreciate it.

2. Always prepare for audience discussion. Executives like, want, and expect *interaction* during a toptalk. They don't care to sit and listen to someone jabber for 30 minutes without the opportunity to ask questions, make comments and recommendations, and discuss points among themselves and with the toptalker. This is a required prerequisite to their making a decision regarding your proposal or plan. How much interaction time should you allow for? If they're hearing about your topic for the first time and you're asking them to make some decision or some level of commitment to it, you'll need to give them more time than if they're fairly well-informed about your proposal.

As a general rule of thumb, if you're permitted a total of 30 minutes on the agenda schedule, I typically allocate 15–20 minutes for my talking portion and 10–15 minutes for interaction time (either during the toptalk or after my talking portion). If I anticipate resistance, or concerns about my proposal, I'll speak for 10 minutes and devote 20 minutes for discussion because they'll be peppering me with questions or possible retorts. I'll need more "maneuvering" time to persuade them. If they're a docile audience and very familiar with my information and favorable toward my anticipated request for approval, however, I'll plan on about 25 minutes talk time and 5 minutes discussion time.

3. Build in several levels of detail into your presentation and be prepared to shift gears quickly. If you want "toptalk insurance for protective coverage" to help guarantee getting your main points across to your audience, you want to build in flexibility and adaptability into your content by creating *three levels* of information content (shown in illustration 4-5. The first level should be a condensed, summery version of your toptalk because you need to always consider the probability that you'll be asked to "keep it short" since "we're really behind schedule today." For example, if you originally planned on spending 20 minutes talking, design one version of your presentation to last 10 minutes *or less* covering only the critical highlights and priority information of your presentation. Even though you won't be able to cover the details to the extent you'd like to, this "emergency" shortened version should provide enough overview points to generate interest and enable you to come back at the next meeting to fill in where you left off.

The second, or planned (normal length) version of your toptalk contains all the information of the shortened version, but with sufficient detail and information to *adequately* support your major points. One effective way to do that is to create visuals aids that consist of summary information (for the condensed toptalk) and visual aids with follow-on details that flesh out the highlight points.

The third level of detail is to have information and accompanying visual aids *in reserve.* This will enable you to deal with questions that go beyond the level and types of information you've planned to present. This consists of even more detailed information on any major point you are making or information about topics not directly related to your presentation, but that might elicit questions too. For example, let's say you are giving your normal length version of your toptalk and you're covering the implementation plan for your new marketing program and an audience member asks, "Can you describe the specific activities you have planned over the next six months to get your program going?" Because you anticipated that question, but didn't feel the need to spend time on it unless someone asked, you nevertheless prepared yourself with reserve information—more details—on your visual aids to cover it.

Modular Concept of Content Design

Illustration 4-5
"Attractiveness Factors" of Your Proposal or Plan

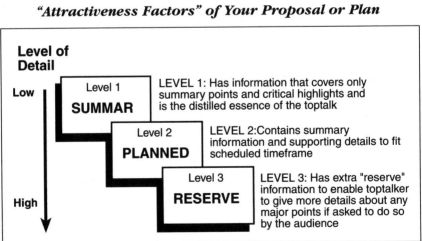

When you hear someone refer to a toptalker as presenting a great plan, ideal solution, optimum proposal, excellent approach, superb proposal, or wonderful idea, what do these mean? What makes an executive audience choose one idea, project, or plan over another? What specific factors color their decisions and motivate them to support a toptalk's objectives? There are a number of criteria that executives are generally concerned with whether it's a plan, major physical or operations expansion project, innovative idea to be considered, or a new venture to enter into. By understanding these considerations, you can design your strategy and content to adequately address them. When listening to a toptalk, the executive audience members are asking themselves if the presenter is reaching the conclusions they want him or her to reach. Is the toptalker balancing the right considerations, and are the issues being raised the ones that the audience thinks are priorities? Does the person recognize the constraints the group is operating under? Following are some key proposal considerations executives evaluate during a toptalk:

Short Timeline. This refers to the time it will take to get the project or plan implemented. The shorter the time period you can solve a problem, get a project completed, or take advantage of an opportunity, the more the group is willing to support it. In today's rapidly changing world, business executives are fearful of putting their resources into long-term projects (5+ years)– especially where technology is changing—unless they're assured of getting a safe return on their investment.

Flexibility and Adaptability. It was the Roman writer Publilius Syrus who said, "It is a bad plan that admits of no modification." The more your plan or project can be readily shown to adapt to changing technological, market, economic, competitive, or other situations that might impact it, the more comfortable people will feel about endorsing it. Executives are hesitant to lock themselves into a rigid plan or project that is costly and difficult to change once implementation is under way.

Minimum Disruption to Operations. Decision makers know that innovation and progressive change will cause a certain amount of discontinuity in the operations of the business. But they want to know that your plan or project will keep disruptions to an acceptable—"reasonable"—level. For example, if a toptalker is advocating implementing a new parts distribution system that will improve accuracy, speed, and efficiency, but will require some "pain" in the transition from old to new, executives will want to be assured of a carefully laid out plan for the changeover process that causes minimal morale problems, operations glitches, and customer complaints.

Short- and Long-term Benefits. The pressure for executives and managers at all levels is always on meeting short-term quarterly production and financial goals as opposed to planning for longer-term growth. If your toptalk proposal can meet both short- and long-term needs of the organization, it will have much added value.

Good Alignment and Strategic Fit. The more your idea or project can be shown to fit within the defined vision, mission, strategic priorities, and directions of the organization, the more, it will be seen as timely and appropriate. If your proposal or plan flows in accordance with the values, beliefs, philosophies, and operating guidelines of your audience, it will stand more of a chance of being accepted. Organizations typically have periodic (sometimes changing) "hot buttons" that focus their attention, motivation, and effort. It might be beating a certain competitor, a push for dramatic cost-cutting, a desire to be the leading-edge innovator, or a rush to grab marketshare. If you can show a cause-and-effect connection between your proposal and helping the audience meet one of their hot-button goals, you'll garner their support.

Attractive *Relative* Return On Investment. The shorter the payback period of your project, the greater the return on investment it brings, the more cost savings or revenue generation and profits can be shown for your project or program, and the higher the costs-to-benefits ratio, the more attractive it will be to your audience. You need to determine and meet the financial justification criteria that the board deems acceptable (e.g., all capital expansion projects must meet an internal rate of return of at least 15 percent). All companies have their own set of financial criteria (typified by financial ratios, net present value calculations, break-even points, etc.) that they use to evaluate the worthiness of that investment. Remember that if you're asking for funding of a major project or program, you're also competing with other potential uses of those funds. Executives are evaluating your project in relative terms by viewing "opportunity costs" —what they might lose or gain by choosing to fund your project over others.

Acceptable Resource Requirements. The fewer resources (people, equipment, plant, money, supplies) that you can show your project requires, especially if those resources have to be pulled from other priority areas in the organization, the more receptive your audience will be toward it. If your plan is resource-heavy, you'll have to compensate and justify it by highlighting its importance and (tangible and intangible) returns on investment. Executive audiences always want to know how much your project will cost and what resources are needed. Therefore, it's important to use conservative figures (where the ratio of legitimate/realistic costs to proposed costs is perceived as accurate) that will instill confidence in the audience.

Tangible and Intangible Benefits. Executives prefer that you not spend precious time focusing on the features or details of your proposal or ideas. Instead, concentrate on the anticipated positive results, outcomes, goals, and overall benefits of your proposal. Tangible benefits (e.g., increased productivity, efficiency, quality, greater innovation, improved customer service, reduced waste, or greater profits) are those that can be quantified, measured, and evaluated. But also include the *intangible* benefits such as improved morale and motivation, greater prestige for the organization, or better public relations.

"WIIFM" Message. Paul D. Lovett, writing about meetings in the Harvard Business Review notes, "Decision makers are as often motivated by friendships, concerns for popularity, and self-interest as by the cold, hard facts gleaned from rigorous analysis."[1], Whenever possible and however appropriate (saying it overtly or subtly), indicate how members in your audience will directly or indirectly benefit from supporting your program or proposal. When making a decision, people often wonder, "What's In It For Me? (WIIFM)—how can this project help me and my department or division, for example. You've got to try to appeal to personal motivations.

Politically and Culturally "Correct." As a toptalker, if you design your proposal in a way that accommodates in-house politics and fits within the culture of an organization, you stand a greater chance of people uniting in support of it. You may have a solid worthwhile proposal that may be rejected because the audience feels it won't survive the political gauntlet.

Milestone Measurements. Executives like to know about the ongoing progress of their decisions. Suppose your plan, project, or program has an operating life or implementation time of two years, for example. During your presentation, communicate that your plan has milestone dates in there to measure whether everything is on target or how far off they are. This gives the executives an opportunity to reassess their original decision and decide to cut off the project, help modify it, or let it continue as is. Milestone measurements add a safety factor into a proposal.

Success Factors and Risk-to-Gain Ratio. The more clearly your toptalk spells out in detail the characteristics that you've designed into it that help to ensure the complete success of your project or program, the more readily the audience will make a commitment to support you. Executives want to know that the objectives of your plan will be safely met. Saying something like, "There are six specific reasons why we feel that this new marketing program will be a resounding success. One . . ." Another way to persuade them is to explain and describe the risk factors and the potential gain factors of your proposal in a way that clearly minimizes their concern.

Solid Plan. Your proposal has a better chance of approval when the audience perceives that you've done your homework excellently—that you've performed a comprehensive and accurate analysis and created a thorough and effective plan where all critical factors have been meticulously thought out. Your plan shows all the detail and smart strategy and contingency steps to handle problems, setbacks, resistance, and other factors that might threaten its success.

Six: Rehearse Your Toptalk

My experience tells me that just about everybody agrees with the concept of rehearsal before an important presentation. Yet, few actually do it to the extent they should. Some tell me they feel foolish talking to themselves, others have said they don't have time, and some note that they're more dynamic when they do it spontaneously. The fact is: *rehearsal is critical before a major toptalk.* That's where you take your presentation on a "shakedown cruise" to get the kinks out and to get a good understanding of the flow of material and to determine where to put vocal emphasis, how much time to spend on each visual aid, how to smoothly shift into giving more detail if asked to.

When you rehearse several times, your confidence level goes way up. You absorb the information into you and you become a master of it. As a result, you can be YOU—more natural, dynamic, conversational, and overall more effective. Actually, by rehearsing, you appear to be more spontaneous as opposed to stilted or wooden. You don't have to intensely concentrate on what to say next, which stifles your personality and poise. With rehearsal, everything falls into place and goes more smoothly. *Rehearsal is insurance.*

If you're dead against rehearsing your presentation word for word—as if you were actually giving it—at least consider just mentally going through it several times by thinking about what points you will cover and what questions to anticipate. If anything, you must carefully rehearse your introduction word for word because that's needed to get off to a fine start. And rehearse your conclusion because it's natural to appear a bit nervous when asking for audience approval of your plan or proposal.

Chapter
FIVE

Overcoming Boardroom Speaking Fear

No good work is ever done while the heart is hot and anxious and fretted.

—Olive Schreiner

Several years ago, I received a telephone call from an anxious marketing executive from a leading Silicon Valley software company. While he tried to blanket it with a deliberate, controlled style of speaking, you could feel the tension rippling from his voice. He probably wasn't aware of the sound of his pen's vigorous tapping against something as it formed an urgent cadence with his words, "I'm calling because I need some assistance quickly. I got your name from Ken 'C' who belongs to our Executive Forum Club in our city. He said you helped his company's team to design and give their tough boardroom presentation last year. My group is putting together a very creative and aggressive new marketing plan to present to our CEO and the board of directors in three weeks and I'm wondering if you're available to help us. Our approach is different from anything we've ever done, and I believe it can slingshot our company past our two major competitors within the next 18 months. A whole lot is riding on this potentially big-win, but higher-risk plan that will be scrutinized to the nth degree by the board. To be frank with you, you might say my program development team is in a state of repressed panic, if you know what I mean."

I knew what he meant—I've been there many times myself. What he was really saying was that HE, not just his imaginative marketing plan would be *scrutinized.* After relaxing a bit and describing his background and the details of the far-reaching program, I found him to be a competent and otherwise confident manager. He was experiencing anxiety when confronted with a daunting task and potentially tough audience. He was one of hundreds of people who have voiced to me their fear of speaking before groups—particularly influential ones. He and his team were coming down with a strong case of "scrutinitis"—the dread fear that everything they say and do will be minutely examined with a super critical eye and probing inquiry. It was the English statesman, orator, and author Edmund Burke who put this paralyzing effect into perspective, "No passion so effectively robs the mind of all its power of acting and reasoning as fear."

Speaking jitters affects *all* of us to a degree. I *still* occasionally get deep pangs of it before important speaking events. I've seen otherwise stainless-steel-spined executives turn into "jelly legs" when speaking before a new audience. Almost everyone feels vulnerable—out there on a limb—when the spotlight's turned on them. The more important the group and the more critical the outcome, the greater the feeling of having a "near death" encounter. My research and experience tells me that that people typically worry about five areas when it comes to a toptalk: (1) making mistakes (even small ones); (2) not having all the answers; (3) damaging their careers; (4) freezing up or appearing nervous; and, (5) being boring.

Creative communication leadership necessitates that we speak in a relatively poised and relaxed state, and that's why I believe it's necessary to talk in detail about the reasons and solutions revolving around speaking anxiety. This chapter will cover the reasons, symptoms, and remedies for dealing with the fear of speaking to groups.

HOW TO TURN STRESS INTO TOPTALK SUCCESS

Eons ago, our ancestral beings (Neanderthals and Cro-Magnons) evolved to develop a powerful and quick response to danger in order to preserve their species. Those who roamed the earth and had to face daily physical dangers (e.g., mastodons, roving sabertooth tigers, and erupting volcanoes) would experience a sharp survival response. Faced with immediate impending danger, the body's mechanism would almost instantaneously prepare itself—physically and mentally—to stand tall and fight to the death or run with boosted speed and agility to quickly escape the threat from man, beast, or environment. This "fight or flight" response syndrome (first described by Dr. Walter B. Cannon, a celebrated professor of physiology at the Harvard Medical School at the turn of the century) was an inborn response to short-term stress that persists today in a form quite similar to that of our prehistoric cousins.

The fight-or-flight response is also triggered by a different threat related to speaking in front of influential groups—a psychological, emotional, and mental threat. If we think there is a possibility of our toptalk "bombing," we create a vivid image of our reputation, our prestige, or our livelihood disintegrating before our eyes. When we perceive this "catastrophic event" of losing the respect, affection, and trust we crave from an audience, our body, which is conditioned by millions of years of evolution, responds as if there were a *real* life-and-death threat. As black foreboding thoughts permeate our mind, a "siren" goes off in our brain (like an alarm signaling DANGER!), sending a rushed message to various glands in our body. The hypothalamus signals the pituitary to secrete ACTH (adrenocorticotrophic hormone) into the bloodstream. The ACTH reaches the two adrenal glands, located at the top of each kidney, stimulating them to secrete extra amounts of epinephrine (commonly known as adrenaline) and norepinephrine into the bloodstream.

Adrenaline, a powerful stimulant, rushes to the heart, skyrocketing the heart rate and pulse up to 200 beats per minute—about triple the normal rate. Blood pressure increases, breathing rate speeds up, and the flow of blood is increased to all muscles and vital organs, including the brain. The digestive tract slows to a halt to reserve energy for other "higher priority" organs. Metabolism is sped up and there's a sense of heightened hearing, smell, and touch. The "body machinery" is supremely ready to fight or run and this response occurs practically in the blink of an eye. But where's the fight and where's the danger when we face an audience? As the famous psychiatrist and psychologist Carl Jung said, "It all depends on how we look at things, and not on how they are in themselves."

The Shake, Rattle, and Roll Symptoms

There are strong, multiple symptoms that occur when you get an *adrenaline rush* triggered by the fear of speaking. I call it the "shake, rattle, and roll" syndrome, where emotions and body parts go into a kind of massive jingling state of dis-euphoria. Adrenaline is produced in direct proportion to our anxiety and fear. When the heavy adrenaline rush occurs combined with hydrochloric acid being released in the stomach (as another by-product of stress), it makes us suffer nausea or vomiting. At this point, the butterflies you were previously feeling in your stomach turn into killer bees. It's time to dial 1-800-NO PANIC.

There is a whole range of mental, emotional, and physical symptoms and manifestations caused by speaking anxiety either before or during a presentation. Some of these may seem comical to those watching in the wings, but they're traumatic to people going through it. Nervousness and anxiety can surface its ugly head in a multitude of appalling forms as the following illustration shows.

Illustration 5-1
Symptoms of Speaking Anxiety

- lump in throat
- hard swallowing
- "mortician's face"
- stammering or stuttering
- lack of appetite
- insomnia
- general feeling of malaise
- death grip on podium
- general clumsiness
- fast-pounding heartbeat

- excessive dry mouth ("cotton mouth")
- frequent licking or smacking lips
- uncontrollable mouth twitch/tick
- fixed "glazed" look
- diarrhea or nausea (or both!)
- shaky knees and feeling of instability
- heavy perspiration (hands, underarms, forehead)
- frequency of urination
- hyperventilation
- dizziness or lightheadedness

- erratic pacing (like caged animal)
- muscle aches (mainly lower back)
- depression or irritability
- trembling all over the body
- inability to slow down or relax
- operating in a "daze and haze"
- feeling like a failure or worthless

- rigid (mannequinlike) posture
- extreme self-consciousness
- self-pity, self-criticism, self-doubt
- inability to concentrate (or total mental "blackout")
- cold and clammy hands
- overall haplessness
- vague fear something bad or unpleasant will occur

Stay "In the Zone"

Look at most dials or instruments on a machine, in a vehicle, aircraft, or other operating equipment and you'll find an acceptable operating range of performance to stay within. The temperature gauge in a car, for example, monitors how hot the coolant mixture is. When it's too cold, your engine may buck and your gas mileage suffers; too hot and your car overheats and can stop dead. For best performance, the temperature should fall within an acceptable (designed) range. The same concept applies to other operating parameters of other types of machinery. And, it's a metaphor for a toptalker's performance as well.

Human beings run at peak performance both physically and mentally. Very similar to the principle of optimum machine performance, athletes, for example, talk about being "in the zone" or "being in the flow"—that moment of peak performance being defined by a state of total attention and focus on maximum achievement. Champion athletes such as those in the Olympics know that too much adrenaline, worry, and fixation on *not* failing instead of *focusing on succeeding* can bounce them right out of "the zone." The best athletes who face this daunting competition (where hundredths of a second or a lead of inches can mean the difference between winning and losing and the pressure of letting down one's countrymen and families), are amazingly adept at bringing themselves to the peak of readiness *without* psyching themselves out.

Stress for Success: The Trick Is to Harness It and Channel It

The same concepts apply to your toptalk performance. Too much adrenaline-caused stress will create unmanageable panic—a kind of human "core melt down" that will cause a person to blow his toptalk to pieces; too little tension (a person is SO relaxed, *he's not worried at all!*) will cause him to be unenthusiastic, dull, and lifeless, and seemingly apathetic about his topic or audience. The ideal performing range (being "in the zone") is to understand that a moderate amount of performance tension is both natural and actually desirable.

Psychologists together with scientists in a number of medical fields are finding out that the way people relate to stress can make a major difference in the outcome of a sports or entertainment performance, for example. People who are excited about the challenge and opportunity to be recognized for a job well done and who generally feel optimistic, and who prepare themselves to bounce back from failures develop a *positive stress response.* Their body has extra adrenaline and sugar in it that helps to "charge them up" with positive expectations of peak performance. Others, who dread the upcoming event and reinforce this feeling with an endless loop self-message, "I think I'm going to fail," produce a *negative stress response* that not only produces adrenaline, but cortisol, which hurts performance and can lead to feelings of inadequacy and, over the long haul, can lead to depression.

Harnessing one's psychic energy to keep the adrenaline at just the right level will ensure that you project energy, excitement, and presence while still enabling you to maintain the needed amount of inner calm, alertness, and sharp mental focus. You don't want to turn the adrenaline tap off (you need some adrenaline flow), but you certainly want to do without a gusher! Using relaxation techniques and positive self-talk such as those explained in this chapter will help to ensure that you're operating at just the right level—"in the zone!"

BEATING THE FOUR PHOBIAS OF TOPTALK

If you've read any books about public speaking over the last 10 years or so, you've probably read the reference about the bestseller *The Book of Lists*[1] which had shown that the number one fear (out of the 10 major fears) that Americans have is the fear of public speaking—greater than the fear of heights (number two), deep water (number five), or even death (number seven). A survey published several years ago in *Dental Health Advisor* magazine even listed speaking in public as the number one fear (27 percent listed it as the most common source of fear). Visiting a dentist was listed as the number two source of fear with 21 percent "mouthing" that statistic. Fear of heights ranked third. Other more recent studies verify this peculiar distaste for being called upon to address an audience.

But, whether you call it stagefright, performance anxiety, stress, or speaking jitters, the reasons essentially boil down to some type of psychological *fear*—the fear of failing to perform to the audience's expectations, fear of hurting our delicate egos in some way, fear of losing the admiration and/or respect of the audience, fear of letting ourselves down. Some experts see all anxieties and phobias as manifestations of the same fear: *the fear of being fearful*. (Remember President FDR's famous depression-era caution: "The only thing we have to fear is fear itself"). As George Bernard Shaw said, "There is always danger for those who are afraid of it."

It's almost certain that anxiety increases the more a person views his or her presentation as an important "performance" that will be carefully observed and judged by "critics." In a discussion I had with a group of upper level managers regarding their feelings of being assessed in the boardroom, almost all recall at least one major incident of catching "scrutinitis." As one painfully put it to me, "There have been times when I almost felt like a male version of a Miss America contestant being judged in the major categories."

Instead, when people envision their toptalk performances as *neutral forums* for them to simply communicate good information to the audience and when they picture a positive reaction to their talk, their anxiety levels begin to plummet. It's not easy to do, but many of us need to change our mindset by envisioning that big presentation as nothing more than a natural conversation with the audience instead of some critical, formal, life-or-death, one-shot performance.

The term I use most often relating to speaking anxiety is "phobia," which is described as an *obsessive or irrational* fear or anxiety. The four major phobias associated with giving a toptalk are: (1) stagefright; (2) ridicule; (3) failure; and (4) fear of those in power.

Stagefright Is Phobia One

All eyes are focused on YOU!

The first of these complicated-sounding phobias we face in executive speaking (or any group speaking situation) is commonly called "stagefright," but scientifically named, *topophobia*, which is the fear of performing in front of an audience. Numerous studies have shown that about 80-85 percent of the general American population often feel *uncomfortably* anxious about speaking in public. It's surprising to know that confident successful professionals in all fields are afflicted—to some degree—by this psychological malady. Attorneys, politicians, public relations executives, entertainers, evangelists, salespeople, and others are not immune to its biting sting. Even the fellow giving a toast at his best friend's wedding gets the shakes in front of his loving and supportive friends and family.

Do we know why people get stagefright? To date, no precise cause-and-effect relationship—no proven theory—has been established. Are certain personalities more prone to this type of speaking anxiety? Psychologists and psychiatrists have not been able to find a set personality pattern in those afflicted; some are confident, outgoing, and articulate, while others are introverted and retiring.

The feisty, "kick-ass-and-take-names" former CEO of Chrysler, Lee Iacocca, was apparently a shrinking violet in front of audiences many years ago, but took formal speech lessons, and this was credited with helping him surge ahead in the automotive industry. Fidel Castro surprised an interviewer several years ago when he confessed, "Let me tell you something that people may not believe. I HAVE stagefright!" This from a man who would speak for hours displaying nothing but raw power in his voice and bravado in body language as he was bellowing veiled epithets against Yankee imperialism. And Winston Churchill, one of the twentieth century's most articulate and stirring speakers, actually collapsed out of fear during a House of Commons speech early in his career.

Roger Ailes, speech writer and media consultant for U.S. Presidents, tells of a poignant stagefright incident in his book, *You Are the Message.*[2] When Ailes was an executive producer of the Mike Douglas talk show, he recalls how a tough Marine Corps general who was a Vietnam Congressional Medal of Honor winner suddenly froze up five minutes before the show in a fit of extreme stagefright and said he *would not* go on. Ailes told the general that unless he went out there, he would tell the millions of viewers about it. Instead of retreating, the general charged ahead in a somewhat shaky fashion, but recovered nicely after several minutes. As Ailes tells it, the general braved machine-gun fire, booby traps, artillery shells, and death all around him only to be terrified by a receptive, friendly audience and a set of television cameras facing him.

Courageous presenters and performers who experience stagefright fight past their fears and anxieties. Some have *reduced* their stagefright; others have successfully learned to live with high levels of it. And some fortunate others in the limelight, like Robin Leach, host of the television program *Lifestyles of the Rich and Famous*, proudly notes that "I've never had it." Perhaps it's all the champagne, caviar, and yachting that keeps him mellow.

In our survey study, we asked the responding executives this question: "In general, when you have to give an important formal business presentation (or when giving a public speech), how would you best describe your typical feeling before giving your talk?" Two percent replied that they experience *extreme stagefright*; 22 percent had a *moderate degree* of discomfort; 59 percent said they usually had a *mild feeling* of apprehension; and 17 percent said they usually experienced *no* stressful emotions. All told, a total of 83 percent, then, experienced some varying degree of topophobia.

Now, these figures reflected executives usually speaking in front of their peers or subordinates. It would seem to bear out that an executive's stagefright would almost always be *greater* when speaking in front of noncompany groups (that are new to them). These and other statistics show that fear of speaking is perfectly normal. But it's the crippling, harmful degree of it that can, unfortunately, dictate the limits of one's career or overall accomplishments. Not corrected, stagefright leads to stage*flight*.

We also wanted to find out how executives reacted to people who displayed some stagefright in front of them, so we asked them this question in our survey: "If a speaker displays slight-to-moderate nervousness during portions of his or her presentation, does that *negatively affect* that person's credibility or professionalism with you?" We asked them to check off only one of four response choices—56 percent agreed with the statement that, "No, a little nervousness would not necessarily hurt the speaker in my eyes," and 5 percent chose to agree with this statement, "No, a display of nervousness would not bother me at all or affect my impression of the speaker."

Nearly a quarter of the respondents, 23 percent, very much cared about a confident job by agreeing with this statement: "Yes, the speaker would project a weak or otherwise negative impression of himself or herself to me," and 16 percent were still judgmental, but a bit less critical by saying that, "Yes, the credibility or professionalism of the speaker might be slightly tarnished in my opinion." The implication from both the study and my discussions with executives is that most of them are relatively forgiving of minor nervousness from a presenter, but tend to reserve more respect for those who exhibit confidence and calm and who command presence in front of them.

Ridicule Is Phobia Two

Sticks and stones will hurt your bones, but words and looks can harm you too

The second type of speaking-related phobia is scientifically termed *katagelophobia*, which is the fear of ridicule. Human nature is such that we will go to practically any extremes to place our egos in a safe, protected emotional cocoon far from the slinging spears of our (imagined or real) attackers. I've had some people tell me that their executive audience sliced and diced them and their presentation like a furiously churning food processor. One seasoned advertising executive in his late forties told me, "I thought our creative theme and program would bowl over even these hard-core important clients. They were absolutely brutal in their attack—the worst I've experienced since I was in my twenties. I felt so shocked, vulnerable, and embarrassed, especially with my boss there. I can't tell you how that affected my self-esteem for months afterwards. I dreaded the thought of my next tough, high-level customer presentation."

Comedians call a performance with a tough audience a "hell gig" where heckling or dead silence replaces raucous laughter and applause. Bombing in front of an audience causes a presenter to bring on himself or herself immediate and deadly *self*-ridicule that further accelerates the performance decline. From my experiences, I've found most executive audiences to be appropriately demanding in terms of expecting high quality in the toptalk, but they certainly don't qualify as "corporate hell gigs." Actress Celeste Holm said, "We live by encouragement and die without it—slowly, sadly, angrily." But sometimes that craving for 100 percent audience acceptance is unhealthy and oftentimes unrealistic.

Sometimes ridicule from the audience can take many other, less direct, but still painful forms. One is when the audience simply takes over from the presenter and ignores all attempts by him or her to "take the floor back." Sometimes, the audience (in what may seem like a collective action) can give out strong negative body signals that shout, "I'm bored," "You don't know what you're talking about," or "That was a stupid thing to say."

Many psychiatrists and psychologists believe that stagefright is a learned response as a result of an especially bad experience (or several of them) during a performance. They believe that there is a certain "trauma" to one's ego when a person does poorly in front of a group (especially a group that is seen as important to the speaker). Psychiatrist Joseph Wolpe, the famed founder of behavior therapy and author of the popular book, *Our Useless Fears*,[3] believes that the bedrock of the fear of public speaking involves early experiences that were unpleasant. He feels that it's usually a history of their having been the center of attention in such a way that emotional stress resulted. One poignant case in his book told of a twelve-year-old girl who stood in class to read but misread a word in the sentence, giving the sentence an obscene meaning. Everybody laughed, and she was deeply embarrassed and became fearful of any public exposure after that.

Often we focus on the possibility (worse yet, *probability*) of ridicule. Examples of counterproductive self-talk about the fear of ridicule from an audience might go something like these:

> I know that one of them will come out with some wise-ass comment and that'll mess me up.

> If I get a little nervous, I know they won't respect me. I won't come off as professional and credible.

> They expect people to have all the answers and if they don't, they chew them out. It's so embarrassing!

People who are generally sensitive to any constructive criticism are especially concerned about losing face in front of a group of people (particularly if they have to work with them on a regular basis). Often, like other fears, the perception is a negatively exaggerated substitution for reality.

Failure Is Phobia Three

"Fail" is a terrible four-letter word for most of us.

The third and most impressive and complicated sounding phobia is *kakorraphiaphobia* (try to pronounce it!), which is the fear of failure. When it comes to executive presentations, this indeed may be the biggest and most critical phobia. Picture a successful up-and-coming manager who has been invited to the company boardroom to give an oral report on her innovative plan for improving the company's stalled distribution system. She feels that the reaction to her plan will either dramatically accelerate her career success or cause it to nose dive into an abyss. She's sacrificed all these years to get where she is and she doesn't want to jeopardize her hard won victories in front of all those executives. She wants to succeed—she wants to be seen as a "heroine." But as one-vice president of sales for a major New Jersey-based pharmaceutical company put it to me, "Being a hero is about the shortest lived profession on earth."

Many of us feel it's a clear-cut win/lose or up/down situation with little in between. Blowing a presentation in front of a group of your local club's friends is not the same as falling short with the power brokers who can make or break your career. So this type of pressure and fear of failure, especially for the ultra-ambitious types, can seem overwhelming at times. Barbara Streisand gave a concert in New York City's Central Park in 1967 despite a death threat she received before performing. That caused her to forget her words in front of 135,000 people. She revealed that she went blank. That "failure" in her mind caused severe stage fright. As a result, she refused to appear at live performances for over 20 years.

"Catastrophizing" is a psychological powerhouse that spews forth *H-I-G-H S-T-R-E-S-S*. This involves using our imagination to carefully craft foreboding scenarios that visualize the maximum damage that will occur to us, even as a result of simple mistakes. People who expect the worst will unintentionally "feed" their subconscious minds to actually make it happen. They anticipate and fear failure—and it comes about. As crazy as it may sound, it then confirms to them that they were right in the first place. Catastrophizers should take Friedrich Nietzsche's philosophy, "What does not destroy me makes me strong."

Perfectionists are especially susceptible to catastrophizing. The slightest setback or minor mistake is seen as a total dismal failure. When the executive committee voices some reservations about a proposed plan, for example, some presenters see this as a "no" and take it as a personal rejection, sending them into a downward spiral of depression. However, a more realistic person might see it as a situation that can be salvaged. The optimistic person sees the reservations as obstacles that *can* be overcome with some modifications to the proposal and a reworked strategy to resurrect it with that committee at a later, more opportune time.

People who dwell on failure or mistakes often put themselves through the mental wringer called the "Should Syndrome" both before and after their presentation. This amplifies pressure on them because it focuses on their real (or imagined) shortcomings. The unrealistically high expectations of themselves are almost always unachievable and they see this as "failure," which makes them feel guilty when it is not accomplished. For example, many people will give themselves judgmental messages something like these:

I *should* prepare more for this big presentation, but I'm so busy with other pressing priorities.

I *should* have been more assertive in my request for funding.

I *should* have rehearsed more—I would have been smoother.

What's wrong with me? I *should* have expected that tough question being brought up.

Perfectionists are almost never satisfied with their accomplishments and seldom feel good about themselves because they can never reach the impossible goals and expectations they set. Ask any psychologist or psychiatrist what a contributing factor toward depression and anxiety is and they'll tell you that being a perfectionist is certainly one.

Unnecessarily subjecting yourself to mental anguish for not being perfect or for not achieving enough is not constructive or productive. A more healthy approach is to feel good about what you've done, examine the areas you need to improve upon next time, and just do it without a lot of fanfare and fluttering. Too much introspection, judgment, and self-denigration just adds muscle to building anxiety for future toptalks. I was consulting with and lending moral support to one high-strung executive who typified the perfectionist. As he was about to enter a client company's boardroom, he "jokingly" said to me. "Well, here goes nothing." Guess what? An hour later I found out he was right. Next time you catch yourself putting yourself down or knocking yourself with, "I should . . . I should have . . . I shouldn't," take this advice: *Don't should on yourself!*

Fear of the Powerful Is Phobia Four

Big Shot Versus Little Tot

The fourth phobia is one I call *execuphobia*, which is a fear of being in front of a group of executives or other important and influential people. In many situations, a presenter is going before decision makers to ask them for something—approval or funding (e.g., of a project). Some people with whom I've discussed this fear have compared it to a child going to a parent to ask permission to do something. Most of us are still intimidated by those who tightly hold the reins of power. *Don't let them scare you!*

Dr. Joseph Wolpe reiterates what most of us feel—that two common fears about public speaking concerns the number of people in the audience and the "authority-figure" dimension of the audience. In other words, some aren't fearful when they speak to 10 people, but the prospect of speaking to 200 curls their toes. Other people are relatively at ease when they speak to subordinates, but clutch up (in a kind of psychological fetal position) when facing their bosses.

In execuphobia, people often unconsciously start to tear themselves down using negative self-talk (which might be subconscious) that unfavorably compares themselves to members of the important audience. They set negative expectations leading to feelings of inferiority and insecurity. Examples of execuphobia negative self-talk are:

> They're all so successful and I'm not.
>
> Why should they listen to me? After all, I'm just a senior engineer (a salesperson, a division head, etc.).
>
> They must know so much more than I do.
>
> They're very powerful. I have to try to impress them.
>
> They look and act so . . . well, *important* and supremely self-assured. I'll be nervous around them. I know it!

If we believe our executive audience to be somehow superior, wiser, judgmental, or perhaps even confrontative, then our anxiety will increase. Instead, when dealing with a very high-level audience, you need to project the natural confidence of being "one of them"—to have them accept you as a peer in terms of credibility and maturity (if not experience). Take the advice of the famous baby doctor, Benjamin Spock, who told first-time mothers, "Trust yourself. You know more than you think you do." The same applies to knowledge about your topic and what to do in front of that important group.

PROVEN WAYS TO BEAT SPEAKING ANXIETY

So much that has been written about dealing with stagefright involves quick-fix "techniques" to reduce the symptoms. Later on, we'll cover those. They are, indeed, useful and are proven to be effective in a variety of low-to-moderate speaking anxiety situations. But I believe that if a person is *usually* experiencing *very high-lev-*

els of anxiety before speaking to groups, stress-reduction techniques will have positive, if somewhat *limited* value in addressing strong psychological obstacles that are probably at the forefront. The previous material gave us general insights on phobias, and we need to go further to try to analyze the possible reasons "why" such fear grips us. We need to take a close look at our overall attitude and perspective about life, how we view our standing and relationships with others, and most important, how we see ourselves.

If we believe that speaking anxiety is caused by our victimizing ourselves through negative thinking and self-talk (i.e., thinking ourself into fear via incorrect inferences and unrealistic perceptions versus realities), then we need to catch ourselves "in the act" and learn to reprogram our thought processes over an extended period of time. We can, in essence, "rewire our head" to eliminate faulty thinking. This is the major principle behind *cognitive therapy*, an effective psychotherapeutic approach pioneered by Aaron Beck, M.D., a psychiatrist who has been accorded great renown as a result of his development. Cognition means *thinking*, and self-help takes a lot of constant hard work and perseverance since many of our distorted thought patterns have been methodically wired into our brain over a lifetime of experiences. But it can be done, sometimes by self-disciplined effort and other times with the help of psychologists specializing in performance anxiety problems.

The first step in the rewiring-our-head process is to identify and analyze our thoughts, beliefs, and feelings and ask ourselves if they really represent reality. We need to recognize that negative, limited, or insecure thinking is not only damaging, but self-reinforcing. We need to step back and clearly understand how we interpret situations that are challenging to us (i.e., do we see the glass half full or half empty or do we just see a glass with water?). Do we see a disguised opportunity or a problem? Do we see all audiences as somehow threatening? The next step is to replace negative perceptions with encouraging, positive, realistic thinking.

Ask yourself if you frequently think and feel the following and then record over those thought patterns with a new positive and constructive-based script that will set positive outcomes, focus on your strengths and accomplishments, and build your self-image:

- *Black and white thinking.* Are you a victim of the "no-such-thing-as-in-between" thinking? Instead of viewing life in terms of *absolutes* such as success/failure, win/lose, or right/wrong, begin looking at things existing on a spectrum with a large number of possibilities existing. Free yourself from extremist thinking by seeing a range of situations or possibilities existing with a mix of strengths and weaknesses, pros and cons, and rights and wrongs.

- *Pedestal/gutter positioning.* Are you always comparing yourself to others? Do you drag yourself down in little ways while elevating others? Do you exaggerate your own mistakes or weaknesses while dismissing those of the executives you're presenting to? Instead, see yourself as having special worthwhile qualities or achievements that others don't. Feel proud of that! Also remember that those who may appear impressive may spend tremendous amounts of time and energy devoted to "image management" to hide their faults and weaknesses and to embellish their perceived strengths.

- *Foreboding black clouds.* How do you first envision things turning out—for the better or the worse? Do you concentrate on and worry about all the things that might go wrong or do you ask yourself what you must do to succeed? How do you generally view your future - with promise, uncertainty, or with dread? If you predicted a problematic outcome for your toptalk, for example, and it comes to pass, do you confirm your self-fulfilling prophecy by saying, "See, I was right.... the presentation went bad!" What's needed is to visualize success, achievement, and positive results. It is a proven fact that visualizing positive outcomes will get the subconscious mind working on achieving what we believe and trust will happen.

- *Jumping to rash conclusions.* With little accurate information available to you, do you frequently jump to conclusions that usually prove ill-founded? Do you tend to exaggerate what someone says and blow it out of proportion? Do you misread cues from your audience and see them as negative? Do you find yourself assuming a lot more of a situation than you should? What's needed is to analyze the situation by checking your assumptions with people instead of mind reading, guessing, or wildly speculating.

- *"I don't deserve it!"* Do you find it difficult feeling good about your overall accomplishments at work? Do you sometimes feel you don't deserve success or that you're fooling people regarding your competence and expertise? If you've done an outstanding job with your toptalk performance, for example, do you pass it off as a "fluke"— something that you cannot normally achieve *consistently*? Or, if people compliment you about your presentation, do you feel they are either being politely insincere (to make you feel better) or that they are somehow wrong to feel positive toward you or what you've done? Instead, feel good about yourself and believe that what others say about you in a complimentary fashion is genuine and warranted.

- *Negative Nitpicky.* Are you the type to endlessly dwell on a single small thing you did wrong or some minor negative remark made by someone at your toptalk to the exclusion of all the other overwhelming positive things done or said about you? Do you knock yourself for that one insignificant thing you forgot to mention during your briefing? Realize there will usually be someone who is not satisfied with your presentation. Don't put yourself down for not being perfect. Look at all the good things you did instead. Focus on the 90 to 99 percent of the good things in your toptalk.

I recommend not only reading, but thinking about and applying the principles of positive living from that wonderful, timeless classic book, *The Power of Positive Thinking* by the late Norman Vincent Peale, which you can get in practically any bookstore.

Anticipate . . . Be Prepared . . . Check It Out

It's a well-known fact that the more prepared you are and the more you know your material "cold," the less nervous you'll be. Knowing your information better than anyone else in the room will give you added confidence. Next, it's important to anticipate all types of questions and be prepared to answer them. Your presentation should be organized in such a way that you can easily digress to go into more detail on any area connected with your material. You need to rehearse your presentation several times in front of friendly, but competent "critics" who can give you constructive feedback on your speaking skills and content. Even Presidents of the United States carefully rehearse their speeches and press conferences with their staff prior to important speaking events.

One of the major reasons for escalating anxiety is not knowing what we face—the fear of the *unknown* or the *unpredictable.* As Norman Cousins said, "Where man can find no answer, he will find fear." Before I speak to an important audience, I try to get a feel for the people, the room, the equipment, the overall environment and meeting situation—*I want to know exactly what I'm facing.* If I'm presenting to a larger group that's listening to several presentations and I'm the third speaker on the agenda, for example, I'll sit or stand in the back beforehand if possible (so I can see most of the audience), and I'll scan the group to watch their reactions to the speaker before me. I'll look at their faces and try to visualize them as nice people whom I'll enjoy being with and people who will enjoy listening to me.

Do you remember the last time you went to a training event or outside meeting, for example, and you were in a group of strangers? You felt a bit uncomfortable, until sometime later (probably in the afternoon of the first day), you became closer with the people after getting to know them. The same applies to a group you're about to speak to for the first time. See if you can make some chit-chat with them ahead of time face to face so you're not meeting strangers.

As you begin your presentation, you may be lucky to spot a friendly face in the group smiling at you and perhaps nodding in an approving fashion at you. Focus on that person for a while until you begin to relax more and then give equal eye contact to the other members of your audience—you don't want to neglect them. That "guiding light" person can give you some needed emotional and psychological support to help you get over the initial hump of nervousness.

If you can, go through a last dry run of your entire presentation in the room with the equipment you'll be using. Look around and visualize just how successful you'll be when you do it "live." Finally, develop contingency plans and play "What if . . . ?" games with yourself such as: What if the projector breaks down? . . . What if they want to delay the decision? . . . . What if I were asked to cut my presentation time by 50 percent? . . . What if the main decision maker walks out five minutes after I begin?" Think of every possible situation that might jeopardize reaching your objectives and develop some effective options to deal with them. By being prepared at that level, it will make you feel much more secure that you're in control. Great preparation puts out the fire of anxiety—it's a "fear extinguisher."

Don't Hyperventilate . . . It Makes You Hyper!

The simple act of *proper* breathing can help to lower prespeaking stress and put you in a more desirable psychological state of mind. . . and MUCH more. But the problem occurs when we get all frizzed up and we begin to hyperventilate, which then sends us on a roller-coaster ride of tension. *Hyperventilation* is a medical term and condition brought on by an anxiety attack. A surge of adrenaline usually triggers a gasping reaction that creates a feeling of "air hunger." The sufferer feels that he or she can't breathe, which boosts anxiety. The natural reaction is to unconsciously take *shallow, quick breaths* (if it's more than 14 breaths per minute, you're generally breathing too fast), which results in a variety of unpleasant symptoms that make a person feel tense, jittery, and often light-headed. A downward emotional and physical spiral then results.

When a person hyperventilates, he or she expels more carbon dioxide from the body than normal, leading to a number of chemical reactions. While many people are aware that carbon dioxide is a waste product of the breathing process, it performs the important function of keeping the blood's pH (acid-alkaline levels) in proper balance. Robert Fried, Ph.D., writing in *The Hyperventilation Syndrome*,[4] notes that when breathing is rapid, the carbon dioxide is exhaled before it can do its job. So blood and other body fluids become too alkaline. Because the pH balance regulates the flow of calcium into body tissues, a variation can cause an excess of calcium to rush into muscles and nerves, heightening their sensitivity and making you tense, nervous, and shaky. As a result of the acidity of the blood plummeting (which rises or falls in relation to the level of carbon dioxide present), it provokes symptoms that include tingling or numbness in the lips, palpitations, chest or upper-abdomen pain, spasms in toes or fingers, blurry vision, or faintness. *Bad stuff!*

In addition to affecting blood chemistry, shallow breathing brings on a double whammy—it can actually reduce oxygen to the brain by as much as 20 percent, leading to headache, dizziness, and light-headedness. While the brain comprises only about 2 percent of total body weight, it uses up 25 percent of the body's oxygen. While a short-term loss of oxygen to the brain can affect concentration and mental acuity, a long-term deficiency of oxygen (brought on by a lifetime of unconscious hyperventilation) to the brain can speed up loss of brain cells, affecting overall brain efficiency and causing premature aging of that critical organ. Dr. Fried estimates that at least 25 percent of the population are chronic hyperventilators. This causes breathing muscles (the diaphragm and abdominals) to weaken over time so they can't function properly. It's a viscous cycle of weakening!

I used to think that the advice of breathing into a bag when a person is hyperventilating was an old wives' tale. But there's a definite medical reason for it: As the sufferer breathes into a bag for several minutes, the person will be able to inhale expired air with a *high proportion* of carbon dioxide, and thus the pH balance of the blood will return to normal. But I doubt if it's a good idea to begin your executive presentation with a paper bag firmly clutched to your mouth. Besides, even if you didn't mind looking strange, it would be difficult for your audience to decipher your muffled sounds!

Breathe DEEP for a Sign of Relief . . . and Much More

There's a great "technique" available for you to lower your anxiety level and keep it lowered. And you can use it *anywhere at any time* when stress erupts. It can give your voice improved quality with much more resonance and power to "project" instead of shout. It will prevent hoarseness and sore throat from too much or too vigorous speaking. And it can increase your energy and make you feel more physically fit. This natural breathing technique is used by stage actors and singers, athletes, martial arts experts, professional speakers, and others who want to enhance their physical and mental performance. Yoga practitioners, for example, have long known that proper breathing provides a powerful link between body and mind. A Yoga proverb states, "Life is in the breath; therefore he who only half breathes, half lives." In Yoga, the *prana* or *life force* is the subtle life-giving element extracted from the air we breathe and the more life force you have, the more "alive" you are.

This breathing technique is known by a number of terms: *deep breathing, diaphragmatic breathing, or abdominal breathing.* Most people don't give much thought to breathing since it's *so* natural. A few minutes of conscious deep breathing right before your toptalk can lessen tension, focus your energy and concentration, and give you a heightened sense of confidence and control.

When you inhale properly, the diaphragm (commonly called the "breathing muscle"), a large membrane sandwiched between the lungs and the abdomen, contracts downward so that the lungs have ample room to expand. When you exhale, the abdominal muscles push the diaphragm up against the lungs to help push air out. When you inhale deeply and completely, the diaphragm and abdominal muscles work to maximum capacity. If a person constantly breathes in a shallow manner, these muscles weaken losing the strength needed to accommodate deep, full breaths. With shallow breathing, the diaphragm and abdomen are constricted and the chest takes over. Chest breathing only allows you to inhale and expel only about *one cupful* of air with each breath; deep abdominal breathing draws in *ten times* that amount

Besides relaxing us, as we perform abdominal breathing while we are speaking, a greater volume of air is expelled, giving our voice a deeper, richer, more resonant—*confident*—sound. The reason babies can cry *so* loudly for *so long* and the ability of dogs (even small ones) to bark with such ferocity is because they instinctively use diaphragmatic breathing. Instead of shouting, which is harsh, "tinny" sounding, and strained, we can project our voice to reach far into the audience. Stage actors have long known this technique and Greek and Roman orators, using deep breathing for projection, could talk to large audiences (in the thousands) and still be heard clearly. The public address (PA) system they used back then was "powerful air" (PA).

The diaphragm and abdomen work together to "shoot" a massive column of air that extends from your beltline to your throat. A loudspeaker cone operates on the same principle of moving a mass of air to create sound. Lower frequencies (deep bass tones) require a *larger* movement of air, while higher frequencies (treble tones) don't. If you've ever removed the foam or fabric screen from a loudspeaker cabinet and watched while music is being played, you'll notice how the woofer (the largest speaker for low tones) *visibly* vibrates—oscillating in and out while you can barely see the mid-range frequency speaker move and not see the smallest size high-frequency speaker move at all (it does, but you cannot see it). The human voice is indeed capable of lots of power. Using diaphragmatic breathing, winners of publicized "shouting contests" in this country and in places like Japan have registered OVER 117 decibels of sound, which is approximately 20 percent louder than a chain saw or jack hammer and almost as loud as a jet plane at takeoff!

How to Breathe Deeply

Sit or stand using good posture. Begin by inhaling *slowly* and *deeply* through your nose. It can take up to 10 seconds to fill your lungs to capacity. As you are inhaling, your belly should be expanding fully, your chest should remain still (as you are getting started, you may want to place one hand on your stomach and one on your chest noticing that your hand on your stomach moves outward as you breathe in and your chest hand remains motionless). You should be very aware of the movement of your stomach. Unfortunately, many people actually do the opposite—they tend to tighten their stomachs as they breathe in, and this causes physical and psychological tension to increase.

Next, exhale *slowly* and *deeply* through your mouth, pursing your lips as if to whistle. By positioning your lips this way, you can control how fast you exhale. You want to keep your airways open as long as possible. Remember that as you exhale, your stomach is now deflating (you're pulling your stomach in) while the diaphragm (large muscle under your lungs) expands pushing air out. When your lungs feel empty, begin to inhale again.

You can control the "fullness" intensity of breathing by how long and how deeply you breathe in. Try it several times a day and do it for about a minute at a time. When starting out, you may get slightly dizzy because of all the extra oxygen you take in (so avoid doing it while driving or even walking.). If you get any stomach cramps, stop immediately. If you're recovering from any surgery or muscle injury or have any medical problems that might be affected by this level of breathing, check with your doctor. Breathing deeply can also help you fall asleep faster. Overall, it has many great benefits.

OTHER PROVEN WAYS TO BEAT ANXIETY AND TENSION

Here are some other ideas on how to lower overall anxiety both before and during your big presentation. The following ideas are designed to do one or more of the following: (1) drain (empty) stress; (2) cover it (cancel it out); or (3) get yourself in a positive, relaxed frame of mind by doing something you find enjoyable.

PRAY. I tried every technique (I recommend to others) to relax myself before an important motivational talk I was to give at a big meeting of a major computer company's salespeople and managers in Chicago several years ago. No relaxation technique worked since I was unknowingly giving myself *tons* of negative self-talk. Five minutes before getting up to speak, I was in a state of sheer raw panic and I prayed that God would work a *miracle*. I was skeptical. Guess what? He came through . . . and I did a great job from the very start. It's worked every time since. Because I wasn't very spiritual back then, prayer was my last resort; today it's my first. Larry Dossey, a physician and author of the book, *Healing Words: The Power of Prayer and the Practice of Medicine*,[5] cites more than 130 scientifically verifiable studies done within the last 30 years (with a variety of different religions and prayer styles) that show prayer's overwhelming benefits to help people with anxiety, high blood pressure, and numerous physical and psychological ailments.

STAND BEHIND A PODIUM. This advice goes *contrary* to what most authorities on presentation skills tell people. They recommend that the speaker move away from a podium and get closer to the audience to develop more rapport with them and to generate a stronger stage presence and confident image. In this book, we recommend that also. But . . . IF someone is SO conscious of his or her body shaking and weak knees about to give way as one stands in full ("naked") view of an audience, this is hardly conducive to showing confidence. How can speakers possibly develop rapport with the audience if they feel more vulnerable in full view of them? They can't! So, my advice is this: If you're *very nervous*, "shield" yourself behind the podium when you begin your presentation. After your initial tension dies down, *then* move away from it. It's better to temporarily "hide" behind the podium when you start than to expose your nervous self to the audience and risk losing all your composure.

NO CAFFEINE. Your adrenaline provides you with enough stimulant before your presentation. Don't "wire yourself for 25,000 volts" by drinking several cups of coffee or tea. Drink a decaffeinated beverage and treat yourself to a cup of coffee or tea afterwards.

BE YOURSELF. BE SPONTANEOUS. Present your material in the way you normally talk. Don't focus on being "oratorical" in terms of public speaking. Be conversational, natural, and genuine. Make the members of the audience feel that they are being spoken *with* rather than spoken *at*. Let your personality shine.

EXERCISE. Exercise can burn tension away quickly. Even a quick walk right before your presentation can help. Before major speeches, you may want to exercise in a more vigorous way (assuming your medical and physical condition permits). I normally run 3 miles every other day, but run 6 to 7 miles the day before or the morning of a major speech.

MUSIC. Listening to your favorite music can calm you quickly or can perhaps inspire you. Why not bring along your portable cassette or CD player with you to play music prior to your presentation?

HUMOR. Get laughing in any way you can. Visit a comedy club the night before your big presentation. Call up a friend who makes you laugh. Recall the most amusing situation you've experienced. Laughter causes the body to generate its own powerful painkiller and tranquilizing drugs called endorphins (which means "morphine from within"). Endorphins have been found to be a natural drug three times more powerful than morphine to relax us quickly.

MASSAGE. Have your spouse or companion give you a long massage as near to the appointed presentation time as possible. Or, treat yourself to a thorough session by a licensed masseuse.

HOT TUB. Enjoy luxuriating in a soothing bath with the warm jets of water kneading the tension away.

RELAXATION AUDIOTAPES. Listen to any number of audiocassettes on the market that are made especially to relax you. While I believe in the concept of mediation or the "relaxation technique," which is a variation of eastern-style mediation, I also believe that most people, including myself, find it very difficult to spend the time and energy to meditate. However, listening to a relaxation tape is more passive in nature and takes much less discipline and requires no training as in mediation. Yet, it produces relatively good results.

LOVE MAKING. It works every time—a special romantic dinner before and a long drawn out wonderfest of loving affection and intimacy will do wonders. It will drain your nasty emotions and replace them with a warm afterglow and feeling of serenity!

MOTIVATIONAL/INSPIRATIONAL. Listen to an audiocassette or view a videotape of a motivational and entertaining speaker. Get fired up with a *Can Do!* attitude.

LOOK GREAT. When you are dressed in your very best and groomed to perfection, you'll feel good about yourself and your confidence will soar.

GAMES/HOBBIES. Play an enjoyable game that relaxes, not stresses you out (that's why I avoid golf at least two days before I give a big talk!). Playing cards, sports, board games, miniature golf, video games—any engagement in pleasurable hobbies or pastimes will help you relax.

Now that you have the idea, think of other creative ways to get your mind off the big event and relax doing something pleasurable and enjoyable.

Chapter SIX

How Your Toptalk Can Make a Winning Impression

You are the message. Everything you do in relation to other people causes them to make judgments about what you stand for and what your message is.

—ROGER AILES

You've heard it many times before: Research studies show that we begin to make up our minds about someone after only 10-15 seconds of meeting him or her. That's definitely true of a toptalker. There's an *intuitive assessment* we make. Most people call it it a "gut reaction," because we don't actively analyze the speaker. We just receive quick (sometimes poignant) flashes of insight and feeling. After all, that's what intuition really is: knowing without knowing *how* we know. It's critical that a toptalker make an excellent first impression with his or her high-level audience and maintain it throughout the presentation.

This chapter will describe the important behaviors and traits that a toptalker needs to display in front of executives (or any group) and will cover ways to improve your overall image, charisma, presence, and impact that you make on your audience.

HOW TO MAKE PEOPLE BELIEVE IN YOU AND YOUR MESSAGE

There's a saying in the television industry, "Perception IS reality." We need to clearly understand how people perceive us and our messages. The overall credibility (competency, trustworthiness, and enthusiastic conviction) of a presenter in front of an audience has to do almost totally with how the group *perceives and believes* the speaker to be regardless of the actual knowledge, skills, motivation, and overall expertise that a person has. Otis Singletary, former chancellor of the University of Kentucky, put it, "Whatever people think, is."

Helen Perry, a corporate image consultant based in Houston, tells her seminar audiences that we can form up to ten important assumptions about someone just after meeting them—things such as their trustworthiness and moral character, degree of sophistication, education level, economic status, leadership potential, social skills, communication ability, and motives, among others.[1] It's critical then that we carefully manage and sculpt our image in our business and social lives.

Speaking Podium Can Become a Pedestal

The "speaking platform" is one of the most efficient behavior forums to enable people, if they do an exemplary job, to very quickly and completely display many of their fine personal and professional traits and skills to an audience. You can perceive so much about people by listening to *what* they say, *how* they say it, *how they act* while speaking and relating to the audience. And . . . how they are dressed and groomed.

Being a very polished and dynamic toptalker can boost the image and create a sterling impression of a person sometimes *beyond* the reality of who he or she really is. As Lowell Thomas (famous radio broadcaster and journalist) pointed out, "The ability to speak is a shortcut to distinction. It puts a man in the limelight, raises him head and shoulders above the crowd, and the man who can speak acceptably is usually given credit for an ability out of proportion to what he really possesses."

On the other hand, a very competent, smart, and dedicated individual with below-par communication skills, appearance, and "presence" can, unfortunately, have a less credible impact when first presenting to a new group. It may seem superficial and unfair, but great ideas and their potential fortunes have fallen victim to the foibles and weaknesses of the person presenting them. We typically remember people's negative stand-out traits and appearance more than we do their names. Humorous writer Oliver Hereford pointed out over 70 years ago: "I don't recall your name, but your manners are familiar."

HOW TO SHOWCASE YOUR PROFESSIONALISM

What can you really gauge about a person when he or she is up in front of a group for, say, ten minutes? Can you tell if that speaker is poised, confident, organized, articulate, friendly, intelligent, and open-minded? Or can you tell if he or she appears to be high-strung, negative, opinionated, arrogant, or perhaps a bit of a showoff? Is the person shaky in front of the executive committee—seeming out of place or maybe trying *too* hard to impress? Or, instead, is the person totally relaxed with the decision makers, appearing to be one of them?

Or is the presenter a mechanical "robospeaker," as one chief financial officer from a midwestern machinery manufacturer described one person to me: "He looks and talks like he just fell off Edgar Bergen's [famous ventriloquist] lap." Finally, how is the person "packaged"? Does he or she have high-quality, appropriately stylish clothes, impeccable grooming and makeup, or does some little "flaw" give the impression of not caring enough?

The fact is you CAN and DO form a somewhat *representative composite* of a person's personality profile, values, emotional state, and skills inventory while he or she is presenting. Many people fail to realize that they are not just carriers of information—they ARE the message. It's been widely taught since the golden age of Greece and the Roman empire that *who* says something is as important to the audience as *what* is said. Who you come across as can speak so loudly it can drown out what you're saying.

Do a great job in front of executives who have never seen you before, and you can shift to the fast lane in your organization's career track. Likewise, a presentation can be a forum to spotlight you on center stage for the audience to microscopically scrutinize your limitations, weaknesses, or negative traits. A bad performance before the power brokers can transform you from champ to chump and put you in the corporate penalty box for a while until you redeem yourself and until their memories fade. Break some taboos or make some major errors in judgment while you're at the boardroom podium and you might just be hurriedly updating your resume. It's tough getting over a poor first impression: Once the toothpaste is out of the tube, it's hard to get it back in.

Don't Mistake Image for Mirage

A vice-president of a Dallas manufacturing firm told me of his colleague, a sales executive, "He's lives and breathes 'image.' I don't think he knows who he really is. When you peel away the plastic . . . you find more plastic." A professional image should NOT be an illusion, but a representation of the best picture of who you *really* are and what you're capable of. It shouldn't be window dressing or superficial gloss, but a display of the real merchandise within. Image is part of who a person is—how he or she thinks, feels, acts, and lives. It consists of how you speak, your body language, business etiquette, social skills, your dress and grooming, and any other behavior that affects your professional credibility. *Your image makes a statement.* It's up to you to decide what that is. That's why I recommend that people put their best foot forward in front of an audience and project an image that is appropriate to the situation, audience, and culture of the organization you're presenting to. Smart toptalkers fill the roles they are playing superbly and go to great lengths to shape themselves into the professional leadership image that gets results.

Virginia Horton-Bettman, president of Best Suited for the Executive Image, notes, "Image is not a gimmick, a game, a trick, a lie, or a substitute for knowledge or ability. It is a communication tool, a part of your skills package, and your billboard for advertising who you are, what you do, and how well you can do it."[2] Andy Sherwood, successful executive recruiter in New York City, told me that people who project a good "executive image" are those who are relaxed, confident, well-dressed and who represent themselves as successful people.[3] "The Dress For Success" guru, John T. Molloy, says, "An image is the sum total of many features. The way that a successful person carries himself, the sureness of his posture, the energy in his gestures, the authority in his voice, all play a part. Without seeming to, he makes his presence *felt*.[4]

Corporate image consultant Helen Perry notes that people's dress and appearance *speak before they do* and can tell a whole story before they even reach the podium. When you're first seen by your audience, they'll take your measure in one sweeping, take-it-all-in glance. John McGrath, director of management communications for Argonne National Laboratory and a speech writer and executive coach, cautions, "Your presentation actually begins the moment you walk into the room, not when you approach the lectern. How you act, sit, what you say, how you manage yourself way beforehand *is* part of the presentation. If your demeanor when you first arrive is different than that which you demonstrate later, the audience won't believe it. For example, a person who appears shy while waiting to speak and then suddenly turns into a human dynamo will make the audience think he's acting."[5]

Those Two Hidden Agendas During a Toptalk

Executives often have hidden agenda items when listening to a speaker they've never seen or heard before talk about his or her project or proposal. The first one is to size up the person behind the idea—to make meaning of the human-to-human contact. Afterall, if people simply needed information, a written report might do. Members of the audience are asking themselves various questions such as:

How do I feel about this person?

Do we have things in common?

Do I agree with what he is saying?

Would I like to work with that person or get to know him or her better?

In essence, each audience member, whether they know it or not, asks: "Does this person positively impact me and am I comfortable with him personally and professionally?" The second underlying agenda item involves executives evaluating the "can-do-ness" of the presenter. They wonder about things such as:

Does this person have the *'right stuff'* to get the job done?

Can we depend on her to deliver what's being promised?

Do I want to do what he is advocating?

Can this person benefit me in some way?

If the toptalker is asking the executive group to approve and fund a new project, they're analyzing the ability of the speaker to successfully implement the plan that he or she is proposing. Make no mistake about it, executives are a perceptive lot—they know human nature well. They know that it's one thing to be a good communicator and persuader. There are people out there who can sell dental floss to folks with false teeth. But selling a concept, plan, or project on paper is not the same as demonstrating the ability, mettle, and resolve necessary to successfully *implement* the idea or project when all sorts of threatening obstacles crop up.

A Toptalk Symbolizes What's to Come

An executive presentation is a *microcosm* of a speaker's project or proposal and a barometer of how he or she will carry out the proposed plan or project. An executive presentation tells a lot about the planning, strategizing, leadership, communicating, conviction, human interactions, creative problem solving, and organizing capabilities of a speaker. If that person makes numerous or obvious mistakes, displays faulty thinking or poor judgment, or otherwise fails to impress the executive audience with something as *relatively simple* as a 30-minute oral presentation, what does that say about his or her ability to implement a major project with all its varied complexities?

A speaker who precisely sticks to the allotted time schedule and agenda, who anticipates tough questions and has thought out very effective answers to them, who appears supremely poised and confident, who provides and effectively communicates the exact information the audience needs and wants, who commands the respect of listeners, who handles adversity well in the boardroom discussions, and who projects a total professional aura WILL make a strong positive impression on the audience. Only then will the project be approved, the idea accepted, or the plan funded. In that regard, the executive presentation is like a test—YOU have to pass before your ideas get a grade.

A Winning Combination: Substance and Style

If impressing an executive audience is one of the indirect goals of a speaker, how does one do that? We wanted to find out what made senior decision makers sit up and take notice. We used written surveys and one-on-one interviews with them. In our survey questionnaire, we listed 27 personal and professional traits. We asked the respondents to check off "*the five most important traits that a speaker should exhibit during his or her presentation to you.*" Here are the top five (the numbers represent the percentages of people who voted for that trait as one of the top five*):

1. knowledgeable   79%
2. organized   71%
3. logical   55%
4. confident   43%
5. thorough   31%

Another question in our survey listed 17 diverse skill areas that applied to giving a presentation. We asked the executives to identify which area was "very important," "important," "undecided," or "not important." Nearly all—98 percent—said *knowledge of topic* was "very important" with the remaining 2 percent saying it was "important"; 79 percent said the *ability to be concise, yet thorough, complete, and accurate* was "very important," 19 percent said it was "important," and 71 percent said that *fluency and clarity of communication* was "very important," with the remaining 29 percent giving it an "important" rating.

The Verdict: Know Your Stuff!

It was abundantly clear that the survey respondents were consistently saying that knowing your topic and knowing how to communicate it efficiently and effectively were seen as critically important for a presenter to demonstrate. If given a choice, executives will favor *substance* in a presentation over *style* (the way the information is presented). One CEO from a small manufacturing company we surveyed put this issue in perspective by quoting Mark Twain,

"Thunder is good, thunder is impressive; but it is the lightning that does the work." What they were expressing was that, without solid substance, a great speaking style and image is hollow. Buck Rogers, famed (retired) IBM marketing vice-president, told me he was a great believer in enthusiasm (and is a highly dynamic and polished speaker himself), but . . . "enthusiasm without homework doesn't cut it. I've even told people. 'When you really know what the hell you're talking about, come on back!'"[6]

Numerous decision makers have stressed to me that they want substantive (highly meaningful, accurate, concise, and well-organized) presentations because they've experienced *too many* that are deficient in those areas. They want information communicated simply and clearly to enable them to make easier and more effective decisions. One regional sales manager of a Connecticut chemical company who apparently had a bad batch of presentations given to him recently vented to me, "I might tolerate some fluff from my managers, but when they give me lint, I go ballistic."

Why Not Do a Great Job on Both Substance and Style?

While substance creates the critical foundation of a worthwhile toptalk, speaking style is, indeed, important. After all, who wants to listen to dull presenters all day? There's often an undertow unconsciously working on executives that affects their judgment during especially impressive presentations. In interviews with senior managers, they've pointed out that the speaker who was an impressive "speaker" could move the audience beyond just focusing exclusively on data, information, or words. Respondents in our survey said use of dynamic body language (gestures, body movement/posturing, facial expressions) and vocal intonation were considered very desirable for a presenter to have.

Speaking style was responsible for one man who moved many of us in our country whether you believed in his politics or not. President Ronald Reagan, who left office with the highest popularity rating of any president since FDR, had a sublime style with somewhat less substance, notes Ross Baker, professor of political science at Rutgers University. He writes, "Reagan succeeded where those with keener intellect, better interpersonal skills and greater reflectivity failed. And it was precisely those dramaturgic skills of the old Hollywood actor, dismissed derisively by savvy and blase insiders, that gave Reagan his matchless advantage."[7]

The color and flavor of *how* something is presented, though, clearly has an effect on the outcome of a toptalk. The "trump cards" of style that give added weight to the substance of a presentation are *charisma* and *presence*. The more people possess it, the more their image impacts on a group. Style without substance is empty; substance without style is boring. The overall issue, then, shouldn't be substance versus style; it should be developing *both* substance and style.

HOW GREAT SPEAKERS PROJECT CHARISMA

You've been drawn to them before—those distinctive people who make their "entrance" into a party and electrify the room with their presence, or the dynamos who command attention and exude confidence in any meeting . . . or even (the quiet "inner glow") ones with a more subtle special allure who draw you to them. They've got *charisma*—a certain "something" quality that usually a select few have oodles of. There are those who are endowed with it, perhaps because of fame, money, or power; others just *have it*—it seems to be in their blood. And *you* can develop more of it.

Charisma has the power to arouse emotions in others, and with enough of it people around that person respond with awe, reverence, devotion, or psychological dependence. A toptalker wants to use lots of charisma when giving an emotionally focused or inspirational presentation. People with charisma have been responsible for holding audiences spellbound. No one is immune to a special blend of charisma—it's like human catnip!

Saint Paul originally used the term charisma to refer to gifts or powers that were manifestations of God's grace. Today, we think of it including spicy ingredients such as charm, wittiness, poise, sauciness, confidence, boldness, energy, and dynamism. In his book, *The Essence of Leadership: The Four Keys to Leading Successfully*, Edwin A. Locke and associates cite research that "found that those who were perceived to be charismatic were simply more animated than others."[8] Locke also notes that when charisma is present in a leader, for example, it has positive effects on the motivation, self-esteem, and attitudes of the followers, and that people working with charismatic leaders tend to work longer and are more confident and trusting than those who work with noncharismatic leaders.

Everyone can develop his or her charisma further. Remember: Becoming more charismatic means being more animated toward and responsive with people. Here are some specific behaviors to boost your charisma quotient during a toptalk.

- Vary your voice volume from a whisper to a powerful surge. Project your voice with deep tones (see deep-breathing techniques for voice projection in Chapter 5, Overcoming Boardroom Speaking Fear). Charismatic people also speak faster than the average person and vary their voice volume and tone to emphasize certain key words or phrases.

- While impressive progress has been made in image management over the last two decades, there's still a lot to be said for the SMILE. This one simple behavior is strongly identified with all charismatic people. Broad open smiles where the whole face seems to join in is the best.

- Let your real emotions come out via dynamic and purposeful body movements and varied voice intonations. Charismatic people are enthusiastic, warm, and energetic. Most executives appreciate enthusiasm and energy from a speaker. In our survey, 72 percent said these were "very important" for a speaker to have and 21 percent said it was "important."

- Walk around and into the audience (don't hide behind the podium or remain stationary for the entire presentation). Let your whole body communicate robust energy, purpose, and confidence.

- Use sweeping and forceful hand and body gestures while speaking. The more emotion you want to use to fire up your audience, the greater the number of gestures with their poignant, energetic style.

- Maintain personable eye contact with the audience. With smaller groups look into each person's eyes as if you were talking just to him or her. Executives in our survey said good eye contact with the audience was one of the most important speaking skills to develop: 63 percent said it was "very important" while 35 percent said it was "important."

- Dress and groom yourself in a way that uniquely reflects you as an individual, while still fitting in with your audience. As one sales vice-president from a farm machinery company in Chicago told me, "I like to subtly stand out without sticking out."

- Use colorful, expressive language filled with action/emotional words that stir your listeners and hold them spellbound. Pronounce your words very clearly.

- Develop a flair for the imaginative—show your boldness, daring, and prudent risk taking.

- Move closer to (and even lean toward) the person in the audience who asks you a question. Listen intently (and nod if appropriate) and respond using that person's name.

- Express your opinions frankly, confidently, and directly and respond to the opinions and ideas of others by giving them constructive feedback.

MAKING YOUR "PRESENCE" FELT

Another rare personal quality that can affect the image of a presenter is "presence." If charisma commands attention and affection from an audience, presence commands *respect*. Confidence and past success develop presence, although people (especially actors) can train themselves to evoke a high level of *command presence* in front of a group. Actors Richard Burton and Elizabeth Taylor were prime examples of people who had incredible presence both on and offstage. Burton was said to be able give a breathtaking performance to an awe-filled audience by reading names aloud from a telephone book! His deep stentorian voice punctuated by his crisp articulation and Welsh accent combined and with his mastery of emotional facial expressions made him appear larger than life.

Likewise, author Louise Erdrich said of poet Maya Angelou's inauguration reading for President Bill Clinton, "This woman could read the side of a cereal box. Her presence was so powerful and momentous.[9] And Britain's Princess Diana has impressively improved her presence (voice and manner) over the last several years by taking lessons from famed director/actor Richard Attenborough.[10]

Presence often involves a certain stately appearance and pleasing and dignified bearing as if to be elevated above the masses *by* the masses. Understated elegance might be a part of it too. Jean Paul

Richter described a piece of it: "There is a certain noble pride, through which merits shine brighter than through modesty." The late Princess Grace of Monaco had enormous presence, grace, and style. President John F. Kennedy had *both* presence and charisma. It's my opinion that more successful CEOs, for example, have more of the corporate aristocratic badge of presence than they do charisma.

In the boardroom, having presence means that a person feels and acts on par with the most influential power brokers. Presence implies a person having a certain "regal air" to himself or herself but without any hint of smugness or haughtiness. Feeling very self-secure and "centered" is typically a prerequisite to presence. While certain people seem to instinctively know what to say and how to act in the highest levels of social affairs, most people can develop poise and social amenities. Having presence means not just holding your own, but having the rich, famous, and powerful accept you at face value—without knowing your "credentials." You can also develop more presence with the following suggestions:

- Speak confidently with a thoughtful deliberation and speak more slowly and with fewer dynamics than charismatic types.

- Carry yourself with dignity and poise: Have very upright posture, deliberate gestures that are meaningful, graceful, and subdued. Keep other body movements relaxed, fluid, and low key in animation (e.g., don't dart your eyes around or make staccato-type hand gestures). Eliminate any nervous gestures (e.g., while others are fidgeting in their seats, sit still but look alert and alive).

- Work on enhancing your speech intonation and pausing. Articulate very clearly. These will display that you are very self-assured, confident, and thoughtful.

- Maintain your dignity when the situation heats up. Don't react; respond in a calm, self-assured way.

- Always try to appear composed—don't show you're rushed, nervous, harried, worried, or overly excited. Show you're in control of yourself and your emotions.

- Don't appear solicitous toward anyone. People who want to exhibit a distinguished bearing don't come across eager to please or fawning in the least.

- Develop more confidence by knowing proper business etiquette. I strongly recommend reading Letitia Baldridge's *Complete Guide to Executive Manners* (New York: Rawson Associates).

THE THREE SECRETS TO CAPTURING YOUR AUDIENCE

There's a *rule of three* I've been telling my audiences about for the last 15 years or so that can practically ensure toptalk success every time. When you distill everything down to its bare essence, your ultimate goal as a toptalker is to get your audience to: (1) LIKE, (2) RESPECT, and (3) TRUST you. If you achieve all three, you can practically *guarantee reaching* your objectives. That's true because your audience has to "buy you" first before they buy your proposal, however great it sounds. Keep in mind, though, that achieving all three is *not* easy!

Building solid relationships with the executives at work are needed to form that degree of hard-earned respect, trust, and affection they have for you. Often at executive presentations, the reputation and, therefore, the credibility of a speaker precedes him or her prior to the presentation—and that can automatically set expectations. Newcomers to the boardroom, though, who are presenting to a high-level audience for the first time, need to prepare and strategize for ways to: (1) behave in psychologically convincing ways; and (2) project a fine personal and professional image to quickly grab the minds and hearts of that group.

The concept of (like + respect + trust) is profound in its simplicity because it essentially encapsulates what it takes to get the audience *totally* on *your* side. You need to quickly and tightly "connect and stay hooked up" with your audience. You have to achieve all three of those relationship-critical criteria. As a way of further thinking about this concept, examine how you might rate past presidents such as Eisenhower, Truman, Kennedy, Johnson, Nixon, Ford, Carter, Reagan, Bush, and Clinton in terms of the like, respect, and trust factors. Whom did you like the most and why? Whom did you most trust among them and why? Who earned your deep respect and commitment? Finally, whom would you give the highest *overall* like + respect + trust score and why? Let's examine each of the three factors.

Getting Them to Like You

One of the first desirable goals in a presentation situation is to get the audience to *like you*—to feel some kind of affection or closeness to you even from the very moment you step in front of them. Once this happens, the job of getting them on your side will be much easier. You want to develop a good rapport with them or, if necessary, quickly take them off the defensive (or at least away from a position of apathy).

A presenter can have the greatest message in the world and can be an accomplished speaker, but if his or her personality or manner clashes with or otherwise bothers the audience, they quickly turn the "off" switch on their minds and hearts. Their antipathy toward the speaker almost totally prevents any admittance of even beneficial and psychologically strong information. Picture the last time you were in a meeting and someone you disliked came up with an idea or suggested a plan of action that you logically believed had strong merit to it. Did you *willingly* support it ? I doubt it. It's hard to swallow, but we humans are more emotional and reactive than we care to believe and that makes us *subjective* evaluators more than we are *objective* ones.

Gaining the Audience's Affection Can Gain You Points

Depending upon how much an audience likes you, it can forgive certain minor-to-moderate weaknesses or honest mistakes you make. We can rationalize or excuse almost anything if we care about someone. The opposite is also true. For example, you and I have seen enough "technically perfect presenters." They're people who did everything right according to the stock books on "How to Give That Great Presentation." They smiled, had very effective speaking skills, and their content was excellent, but somehow they across as being perhaps self-centered, insincere, or too coldly mechanical. Chances are the audience didn't genuinely cozy up to this alleged paragon of choreographed excellence.

Instead, people prefer listening to those who project warmth, genuineness, and humanness—mistakes and all. I'm not saying that if you're one of the incredibly fortunate humans loved by all men, women, and beasts you can slack off on improving your group speaking skills and image because of the forgiving nature of your adoring group. No! I'm saying that if you have excellent people-attracting skills, use them more to your advantage.

However, if you're part of the majority of people (including myself) who do not elicit an immediate outpouring of spontaneous affection from others, you need to actively work at *establishing* rapport with every new audience you present to. Here are some suggestions to help endear you to the boardroom crowd or to any audience:

- Relax . . . BE YOURSELF. . . Be comfortable with your audience; don't act intimidated; they want you to be at ease. After all, who likes to see a presenter shaking like a crackling leaf in the wind?

- Smile sincerely and have friendly eye contact with all members of your audience (this increases trust too).

- Have a purely natural conversation *with* your group—talk *with* them not *at* them. You're not a stiff and formal orator— you're a personable communicator! Today's real "eloquence" forgoes eloquence.

- If it's relevant to your points and you're naturally good at it, appropriately weave humor into your messages.

- Move into and around your audience to show that you want to "get close" to them; use hand and body gestures freely (this makes you come across as more natural and warm).

- Use tact, diplomacy, and subtlety to deal with touchy issues; be on guard not to display a "know-it-all" attitude in the quest to make a good impression.

- Briefly compliment members of the group on any recent achievements, promotions, or awards they received; thank them for any assistance they've given you on the proposal you are presenting.

- Avoid anything that might annoy, offend, irritate or somehow turn off the group (see following section on toxic actions in this chapter).

- Personalize your presentation—use people's names when appropriate; give personal examples of points you are making; communicate everything from *their* standpoint—terminology, illustrations, stories. Speak as if you were one of them *with them*.

- Be respectful and encouraging of other points of view expressed; Demonstrate that you are listening with an open mind; be flexible and accommodating to the needs and wishes of the audience.

- By words, voice, body, and deeds, give your audience the impression you want to be with them and are enjoying yourself (or if it's a critical group, at least not disliking) the interaction with them.

Getting Them to Respect You

When we respect someone, we admire him or her; we hold that person in high esteem. The greatest form of respect is to *revere* or venerate somebody. We can respect someone for: (1) *who they are* (their character, personality, spirit, attitudes, beliefs, values) or (2) *what they've done* (major accomplishments, talents, or humble charitable contributions), and (3) *how they behave* (their everyday actions and displayed traits). *Showing respect* to someone is different from *feeling respect* for them. We show respect to the powerful, influential people who control or otherwise have an effect upon our lives; we respect those who impress us—who, we feel, deserve our respect.

When an audience respects a speaker for his or her credibility, expertise, and sense of honor and ethics, they carefully listen to the speaker because he or she is perceived as being worthy or deserving of being listened to. They may not agree with the speaker, but they'll give him or her their full attention and usually a "fair hearing." Here are some suggestions to help build respect for you by your audience:

- Be highly organized, prepared, and knowledgeable about the topic (this is a frequently repeated theme from executives).

- Work on coming across poised, confident, and competent while presenting.

- Have an impeccable and appropriate appearance (grooming and dress).

- Act reasonable, open-minded, fair, and flexible in dealing with the audience and their requests; don't hold grudges against dissenters in group.

- Display a strong sense of optimism and "can do" attitude.

- Be composed and in control when problems develop—don't get flustered by anything the audience says or does.

- Demonstrate being a highly creative problem solver.

- Behave in the most professional, responsible, and mature fashion.

- Be sensitive to and respectful of the audience's values, tastes, desires, and sensitivities (highly empathic).

- Show your commitment and patient perseverance toward reaching your goals; demonstrate that your energy and focus is always on accomplishing the mission.

- Subtly and tastefully mention your past accomplishments that relate to your presentation objectives to boost your credibility.

- Communicate your eagerness to volunteer for challenging assignments.

Getting Them to Trust You

Edward R. Murrow, one of the classic journalists and broadcasters of our century said, "To be persuasive, we must be believable. To be believable, we must be credible. To be credible, we must be truthful." Truth is the essence of trust and the rock-solid basis for the persuasion process and for establishing a positive image with an audience (see more about integrity and honesty in Chapter 7, Developing your Leadership Aura).

Except for the term "love," the word "trust" probably pops up with the greatest frequency in conversations about personal and social relationships. In my discussions with executives on this topic, some felt that to be trusted was almost a greater compliment than to be loved and admired. Whatever priority one places on this hard-to-achieve bestowal, it's *vital* to attempt to gain it in relationships with your audience. When we trust people, we depend upon them, we have faith in them, we believe and have confidence in them. We put a firm reliance on the integrity, strength, ability, and overall good character of that person. "Character is power," Booker T. Washington pointed out.

We believe a trustworthy person to have good intentions (toward us and anyone he or she deals with). We have positive expectations of that person without fear of negative consequences that might result from trusting and relying upon that person. Trust implies a feeling of security with the one being trusted—that the person will "do the right thing" and not let us down. When a presenter, in front of the board, gives the impression that he or she is a self-serving narcissist, for example, the trust level gets sucked into an abyss.

Trust Means Unflinching Acceptance

The greater the amount of trust we have in a person, the more there is *unquestioning acceptance* of what is said. At very high trust levels, we accept it as prima facie. When we do not yet trust a presenter, we require more proof to verify information. We check it and validate the "claims" made. But if a presenter has *consistently proven* himself or herself to be accurate, conservative, forthright, and correct in the communication of facts, statistics, examples, and so forth, we feel a high level of confidence in that person. Earning trust takes longer than getting respect and much longer than developing feelings of affection for another.

Actually, when we respect and trust someone *too much*, a "halo effect" comes into play that clearly affects our objectivity and judgment. That's when we have so much faith and awe in the ability, wisdom, and knowledge of a person that we tend to think of that person as being an almost infallible paragon where even his or her slightest *opinion* might be interpreted as rock-solid fact by us or that his or her judgment is faultless. We believe these people can do no wrong. The halo affect is the polar opposite of cynicism, skepticism, and mistrust. As such, we need to be aware of being *too* unfailingly accepting of everything a person like that says. Being eminently successful and brilliant doesn't mean that person is perfect and omniscient.

Without trust, open and effective communication is absolutely impossible. People are on guard and defensive. They hold back their real feelings and often say the safe "politically correct" thing. Once an atmosphere of trust prevails, fears of rejection, disappointment, judgment, betrayal, and potential harm disappear and a communication environment of supportiveness, acceptance, openness, cooperation, and safety emerge.

Here are just a few examples of personal traits or known behaviors that you can use to build trust with your audience:

- Demonstrate that you're an unselfish, highly conscientious team player who freely gives public credit to other deserving members; work toward cooperating and compromising for the good of the group.

- Maintain strong—direct and friendly—eye contact with your audience; use a conversational voice tone.

- Give frank, straightforward answers without hesitating or equivocating; never give "slick" or manipulative answers; never act as if you have *all* the answers.

- Demonstrate high principles and deep ethical convictions and stick to them regardless of group pressure to change.

- Show effective listening abilities (especially empathic listening).

- Demonstrate good will toward the audience with selfless intentions; emphasize that you have the audience's best interests in mind when asking for their help or commitment.

- Show your consistent reliability and dependability to meet stated commitments.

- Be yourself. Come across as very natural and sincere; don't role play, wear a mask, or "put on airs" in an attempt to impress.

- Display vulnerability by admitting mistakes you might have made or information you don't know about; use other "self-disclosure" so your audience can see your "human side."

- Be totally open-minded to counter-arguments or ideas and be willing to discuss them.

- Display humility. You'll come across as more trustworthy and mature. As Chesterton said, "It is always the secure who are humble."

DEADLY SPEAKING MISTAKES TOPTALKERS SHOULD AVOID

Another useful way to look at image, impression, and perception of the speaker is to know what bothers executives about speakers they've listened to. What mistakes, poor judgments, or annoying, irritating, offensive or otherwise negative things could a speaker say or do during a presentation that would cause executives to *"turn off"* toward that person? Once you turn them off, it takes a lot of energy to turn them back on—it's not like flipping a switch. Here are some actual representative responses from our survey that form an accurate cross-section of *toxic actions*:

- Pompus and condescending
- Attacking another person, group, or company
- Race or gender remarks
- Flippant—not thoughtful
- Argumentative style
- Direct comments to other people at the exclusion of myself
- Monotone voice projection and no enthusiasm
- Strong opinion without regard to the actual facts
- Irrelevant material and inconsequential points
- Someone who has "decided" the best solution and tries to force that solution on his or her audience without benefit of presenting alternatives
- Lack of commitment to the proposed program
- Dogmatic (inflexible) style and opinionated
- Not listening to (audience) feedback and unwillingness to adapt. Some people have the need to give their presentations (exactly as planned) no matter what!
- Individual's ego shows little or limited respect for the audience
- Grandstanding or very negative focus
- Rambled on and on
- Off-color humor, swearing, and loud talking
- Focusing on just one or two people in the audience to the exclusion of others and playing up to the boss—singling out the top person and talking only to him or her
- Reading visual aids word for word from the screen

- Mistakes in material (spelling, errors, inconsistencies)
- Obvious irrationality or lack of effective logic and good judgment

HOW TO DRESS FOR TOPTALK SUCCESS

Clothes make the man . . . naked people have little or no influence on society.

—MARK TWAIN

Topnotch executive recruiter Lynn Bignell in New York City, who has helped place some of the country's corporate superstars told me, "The most important thing is someone's appearance. How you are coiffed . . . how you are clothed . . . how you are *put together*. All of a sudden there is an image. There is an instantaneous (unconscious) decision making on the part of the audience. They're thinking, 'This person looks well put together. Therefore this person must be successful and know what he or she is talking about.' Now if a person's hair is a bit messed, collar's slightly upturned, there's a tiny, but noticeable stain on the tie, or a blouse or shirt is a askew, then all of a sudden this person has instant loss of credibility and they're now fighting an uphill battle. Audiences draw total implications from dress and grooming."[11]

She's right! The audience *receives* the image you're *transmitting* and if it's one of personal power, leadership, and "class," then it translates into status for you. Because they're buying you (your beliefs, values, principles, philosophy, lifestyle) as much or more than they're buying your ideas, your dress and grooming should exemplify what you stand for. While clothes and grooming cannot substitute for performance and overall competence, they're your allies to help convince your audience that you're the perfect person—*the only person*—to get the job done. Therefore, at your toptalk you definitely want to look your best and you want to *fit in* with that audience. To play the part, you have to look the part. And when you do, you'll feel more confident, comfortable, powerful, and in control.

Apparently "Dress for Success" Is Not Universally Accepted

Who really needs to enhance his or her image, though? The answer is that *all* of us can make some enhancement, however minor. When I spoke to some of the country's best executive recruiters, I was shocked and at times amused to hear of their tales of some apparently successful, high-paid men and women who violated the "basics" of proper and tasteful dress and grooming. Poor selection and fit of ties (loud/dull, bad match, hung too short/long, stains), short sagging socks on men that spotlighted hairy legs or runs in womens' stockings, "high water" pants, tight-fitting or too revealing outfits, dandruff on clothes, unshined shoes, fingernails needing repair, frayed clothes, flashy hair styles, too high heels, and improper makeup were just some of the credibility killers they mentioned. It's surprising how some people in such high level leadership positions need to take care of some of the basics, let alone the fine points of dress and grooming.

Christina Ward, president (1994-1995) of the Association of Image Consultants International and a corporate image consultant based in Houston, also told me that among all her clients, she's consulted with a few high-level people who have succeeded in spite of less than impressive clothing and grooming. "It's difficult to convince some people to enhance their appearance when their career has seen a steady upward climb. They're the exception, though. Besides, they might not get the next promotion because the higher you advance, the more you need to pay attention to the fine points of *packaging.*"

Your Packaging Is Not Just for Show

The measured style and appropriate dress and grooming of successful leaders is not just for show. It says, *"I'm a quality person . . . I'm confident . . . I have an eye for fine details . . . I'm a team player . . . I have taste and style . . . and I belong here—I'm one of you.* The right dress and grooming image for you is not something that should be hastily conjured up. It requires a lot of thought, effort, and discipline because you want it to be genuine and you want to stretch yourself to become more than what you were. Your appearance at the executive podium should communicate polish, power, poise, presence, and precision.

The "Look of Importance"—Some Guidelines

Christina Ward suggests that everyone periodically assess their image and make enhancements to it. She believes that the impact of image from dress and grooming is inestimable and that even small enhancements can give worthwhile returns on their investments. In my discussions with her, she provides these guidelines and advice for both the male and female toptalkers:[12]

- **QUALITY.** Buy the highest quality clothes and accessories that you can afford. You're better off with several high-quality outfits than many more medium-quality ones. Perfect *fit and fabric* is the aim. If possible (and if you can afford it), find out where the CEO and other respected leaders in your organization buy their clothes and shop there.

- **STYLING.** Stay with classic styling instead of being "trendy." Understated and tasteful elegance is the mark of the power broker. If you look excessively well dressed (as if to be on the cover of *Gentleman's Quarterly* or *Harper's Bazaar*) it draws attention to your appearance and the subtle implication might be that you're spending an *inordinate* amount of time on *obvious* image management and shopping instead of taking care of critical business issues. Conservative dress does not mean drab. The goal is to be distinctive and individual, but not trendy. Select a combination of colors, patterns, styles, and accessories that are ideal for your age, body shape, and personality.

- **FABRICS.** Stay with classic fabrics (wool blends, silk, 100% cotton), which relay the message of quality. These fabrics also endure and apply to varying climates.

- **JEWELRY.** Jewelry should be unobtrusive, nonflashy, with tasteful classic styling. Men should avoid the electronic "gizmo" and jeweled watches, bracelets, tie clips/tacks, and numerous rings. Women should avoid a bracelet and watch on the same wrist and should wear jewelry that makes no noise or draws strong attention to itself. Stay away from amulets, charms, bangle bracelets, a "big rock" engagement ring, or cluster rings that suggest gaudiness.

- **GROOMING.** Be impeccably groomed. Fingernails should be manicured. Hair needs to be a conservative style for men and women and needs to be neat, tidy, perfectly in place, and with an "efficient" look to it (as if the person didn't spend a lot of time on it, but it looks like a million dollars). Avoid a lot of hair fixatives such as mousse, gels, oils, or anything else that's noticeable.

- **COLOGNE.** Use only the finest colognes that have a delicate scent and long life. Cheaper ("heavy") colognes have a strong short-lived smell and can be distracting, have sexual overtones, or may bother the allergies of people in the audience, especially older executives.

- **MAKEUP.** All makeup tones should be natural (shadows in the taupe, gray, deep-blue, and plum range and matte finish— absolutely no frost). Lipstick and blush should enhance the natural color tones of the wearer and be blended for a subtle effect, never greasy or glossy.

- **JACKET.** Wear a jacket. It lends an image of more formality and seriousness and gives the toptalker power (especially if buttoned).

If you're dressed and groomed just right, people in your audience will spend 30 seconds or so focusing on your effective overall appearance and the rest of the time they'll focus exclusively on what you're saying because they're not distracted.

Executive Image

- Understated elegance
- Tasteful simplicity
- Top quality
- Classic styles
- Distinctive, not trendy.
- Impeccable and meticulous grooming

Considerations for Women in the Boardroom

Sadly, the "glass ceiling" is still installed in the boardroom of corporations in America since only approximately 500 women out of 11,715 (6.2%) are directors in the biggest 500 service and 500 industrial companies.[13] And women who give presentations in the boardroom and other executive meeting rooms are a small minority as well. Unfortunately, women have to exert more effort and be more careful to gain the same amount of credibility as their male counterparts, so appropriate dress and grooming becomes paramount.

Leslie Smith, Associate Director of the National Association of Female Executives (NAFE), provided some insights to me about women presenting in the top-echelon meeting rooms, "There's a good chance she's the only woman there. Men are going to notice she's a woman and she's going to see fifteen suits of the same color—the same cut 'uniform.' Number one, she's going to realize she's out of uniform by the way she's dressed (wearing a suit or tailored dress). Many of the men might be in the 'boy's club'— they see her as a woman first. She wants her brain and words to be taken seriously so she needs to blend in. She has to be careful not to wear excessive makeup, have a low-cut neckline, too short skirt, or too high heels."

Leslie Smith believes that women sometimes tend to select one of two different strategies as it relates to their image. One is to "stand out" as an attractive woman and dress in a feminine, fashionable way. She told me of a woman—a very successful and competent partner in a law firm—who dressed in a somewhat provocative, sensual way. Her attitude was, "I'm noticed because I'm a woman and I get more clients that way" and felt very comfortable with her image. The other strategy Smith believes woman use goes to the other extreme of being *too* boring and blending in *too* much. As she put it, "Some women feel they're in a no-win situation. If they look too masculine, they're criticized; if they look too feminine they criticized. I believe in finding the middle ground."[14]

One thing image consultants and female executives I've spoken with agree upon: For credibility don't overly draw attention to yourself as a woman with the way you dress, groom yourself, or act. An outfit should fit a woman in a way that looks tailored and businesslike, but not tight enough that it accentuates every curve in her body. A female toptalker's goal is to have the audience riveted to her as a compelling speaker and credible professional. They recommend always wearing a jacket to project more power and authority.

For information on working with an image consultant in your location, contact the Association of Image Consultants International (AICI), 1000 Connecticut Avenue NW, Suite 9, Washington, DC 20036. Phone: (800) 383-8831.

Developing Your Leadership Aura

The leader must know, must know that he knows, and must be able to make it abundantly clear to those around him that he knows.

—CLARENCE B. RANDALL

There's one overwhelming factor to get people to wholeheartedly support your idea or proposal. *It's your leadership!* Elite toptalkers display leadership by word, deed, and impression every second they're in front of that group. Creative communication leadership is the ability to tie people to both you and your cause. Corporate leaders around the country told me that it's *not enough* for a presenter to be informative, interesting, or even convincing. If a board of directors, for example, is going to approve millions of dollars or more for an organization improvement plan, plant or capital equipment expansion, or a major new product or market thrust, they want to know that the person asking for approval and funding can *lead* the project or plan through to its successful implementation.

Several years ago, over a two year period, the board of directors of Texaco, Inc., reviewed over 40 projects with a total investment value of $3.8 billion.[1] I'm sure that presenters in that boardroom were *leaders* who communicated the attractiveness of those proposed investment projects which gave the board the confidence and motivation to go full steam ahead. CEO of First Interstate Bank of Texas, N.A., Linnet Deily told me simply, "Leaders are people who make you believe *in them* as well as the information they're imparting."[2]

173

This chapter will cover ways for you to communicate to your audience a stronger *aura of leadership* that will give you extra credibility and influence in achieving your toptalk objectives. We'll sketch a portrait of a creative communication leader.

HOW TO TAKE COMMAND AT THE PODIUM

Two great orators of antiquity were the Roman Cicero and the Greek Demosthenes. One was persuasive, the other led his audience. When Cicero was done speaking, people always gave him a rousing ovation and proclaimed, "What a great speech!" When Demosthene's fiery words ended but still burned within the assembly, people shouted, "Let us march!" And they did. Too many presenters want to "manage" (which derives from the French word for "to control") their audience. *You want to be like Demosthenes*—a great speaker and leader who gets his or her audience to enthusiastically follow—to act—not just agree, applaud, or be "controlled."

In his book, *The Sir Winston Churchill Method. The Five Secrets of Speaking The Language of Leadership*, author and presidential speechwriter James C. Humes says, "A leader doesn't just recite; he offers an insight. He doesn't just recite; he enlightens. A leader is someone whose report is remembered the day after."[3] Poet Robert Frost complements that thought with, "What is required is sight and insight; then you add one more—excite." Leaders get people to board a "streetcar named desire"–a desire to follow.

John W. Garner, an exceptional scholar and leader himself and author of, *On Leadership*, says, "Leadership is the process of persuasion or example by which an individual (or leadership team) induces a group to pursue objectives held by the leader or shared by the leader and his or her followers."[4] A true leader is not someone who gets obedience or compliance or even cooperation from a group; it's a person who gets them to *eagerly commit for as long as it takes* to meet the goals set forth by the leader.

> A toptalker who *leads* his or her audience lays out the path, points the audience in the right direction, and persuades, motivates, excites, and gets them *committed* to quickly move toward the intended destination.

Let's say a manager was giving a presentation to an important group for the first time and they know little or nothing about her. Based upon her performance, it was evident that she was in command of herself, her topic, and her audience. You got the distinct impression she was a person who had a deep desire to lead, to achieve, and to accept responsibility and challenges. Here was a person driven and tenacious enough to refuse to accept the word "failure." Someone you can always count on. A person wrapped in competence and imbued with character.

If you were to read the minds of people who listened to and watched her, here are just a few things they'd probably be saying to themselves: "She did her 'homework' and laid out her plan beautifully." "She got me excited about her project—I want to be part of this! She's bright, competent, and creative. I like her and would enjoy working with her. I strongly believe she can be trusted and depended upon to get the project done on time, on budget, and on target. It's a wonder that she convinced this tough group. She made it seem so relaxed and natural–almost easy!" A strong leader, indeed, makes an impression far beyond that of just a good presenter/communicator—he or she deeply affects people long after the encounter. People intuitively feel good about the experience and being with that leader.

Being a strong public speaker doesn't mean that you also come across as a leader to your audience. The bass drum player makes more noise than other players, but he doesn't lead the orchestra. What does a leader act like in front of a group while presenting? Allen Krowe, vice-chairman at Texaco, intuitively noted, "You know one [a leader] when you see one. It doesn't take very long."[5] But, what do you see and hear? Is it personal charisma, brains, command presence, vigor, assertiveness, die-hard confidence, and having the ability to win loyalty?

Think back to when you saw a particular person for the first time giving a presentation and at some point (perhaps 10-15 minutes later) your *perception* was that he or she had strong leadership abilities. CEO Linnet Deily says, " . . . it's more that overall impression that this is somebody who is *in charge*." [6] Writing in *Executive* magazine, L. P. Williams articulates it further, "Some people simply seem to have an aura around them that inspires trust and confidence. We have faith in them and in their ability to deal with matters in a way that will be satisfactory to us. They inspire our confidence and we grant them our loyalty. These are the qualities that unite followers and that leaders, somehow, in some mysterious way, are able to call forth. Quite simply, we know leadership when we experience it."[7] But, specifically, how did the person communicate the *language of leadership*–the speaking style, spoken words, body language, dress, or overall attitude and behavior in front of an audience that causes someone's intuition to clearly decipher L-E-A-D-E-R?

In my interviews with executives, my analysis of hundreds of presentations I've seen, and by studying the research of respected authorities in the field of leadership,[8] I believe the following traits, characteristics and behaviors that I describe portray the image and substance of a leader at the podium. Together they create an *aura of leadership.*

HOW YOUR NEW LEADERSHIP AURA HELPS YOU GET ACTION FROM YOUR AUDIENCE

Does it mean that if you actually use certain behaviors while giving a group presentation, you're a "leader"? Hardly! You can only "fake it to make it" for a limited time until a situation forces you to display your true level of competence, maturity, and leadership mettle. But, I believe that *not* exhibiting many of the defined traits that follow will indeed detract from a stronger image of leadership that's vital in getting influential groups to support your program or cause. Obviously, if the audience knows of your leadership ability or reputation, you don't have to prove yourself as much. But, if you're facing a high-level group for the first time and they've never seen you or heard about you, then lighting up your leadership aura takes on a magnitude of importance. For example, a research scientist presenting a major venture she'd like to get approval on stands more of a chance if she is seen not only as a brilliant scientist, but as one who can head up or at least play a supporting leadership role in ensuring the success of that costly venture. It's not about *counterfeit* leadership—it's about taking on the role and being it.

Leadership is a very complex, intangible aspect of behavior, and simply saying that if you master certain traits, you'll be a great leader is incorrect and naive. A leader is more than the sum of his or her "parts." Think about it. Who was a better leader, General George

Patton or Mahatma Ghandi? Alexander the Great or Abraham Lincoln? Jesus Christ or Julius Caesar? The answer is that all were effective leaders in their own way and all were different—some with seemingly opposite personalities, drives, and communication styles.

NINE TOPTALK LEADERSHIP CHARACTERISTICS

Noted authorities on leadership Warren Bennis and Burt Nanus tell us that decades of academic analysis have given us more than 350 definitions of leadership.[9] However, in a public speaking situation such as giving a boardroom presentation, I believe certain traits, more than others, tend to paint a commonly accepted image of how a leader acts in front of a group. Knowing what those traits are can enable you to further develop or more strongly exhibit those inherent traits and behaviors in a way that lets you role model leadership in a radiant and triumphant expression.

My research and experience indicates there are essentially nine *core* characteristics or traits that project the image of a leader at the executive podium.

Leadership At the Podium

- Decisive
- High stamina and energy
- Honesty and integrity
- Confident and poised
- Knowledgeable and competent
- Knows and "touches" people
- Big picture and bold thinker
- Visionary
- Passionate

Decisiveness Speaks of Strong Leadership

Leaders take responsibility for and feel confident making decisions. They're willing to step forward when no one else will. Today's executives are paid hefty salaries and bonuses to make those tough decisions using good judgment—decisions that could dramatically affect the welfare and future of their organization. Executive audiences are impressed by a toptalker who can make effective and *quick* decisions based on the requests, questions, or other discussion points at the presentation. Someone who rarely procrastinates when making a decision with an "Ah . . . I've got to think this over" reply.

Implementing major projects requires lots of decisions along the way. So, if a boardroom presenter who will be managing the project seems to hesitate longer than called for, or appears to unnecessarily avoid making decisions, or is encumbered by "paralysis of analysis"—requesting extended time to get and analyze yet more data—the executives may feel unsure of his or her willingness and ability to make decisions. You'll never have enough data or time to make perfect decisions, but you need to make timely decisions, based on your judgment. Every decision involves some degree of risk, and leaders are known for taking prudent risks.

How you say something signals decisiveness. I remember coaching one ultra-pleasant, hard-working executive from a New York City insurance company who appeared "weak" in front of his peers and his board. Here's what he actually asked me, "I've been told that I appear sort of indecisive. I don't know. I'm not indecisive, am I?" On the other hand, I remember observing one executive giving a presentation several years ago, who, when he said "I don't know" two or three times (when asked questions) seemed incredibly decisive and confident in his admittance of not knowing.

To project decisiveness, keep your answers as concise and precise as possible. Sometimes a simple and direct "yes" or "no" shows your direct, get-the-point thinking. Another way to communicate clear-headed decisiveness is to use *enumeration* when responding to an audience member question or request. For example, "You asked how we would handle customer complaints during this major new system phase over. There are four specific ways we would do it. "First . . ." Enumeration shows your use of logical and organized thinking needed for decision making.

Decisive people are willing to bear the burden of making the decision and living with it. Therefore, use the active, personal "I" or "We (team)" in place of a passive response. Example: "Together with my team, I will execute a three-prong strategy to improve productivity in that plant" as opposed to "The strategy to be executed is a three-part one . . ." To add decisive punch to a response, answer questions with such unequivocal words or phrases as, "definitely," "absolutely," "positively," "without a doubt." Examples: "*Absolutely!* I can assure all of you of that fact" or "*Definitely.* We will meet that deadline." A word of caution, though. Make sure these definitive responses are worthy of such strong confidence and don't overdo. And think about every possible audience question, challenge, retort, or request that requires a decision from you. Anticipating and preparing well-thought-out replies will make your answers more fluid and decisive sounding.

Decisive people "want to be the rider, not the horse." During your presentation, assert your leadership by letting the audience know that you want to accept the challenges ahead, that you welcome additional responsibility, and that you're willing to stretch yourself in new decision making directions. Oliver Wendell Holmes, Jr., said, "The reward of a general is not a bigger tent—but command," and command necessitates decision making and that's what you're telling the audience you want.

Stamina and Energy Are the Fuel to Rocket Leaders Toward Tough Goals

Leaders are very hard working. They put in long hours and lots of effort to succeed. People follow energetic leaders who have the will and drive to get the job done in spite of failures, obstacles, resistance, or other hardships. Implementing a tough project with demanding deadlines, complex procedures, and technological challenges, for example, requires a leader having that which is a combination of energy, strength (physical, emotional, mental), and endurance.

Leaders with stamina keep at the job until is done right. It's meeting deadlines, putting up with fatigue, dealing with "impossible" people, fighting the bureaucracy, and making sacrifices. It's pushing yourself to the finish line even when you feel like quitting or slowing down. Successful leaders have reserves of energy they tap into. Their bodies, voices, and attitudes release abundant amounts of energy such that leaders are typically seen as active (even restless), vigorous, and full of life. "They're pumped to achieve" as one vice president of a furniture outlet put it to me.

To communicate a sense of personal energy and power, have a strong upright posture, make use of sweeping and forceful body and hand gestures, and project your voice with powerful volume while speaking at a brisk rate even if you're very tired. In a steady and purposeful way, walk around the meeting room as you speak, rather than locking yourself behind a podium or standing in one spot. Speakers with energy are animated and their body language shouts force and energy.

Check to make sure your appearance and grooming make you appear fresh and vigorous. When everyone else feels drained at the meeting, and it shows on their faces, *smile* in a relaxed way. Giving a presentation at the end of a tough long day, for example, is difficult, so you want to have your facial expressions denote a sense of revitalized energy. It's helpful to videotape yourself at some presentation and analyze whether you exhibit a sense of personal power and stamina in front of a group. Ask respected colleagues to help make suggestions.

You might want to tell the audience that you have the die-hard robustness to tackle the tough roads ahead. An example statement like the following can "alert" the audience to your expected stamina: "Our team is aware of the deadline, our resource limits, and the other challenges and unknowns we face as we try to pioneer this new technology project. We will do whatever it takes—work around the clock and push ourselves beyond what we've ever done to reach this goal. We've got the energy and drive to succeed."

Display lots of optimism and possibility thinking. A person who is pessimistic cannot draw upon deep wells of energy within because of its draining effect. It's difficult to imagine an effective leader who is sad, gloomy, fatigued, disheartened, overburdened, or depressed for too long. They have a great resilience to them that enables them to snap back fully and quickly. Toptalkers need to communicate their sense of energetic optimism at all times. Their language should reflect "can do." Their overall attitude should tell the audience, "I know we'll come up against problems and obstacles, but we'll lick every one of them!"

Honesty and Integrity Are a Leader's Badge of Honor

Mark Twain said, "When in doubt, tell the truth." But, there doesn't seem to be much doubt when you ask executives how vital trustworthiness is from a leader. Canny, Bowen, Inc., a New York-based executive-search firm did a recent survey of 375 directors, chief executive officers, chief operating officers, and other senior executives to determine what attributes those executives considered important for effective leadership. The most important was integrity: 68 percent of respondents said that integrity was *very important*, while the remainder—32 percent—rated it *important.* [10]

In our survey, we asked executives what a presenter could do that would not only turn the audience off, but essentially guarantee that person's failure in front of the executive group (we called it the "ultimate no-no"). The following actual responses from several executives form a consensus: *Lack of integrity kills trust, which kills the presentation!*

> Faking it or outright lying. If I catch a person doing that, I challenge them immediately. They'll never do it again! And, it will take a long time for them to get back in my good graces.
>
> Being indiscreet—breaching a confidence.
>
> Any misrepresentation of the facts (i.e., any action which even hints at dishonesty or lack of complete forthrightness on presenting all the facts.
>
> What really angers me is unreasonable exaggeration, unbelievable numbers or covering up the percentage downside factor, or outright misrepresentation or lying. As far as I'm concerned, the trust factor vanishes right then and there.

A speaker who is a *prevaricator* (one who speaks falsely or misleadingly with deliberate intent) commits the most grievous offense to the audience. Humorist Leo Rosten, in his book *Leo Rosten's Giant Book of Laughter*, facetiously said, "The real secret to communication? That's easy. It's honesty. Absolute, irresistible honesty. . . Once you learn to fake that, you'll make a fortune." But faking it is ultra-risky besides being unethical, and it's the worst thing you can do in front of an executive audience or any other. A senior vice-president from a Boston insurance company put truthfulness in perspective when he quoted a law maxim, "False in one thing, false in everything."

Leadership authority, Warren Bennis defines *integrity* as the correspondence between word and deed. A popular term is "walking the talk" or doing what you said you would do—being reliable and dependable. Integrity involves being honorable, incorruptible, uncompromising (in principles), and upright. Honesty is simply telling the truth, refusing to lie, or otherwise being deceitful, however indirect or subtle. Sterling character symbolizes the reputation of today's leader.

Admitting mistakes or taking the blame in front of an important group, rather than trying to cover up or pass it along to someone or something else, broadcasts solid integrity and shows maturity and courageous character. The CEO of a Massachusetts software company frankly told me he erupted at a presentation with his sales vice-president (who spent more time explaining the problems he faced instead of attempting to solve them) with, "You could get rich manufacturing crutches for lame excuses. You don't need this job." A week later he was gone.

The slightest hint of manipulating the decision of a group will turn them off. Professional persuasion is always admired by executives, but if a presenter, for example, tries to pitch a totally one-sided—slanted—solution without giving the group a well-rounded, accurate perspective including other options or possible approaches, the speaker's credibility will be hurt.

Some presenters make the mistake of "sugarcoating" bad news or problems by sterilizing their words or blanketing the real meanings. Instead of being frank, direct, and upfront, they'll use euphemisms or obscuranta. I deem these "antiseptic presenters" because instead of telling the group, for example, that "the facility at Grogan's Bluff experienced two explosions over the last quarter and production dramatically suffered," they'll say something like, "We're evaluating some variances in production due to recurring nonpredicted incidences." Huh?

People often do that to avoid "being shot as the messenger," but straight talk, even if it's unpopular but needs to be said, earns bonus points for gutsy integrity. Besides, so many senior executives get information that's so filtered, "cleansed," and packaged in a palatable way that it's often useless. Lee Iacocca was renowned and respected for his frank, oftentimes brutal honesty with stockholders, suppliers, and his managers. At least you knew the facts and where he stood. On one or more public occasions with customers, the Iacocca formula: *We screwed up. We're very sorry. Here's what we're going to do to fix the problem. We'll make sure it won't happen again* worked wonders.

Ethical toptalkers use conservative data and other information, for example, when making forecasts as to the expected costs and financial returns on their project or technical performance of their new product or the expected results from their plan or any other situation that the audience will base their decisions on. Optimistically inflated predictions "sold" in a convincing way may get results this time, but will seriously harm the credibility of the presenter the next time (if there is one) he or she tries to get support and approval from the audience. Consider giving your audience *worst-to-best-case scenarios* of estimates and forecasts if you really believe your proposal has impressive potential. For example, you can position it like this, "I'm optimistic that we can, in reality, achieve improvements of a 45 to 60 percent increase in productivity with this new process I'm advocating. But I believe you need to evaluate this project on the highly conservative estimates of a 25 percent enhancement, which we give a 98 percent probability to." This concept of *under*promising and *over*delivering bespeaks integrity and trust. Or, as one executive vice-president of a Boston bank put it, "There's a difference between making good promises and making good on your promises."

Intent also communicates integrity or lack of it. If the audience feels your proposal is self-serving, the intent is clear and will not be endorsed. But if the intent is to benefit others (in addition to oneself) in a more noble and worthwhile way, then the appeal will gain weight. So, it's important for a toptalker to make clear (directly or indirectly) the good intentions and motives (to help others) behind the proposal.

Confidence and Conviction: It's You They Draw Strength From

Leaders exhibit industrial-strength confidence in themselves and in their plans or proposals. They're very secure when dealing with influential and powerful people, assured in making decisions and taking risks, and totally self-certain in pursuing a course of action fraught with skepticism, doubt, and confusion by others. A high level of self-assuredness raises a person's credibility.

Leaders come across as confident in their ability to control affairs. Former Houston Mayor Kathy Whitmire told me, "Leaders share the belief that they, indeed, can make a difference. They have the power, the smarts, the staying power and that's reflected in their confidence."[11] Exceptional leaders exhibit a "superism"—an unshakable, all-encompassing belief and mega-dose of quiet confidence that they cannot fail. They know they'll experience setbacks, problems, and major roadblocks. But their confidence, optimism, and tenacity give them a mastery over everything they come up against.

An audience draws strength from toptalkers who exhibit total faith in themselves and their ability to succeed. For example, when a toptalker is advocating major changes or innovative and risky new development projects affecting the organization, his or her outward display of confidence and conviction can help strengthen the resolve of the group to give him or her support. A leader's unshakable confidence nourishes and sustains the followers' hope that what was promised will, indeed, happen. Strong leaders have this inner cauldron of assuredness that bubbles outward and affects others. And they have a "power look" of being at ease with people and the situation confronting them. The "secret," though, for many of these steel-nerved leaders is that they act as if they're comfortable even when they're not.

Buck Rogers, retired IBM marketing vice-president and now author and lecturer, told me, "The first thing I notice is the self-confidence of the person speaking to my group. Is the person at ease with the audience and does the speaker display a feeling of assurance demonstrated by knowledge of the subject and by poise. You can see it (confidence) and sense it right away."[12] The CEO of a successful Miami retail outlet told me of a marketing manager who swung him over: "There was something about the remarkable confidence she had in discussing her proposal regarding a new major marketing thrust. She seemed to be totally convinced of its potential success. Even under hard questioning, she didn't buckle. She was assertive, decisive, and unflinching in her belief. It's as if she knew something we didn't know—beyond the solid data she gave us. I guess that remarkable confidence had a significant impact upon the executive committee, because we decided to implement her creative strategy, even though we considered it more risky than our past marketing efforts." Actually, she won support through her acts of presumption, where everything she said came across as glaringly true and believable because of how she said it—with absolute conviction and authority.

The saying, "A frightened captain makes a frightened crew" applies to how an audience reacts as well. If a presenter is nervous or seems to lack the courage of his or her convictions, that will immediately be picked up by the audience and plant doubt in their minds. "When a brave man takes a stand, the spines of others are stiffened," Billy Graham has said. Many executives have told me that they are impressed with a person who holds the line and doesn't waver when people in the audience are trying to challenge his or her ideas. Without appearing arrogant, confident toptalkers will say "This IS the way IT IS" as opposed to "I think this is the way it is." It's been said that one of the major responsibilities of a true leader is to *define reality.* Reality, such as telling them, for example, that a major product line needs to be obsoleted to make way for new inno- vative one, or that the company is in a lot more trouble than they believe and drastic action is needed now, is a bitter pill for many to swallow, but it's a sign of forthrightness and confidence.

Warren Bennis, in his comprehensive research, found that out- standing leaders model *consistent behavior* and don't flip-flop on issues. You always know precisely where they stand. Their convic- tions, principles, and cherished ideas won't weaken with discussion, pressure, or self-serving opportunities that go against their moral fiber. Impressive is one who has the courage to buck conventional thinking in the organization by advocating change that bypasses tra- dition and entrenched habit. When a presenter appears to be com- promising his or her position at the least sign of pressure from the audience, then the person's credibility is tarnished. Yeats said, "I always think a great orator convinces us not by force of reasoning, but because he is visibly enjoying the beliefs which he wants us to accept."

Leaders show poise and grace under fire that reflects the say- ing that the English have an extraordinary ability for flying into a great calm. When there's upheaval, confusion, dissension, problems, and stressful events, you'll find the *leader with aplomb* staying placid and in control. That, in turn, has a calming effect on others while reassuring them that this leader is in control and will act intelligent- ly by virtue of his or her steely composure and emotional stability.

To display your confidence, use lots of direct and friendly eye contact with audience members. When people are not sure of them- selves, they have a tendency to look away from others when they're speaking. Don't "hide" behind the podium the entire time you're speaking. Step away from it and engage the audience by purpose- fully moving around the front and sides of the room. And voice tone is very important to projecting confidence. A strong, unwavering, deep tone acts as a high-wattage public-address system, amplifying your image of confidence.

Know your presentation material inside and out, anticipate tough questions and challenges from audience members, and prepare effective replies for each. But when you don't have an answer for a question, don't be afraid or overreact. Calmly and slowly say something like, "I don't know. If you need information on that, I'll get back to you quickly." And use humor when appropriate and show a light side to your presentation even if it's to smile more and show a sense of humor. Appropriate witty remarks, light-hearted comments, laughing when someone in the audience makes an amusing remark shows you're *very* relaxed with yourself and the audience.

Giving a well-organized and polished presentation is impressive enough; handling a rough-and-tumble executive audience in the "pressure cooker" setting in the boardroom where searing questions or bitter rebuttals could be the order of the day can catapult you up to a temporary pedestal (staying there requires a lot more work!). Airline pilots will testify that any experienced pilot can fly fine in great weather with no problems present. But when severe weather situations are experienced or major aircraft systems emergencies develop, the true skill and mettle of the pilot is tested to the max. That's what separates the glorified button pushers (the "autopilot pilots") from those with "the right stuff." Likewise, a presenter's refined grace, ice-cool calm, steely efficiency, and polite patience under fire will win extra bonus points in the "Man, am-I-impressed-with-him or her!" category.

Rehearse your presentation several times beforehand. It will make you feel much more confident. Totally knowing your content will free up your concentration so you can present in a more poised, relaxed, and natural way. Work on reducing any prespeaking nervousness you have by following the guidelines in Chapter 5, Overcoming Boardroom Speaking Fear.

Avoid "weak" language that could affect your image of strong conviction. A presentation sprinkled with words and phrases such as "sort of," "possibly," "maybe" comes across as tenuous or as a safe disclaimer. For example, instead of, "We are looking to possibly wrap up this program by Q4," use a statement such as, "We will complete this program by end of Q4." To project thoughtful confidence, slow your speech rate down and use deliberate pauses to emphasize key phrases and give strength to your convicted points. The tendency when nervous is to talk faster and run sentences together.

Actively encourage interaction with your audience. Encourage questions, comments, suggestions, and even dissent. Let them know that you're not afraid of conflicting points of view and that you realize that certain issues have to be resolved before they make a decision on your proposal. When a toptalker appears to be totally open and comfortable with answering (instead of evading or dreading) tough questions or challenges from the group, this shows supreme confidence. Avoid showing defensiveness, nervousness, doubt, or fear from your voice, facial expressions, overall body language, or the words you use to answer tough questions.

Don't *try* to impress your audience by appearing too cocky or too eager and anxious to please, or by overpreparing, or by blowing your horn too much (which Warren Bennis calls, "Broadcasting Station Identification"). Also don't indicate that you're overly concerned about how the audience is reacting to you or by acting in even minor subservient ways, which can paint a picture of you as being insecure. Nonconfidence can rear its nasty head when you try just a little too hard to prove yourself. If you're doing an effective job, it will speak for itself. I believe that one of the most common mistakes that young aggressive achievers make at their first important presentation is to attempt to "prove" their knowledge and competence. Unfortunately, it comes across that way.

Confident toptalkers don't make their presentations seem like a big deal (even though they are), and they're not intimidated by their audiences, but instead exhibit a steady, secure, and calm demeanor. When unexpected or uncertain situations disrupt your presentation, remain poised and calm. Don't show you're flustered, annoyed, embarrassed, or otherwise shaken when things such as audiovisual equipment malfunctions, the handouts your support person put together have mistakes, or something else unexpectedly goes wrong. The trick is to be cool, but not to freeze.

Being Knowledgeable and Competent Are Staples of Leadership

As I mentioned in the Chapter 6, How Your TopTalk Can Make a Winning Impression, the one trait that impressed executives *most* about a toptalker was his or her knowledge of the topic. I can't stress the importance of this enough. Know your stuff! It's a major ingredient in the leadership recipe and a common theme heralded by almost every executive I've talked with. And it's more than simply being a walking encyclopedia of your topic or area of expertise. In addition to knowledge, competency means being able to transform that information into a plan and exhibiting a sharp ability to execute it. Team leadership, project management skills, problem solving, negotiating, and numerous other skills complement being knowledgeable about a topic.

Lynn Bignell, the prominent New York executive recruiter, gave me this advice to pass on to those giving high-level presentations, "You want to show that you own the material . . . you want to become the information you're presenting It's almost systematic. The more you appear to own the information, the more control you have. And when you know your material inside and out, you can have a more meaningful conversation or interactive discussion with your audience, instead of a lecture."[13] CEO Linnet Deily adds, "Leaders do indeed exhibit a *command or mastery* of the subject they're talking about."[14]

"Doing one's homework" is critical for a toptalker as far as executives are concerned. It's expected—it's really the price of entry into the executive meeting room. Texaco's vice-chairman Allen Krowe noted to me, "No matter how bright, how quick, or how facile you are in your thinking, you're ten times better at all of those things if you've done more homework than others in the group have."[15] Therefore the most obvious way to show your command of your topic is to prepare and then deliver it in a well-organized, logical fashion.

In the quest to show preparation and knowledge, some presenters ("info-maniacs") make the deadly mistake of trying to cram in everything they know about the topic by speeding through it in 30 minutes. In our discussion, 3M's senior vice-president Harry Andrews said, "There is a tendency to overwhelm with data. A person should know the difference between data and information. This usually comes through with the individual's comfort level of the knowledge of his subject. If someone is very well-versed in the material he's presenting, then he will understand what information IS . . . as opposed to volumes and reams of data. I measure that as a level of comfort and it's pretty easy to differentiate the forced comfort as opposed to actual insight or knowledge."[16] Master toptalker Buck Rogers puts it in perspective, "Too many people try to give a laundry list or demonstrate how much they know about the subject. You don't have to do that. The people listening to you realize that you have to have knowledge . . . otherwise you wouldn't be there."[13]

One way to show the mastery of your topic is to able to comfortably and competently talk about it extemporaneously *within an organized format.* Elton Yates, senior vice-president at Texaco, (now retired) told me, "The first thing I seem to notice is whether they're using a prepared script and how they're using it—whether they're essentially reading it or having to refer to it very frequently. This tells me something about whether the individual knows his topic or not. The less that he uses a prepared script, the more confidence he instills in me that he knows what he's talking about. That exhibition of confidence in his presentation is what impresses me the most."[18]

This applies to using visual aids as well. The more a presenter critically depends on data-packed visuals, the less he or she is seen as truly knowledgeable. Another leading executive recruiter, James Cornehlsen, told me, "The most impressive presentation I saw was a person using 20 inch by 30 inch cards on an easel with just one impact word on each. He then talked eyeball to eyeball with people around the table. The guy was absolutely in control."[19]

Knowledgeable leaders set specific goals and create plans to reach them. Toptalkers let the audience know right away what their objectives are, what their proposal is all about, and what they want from the audience. They're "straight-line" communicators—they get right to the key issues without a lot of fanfare or extraneous details.

Another powerful way to show your command of your topic knowledge and expertise is to actively encourage questions, comments, and audience discussion of your issues. First-time presenters in the boardroom try to get through their presentation hoping that the audience doesn't ask them any "tough" questions. There are basically only two reasons a group won't ask questions: (1) the toptalker has done such a marvelous job that he or she has essentially covered everything everyone needs to know; or (2) they're not interested. Questions are to be expected and valued because they show audience interest and they give you an opportunity to remove doubt, confusion, and skepticism. Planning time for audience questions and showing that you're open to addressing anything including challenging questions or comments shows that you have a high level of confidence in your expertise. And when you adeptly handle someone's barbed response or "put-him-on-the spot" question, you elevate your status in the eyes of others and even in those of the "inquisitioner."

Finally, think through every question that might be asked as it relates to the important material you're covering. Important: be prepared to go into more detail in areas that the audience wants to explore more or to defend your position with convincing backup data/information and visual aids. Having planned for information in reserve in case it's needed not only shows that you know your stuff, but also that you're a foresighted person who leaves out nothing.

Leaders Know and "Touch" People

The dazzling powers of personal leadership creates a dependency in followers. They see the empowering leader as a dynamic spokesperson to help them express their feelings, ideas, beliefs, and values and as a moving vehicle to take them where they could not go alone. Wise leaders know of a group's set of unfulfilled goals, dreams, and ambitions. They well know and perhaps share all or part of the audience's smoldering disappointment, suffering, anger, disillusionment, indignation, shame, or embarrassment. They feel the audience's resigned longing for restitution, justice, or vindication. And they echo the audience's sanguine yearning for achievement, glory, progress, and victory. These leaders are touched by people and touch them in return.

The leader who can tap into the secret reveries and rooms of people's souls (where dark fears reside, hopes abide, and a sharp hunger for recognition, power, and control needs to be satiated) can channel it into a source of great collective power and action. People will turn over the reins to a leader who will drive the horses of their discontent away and lead them to the "promised land."

A great leader has a kind of built-in, fine-tuned personal *seismograph* that detects, measures, analyzes, and then responds to even the most delicate vibrations coming from the minds, hearts, and souls of people. He or she will pick up slight "rumblings" that are not yet being felt by anyone else. And then, acting as a loudspeaker, the leader will communicate and amplify the unspoken feelings and secret desires of the masses, as if to release the long pent-up energy of an earthquake.

Napoleon said, "A leader is a dealer in hope." During a toptalk, these leaders get people to believe that there's a solution and a better tomorrow with their plan and guidance. They get the audience personally involved and give them a feeling of authentic power. These leaders get the audience to believe that they can make a difference by their support and commitment to the leaders cause. Above all, inspirational leaders make people feel good about themselves and elevate their esteem and status in their own eyes and in the eyes of others. Toptalkers don't "motivate" people as if somehow to create motivation out of thin air; they discover, tap into, and then channel existing motives of their followers toward the goals they are striving toward.

A leader learns by observing and watching people, by testing his or her theories of human nature, by studying psychology, by exposing himself or herself to diverse human dealings, and by always analyzing what occurred and why and determining how the interaction could be improved next time.

Before your toptalk, do a detailed audience analysis (see Chapter 2, Knowing Your audience). If you're going to appeal to the needs, ambitions, fears, values, insecurities, wishes, pride, and other emotions, needs, and expectations of your audience, you've got to know exactly who they are and what turns them on and turns them off.

Be an active and sensitive listener. I've found that people *totally open up* to a great listener and will tell you very frank and personal details about themselves and often share their innermost feelings and secrets. There's something about an empathic listener (who will not breech confidences) that causes people to quickly and largely develop trust for and quick bonding with that person. People divulge their intimate feelings and experiences to psychologists and psychiatrists because of their rapt caring listening and their asking insightful questions. Good leaders do likewise: they listen and ask meaningful questions to understand and help.

Empathize with your audience. Spend time asking yourself, "If I were the people in my audience and I were listening to my proposal, what would my concerns be? What would motivate me to be excited about it? How would it help me in my job?" While we could never actually do it accurately, trying to put yourself in their bodies, minds, hearts, and souls will at least give you a better understanding of them. "Walk in their shoes" as the saying goes. Think about their personalities and what drives them. Try to feel yourself evaluating situations as they would, cherishing what they value most, and projecting inward what their insecurities and weaknesses are. Ask what image they want to portray of themselves. Ask yourself how each person in your audience might want to be changed by your ideas or project. Be a human seismograph with empathy as the recording needle.

If appropriate during your toptalk, communicate to your audience what you believe they are feeling and thinking and wanting, but perhaps are afraid to articulate for one reason or another. Be their collective voice of discontent, hope, and action. Let them see possibilities through you and be their advocate.

Leaders See the "Big Picture" and Think Boldly

Leaders from antiquity who have left their indelible mark on the world were big and bold thinkers and ambitious doers. King Phillip of Macedonia said to his son Alexander, "You must find a kingdom big enough for your ambition." So he did. Before he died at the early age of 32, Alexander the Great conquered all of Persia right to the borders of India.

Leaders have the ability to see the "big picture" of situations. They're *global thinkers* in that they examine a very large-scale approach or connection to a problem or opportunity. It's as if a person takes a helicopter ride to 30,000 feet and surveys the entire landscape to understand what the full landscape looks like. This lets the leader know what routes, options, consequences, and obstacles are facing him or her.

Toptalkers who think in big pictures don't give a presentation just about their own department or division as if it's a separate entity in isolation. Instead, they show how their project goals or ideas affect other areas of the organization and how the success of his project plays into the overall vision and strategic directions of the organization. Big picture thinkers are not turf protectors—they're empire builders who seek not their own selfish fiefdoms but look to build the organization's empire. These leaders explain the linkages between their ideas and the direction the whole organization is moving in. They grasp the relationship of their work to much larger strategic realities of the whole of the organization and its future and communicate it clearly.

Big-picture-thinking leaders examine the critical broader and longer-term tangible and intangible factors that might have an impact on their ideas, plans, and decisions, such as economic forecasts, possible technological breakthroughs, anticipated social and demographic trends, new market possibilities, impact from competitors, shifting global markets, and the consequences of their own organization's long-term plans. They understand complex interrelationships and their impact on one another. There are persons who peer into the future, think ahead, and plan accordingly. Effective toptalkers are seen as being strategic thinkers and doers as opposed to (smaller-scale) tactical leaders.

Good leaders have timing, and they know priorities. "Everything in this world has its critical moment; and the height of good conduct consists in knowing it and seizing it," said Cardinal deRitz, seventeenth-century French ecclesiastic and politician. Leaders are ones who respond quickly to grab opportunities and take advantage of them. They are possibility thinkers and are very optimistic in believing they can control the destiny of events.

Bold thinking involves doing things in advance of other people, taking risks, pioneering new concepts, being the trailblazer, which all adds up to being an innovator. Leadership is about progress and change and doing what others are afraid to do or are not wise enough to do. Bold thinking involves breakthroughs, quantum leaps, paradigm shifts, and sometimes thinking the impossible.

To demonstrate big-picture thinking during your toptalk, focus on those strategic high-priority issues that grip your audience. Show how your proposal fits neatly into the bigger plans of the organization. Demonstrate that you have carefully done your homework and understand all the possible consequences of your project as it relates to major factors (economy, technology, competition, etc.) that might affect it. Keep a tight focus on the key issues your audience is concerned about and relate how your plan or idea addresses them.

When presenting your bold and innovative ideas and major organization changes, give your audience startling examples and dire consequences of the effect of lack of vision, stifling bureaucracy, fear of innovation and change, late starts, lack of commitment, and intergroup battles that resulted in lost opportunities of an incredible scale for new products and services.

In his book *Tough-Minded Leadership*, author and consultant Joe Botten writes, "Leaders believe negativism is never justified. They know that there are plus and minus elements in many situations but that the minus areas can be made into pluses."[20] The great American military generals of World War II such as Eisenhower, Patton, and Bradley, who had never led masses of soldiers in combat on such an enormous scale, described later their most important lesson in leadership: always be optimistic of victory! As a big and bold-thinking toptalker, you need to exhibit a sense of great optimism in front of your audience by repeating various messages that communicate, "We can do it if we're steadfast . . . if we don't give up . . . if we maintain courage." Tough-minded optimism is often forged in a crucible of experience, tempered by setbacks, hammered tough by faith, and renewed by the hope that opportunities will open up again.

Big-picture thinkers do their homework and read extensively about broader issues occurring in their market, industry, and the economy as a whole. During their presentation, they often show connections of their main points to relevant strategic concepts, philosophies, theories, trends, industry directions, political issues, or other global issues to the main points they are making in their toptalk. Modestly exhibiting yourself as a well-read thinker and well-rounded generalist will help elevate your status as a highly informed individual who has a deeper understanding of worldly affairs and history.

Leaders Create a Vision That Beckons and Enthralls

Make no little plans. They have no magic to stir men's blood. Make big plans; aim high in hope and work.

—D.H. BURNHAM

Alvin Toffler, well-known futurist and writer, would advise people, "You've got to think about 'big things' while you're doing small things, so that all the small things go in the right direction." The big thing that creative communication leaders use to inspire and move others is a grand vision of what might be. It can be a vision of the way the organization will look in the future as a result of the planned change, a vision associated with a new major project, or even a vision of creating an exciting new product or service.

"Visioneers" captivate and rally their followers by creating and communicating spellbinding and enduring visions. Alexander the Great, Caesar, Napoleon, Ghandi, Lincoln, Churchill, Martin Luther King, Jr., and countless other men and women who've changed the course of history did so by creatively painting (with words, symbols, metaphors) for their followers an exciting, vibrant, and worthwhile glimpse of the future eagerly awaiting them. With a sense of preordained mission, these visioneers made a practice of reaching for challenges that were beyond their grasp. They spoke of a destiny, not merely a future.

John Kennedy's 1961 daunting vision of putting men on the moon and returning them safely within a decade of his challenging announcement pushed and pulled NASA to create monumental technological breakthroughs to fulfill that "out-of-this-world" vision. President Bush was one leader, though, who had trouble with what he called the "vision thing," which appeared to baffle him. While an effective leader in many ways, presidential scholars noted that he focused on day-to-day operations at the expense of bold, long-term initiatives.[21]

"Tell-a-vision" has been used by both good and evil leaders throughout history. Jesus was a guiding force in the world for two thousand years. His enduring messages and parables of faith, hope, charity, and love wove visions of the kingdom of God on earth and in heaven awaiting those who would embrace The Word. Hitler's speeches brilliantly mesmerized and incited a nation to its ultimate moral and physical destruction with his intoxicating vision of a glorious thousand-year Reich of conquest and supreme greatness to be savored by all Aryans.

Articulating a Vision Is Important and It Gets Results for Leaders

Several years ago, in a study of 1,500 senior executives in 20 countries (870 of them CEOs) by the Columbia University Graduate School of Business done for Korn Ferry International, they were asked to assess the dominant characteristics that describe today's CEO and ones that will describe the ideal leader of the year 2000. Seventy-five percent, believed that *conveying a strong sense of vision* was important, while 98 percent said it will be important in the year 2000.[22] When James Burke, an IBM director, was leading a search to replace CEO John Akers, he said that above all, he wanted a visionary leader who has a savvy sense of business. High tech experience is not required; passion and integrity are a must.[23] Burke stated that candidates "must know how to get people excited by change. I'd opt for a creative visionary at the expense of having technical knowledge."[24]

Two Stanford professors, James C. Colins and Jerry I. Porris, discovered in their research that vision-driven companies—ones that clearly articulated their mission (or reason for being) and communicated its core values and philosophies so that they were held dearly by their employees—actually performed 8 times better than their competitors and performed 55 times better than the general market.[25] Porris says, "visionary companies stand out partly by setting ambitious goals, communicating them to employees, and following a core ideology—a purpose behind making money."[26]

The more important your toptalk, the more you need to articulate a vision of your idea, project, approach, proposal, plan, or solution. Yet, even "ordinary" presentations can make use of visionary elements that educate, motivate, and entertain. A Chinese saying tells us, "The tongue can paint what the eye can't see." Indeed, a master of toptalk paints a vision, communicates it, gets people to see it, feel it, believe it, and become totally committed to achieving it.

Highly impacting leaders create what I call *intravenous visions* that feed motivational nourishment right into the veins of people's hearts and souls. Ray Smith, the CEO of Bell Atlantic, has an incredibly focused bold vision of the future where television and the telephone system are merged with the hoped-for result of making the nation's number-two telephone company grow dramatically. To symbolically "stay tuned" to his vision, he wants employees to carry a blue poker chip in their hip pockets, as he does, to keep them focused on his blue-chip priorities.[27] "Beware the small dreamer," as one Los Angeles bank senior vice-president warned me.

Seeing and Telling About What Has Not Yet Been Created

An effective vision for a toptalk is a clear, compelling, realistic, and persuasively communicated image of an attractive future awaiting those who support the policy, ideas, goals, and mission that make up the vision. A vision can give a deeper, more profound meaning to a leader's cause. It's not a prediction or forecast, but a description of how things are planned to be, what the future will hold. It says, "Here is what we want to be!" In their book, *Creating Excellence: Managing Corporate Culture, Strategy and Change in The New Age*, authors Craig R. Hickman and Michael A. Silva describe vision as "a mental journey from the known to the unknown, creating the future from a montage of facts, hopes, dreams, dangers, and opportunities."[28]

A toptalk vision is a mental, emotional, and even spiritually based glimpse of a desirable future condition that is somehow better than the existing one. A vice-president of research and development for a Silicon Valley high-tech company put it to me simply, "We're keeping our eye on the future because that's where we're going to be spending the rest of our time." Well-constructed and dynamically articulated visions can draw and uplift an audience by deeply tapping into their hopes, dreams, and aspirations.

Brightly illuminated visions can ignite feelings of responsibility, decency, potential greatness, boldness, power, courage, or they can build a sense of closeness with God. In Proverbs, the Bible tells us, "Where there is no vision, people perish." People need to feel a sense of purpose and meaning in their lives. We all need to feel that what we do counts for something beyond accumulating material goods, grabbing for power, or building artifacts. A communicating leader's inspired vision can nourish a starved or insatiable soul and sustain hope and optimism. Via the right vision, the audience will be mobilized, motivated, drawn together, and committed to press on toward its guiding light. And it can rally people around the organization flagpole when morale begins to sag by saying it's a new year and the slogan is "In with the bold, out with the blues!"

A Toptalk Vision is More than a Mere Statement

When I talk about articulating a vision for your presentations, I'm not referring to coming up with a written formal (carefully worded) *vision statement*, which many organizations have. This is a summary of the role, mission, values, and beliefs of an organization and consists of crafting and linking key words and phrases together. Its purpose is to make clear where the organization is heading and what it deems important. For example, National Aeronautics and Space Administration (NASA) created this vision statement: "As explorers, pioneers, and innovators, we will boldly expand the frontiers of air and space for the benefit of all. NASA defines its mission as a human presence in and beyond earth orbit; scientific knowledge of earth, the solar system and beyond; aeronautics; U.S. competitiveness, and science education."[29] Texaco Corporation's vision is "to be one of the most admired, profitable, and competitive companies, and to make Texaco the leader in its industry."[30]

Vision statements used by organizations are intended to be the focal point for all their plans, strategies, and approaches that are designed to bring their vision into reality. More than a public relations tool or an executive team-building exercise, vision statements should help align everyone to change the fundamental culture and character of the organization.

Two "Flavors" of Visions: Altruistic and Pragmatic

In Aristotle's famous work *Rhetoric*, he says that the most important thing in making a speech is keeping to one overall theme. Whether it's winning, survival, vanquishing the enemy, or doing the impossible, a vision is a great way to do that. During your toptalk, you create and articulate a vision as if you were an *oral cinematographer* making a movie or video about how your proposal will affect the organization's operations and how the lives of people within it will be enriched by playing their orchestrated parts.

Clearly communicating your vision means including several or all of these elements: (1) overall aims; (2) the goals to be reached; (3) the change that's envisioned; (4) benefits to the audience and roles they should play to make it happen; (5) how the action steps required for the vision link together to attain its objectives; and (6) how it should be implemented in a number of situations, places, and ways. Dr. Harry Andrews, senior vice-president at 3M, told me that in communicating a vision, make it simple, far-sighted, and strategic.[31]

Visions vary infinitely in their style and content. There are essentially two primary types of visions you can use in your speech or presentation and you can mix elements of each to create a blend. The first is what I call the *Altruistic Vision* (AV). This type of vision has these characteristics. It . . .

- is more imaginative, abstract, and conceptual in nature; it focuses on a general ideal or principle as opposed to specific goals.

- focuses on universal and timeless principles such as fairness, integrity, love, justice, and trust.

- draws upon deep emotions and spiritual sensitivities of the audience.

- appeals to the highest principles and selfless nature of people.

- is stable and guides people far into the future focusing on long-range possibilities.

- uses symbolism, creative metaphors, poetic language.

- spotlights the most noble and worthwhile intentions of helping people.

- often focuses on battling evil, overcoming "bad" situations, solving major problems that cause human suffering of any kind, or improving the quality of life.

- enlists people to try to do the "impossible" by overcoming insurmountable odds or coming up with breakthrough results.

A wonderful altruistic vision couched as a dream immortalized Martin Luther King, Jr., and what he stood for in his epic speech, "I Have a Dream." That one speech, with its incredibly hopeful message delivered in a powerfully inspiring way, pushed a nation and the world to move faster toward civil rights. An altruistic vision can be very successful when the "soft stuff"—values, principles, and beliefs that represent the things a company stands for—drives the business. Here's an example of one CEO of a computer manufacturer giving his "vision" of the future to his middle- and upper-level managers:

> In 5 years we will increase revenues over 300 percent, cut costs by 45 percent, improve productivity by 60 percent, and reduce manufacturing defects by over 70 percent. I'm so excited and you should be too!

This focus on financial and operational goals is not an altruistic vision and would hardly stir the soul (maybe the pocketbook). In comparison, note the effect an audience would have with this CEO (from a competitor company) who gives her altruistic vision:

> Our precious children are the future of our wonderful country. That's why we are embarking on the most innovative, challenging, and costly research and development project to date, called 'Brain Child.' In

five years, we'll develop the most sophisticated, powerful, low-cost multimedia computers the world has ever seen. They'll be ten times as fast as our most powerful computer is now. They'll be so easy to use that every child in every school, regardless of learning ability, will be able to significantly accelerate their education with interactive software using creative video, audio, and animation. And we'll make them so inexpensive that schools will have one on each desk.

We'll revolutionize education and change children's outlook on life and learning, and even help instill in them deep values that our nation seems to have forgotten. The toughest subjects will be immensely easier to understand, and learning will be more challenging, interesting, and fun! We'll enable children even in the poorest neighborhoods to compete with any one... any where and gain incredible knowledge, insight and confidence at their own pace. All of you here today will be the champions who, through your imagination, sweat, and perseverance, will dramatically enrich the lives and opportunities of our children everywhere by making this bold vision a wondrous part of their lives and yours. Our first step in making our nation a better place begins today. Let me give you the goals and details of our plan . . .

The second type of vision is called the *Pragmatic Vision* (PV) which tends to be based more on an overall business plan. It still paints a glimpse of the future, but it's more strategic and "down-to-earth" in nature. It includes more of the "hard stuff"—plans, strategies, financial forecasts, operating requirements, and organization changes, among others. It has the following characteristics. It . . . .

- is more detailed and specific in terms of objectives, plans, directions, or approaches and is designed to become an organizing force behind decisions.

- is designed to provide understanding, direction, and guidance more than motivation or inspiration.

- often communicates a more results-oriented future that you intend to create.

- is created to be perceived as necessary, attractive, and attainable by the audience.

- is designed to align groups and bind organizations together to converge efforts, cooperate, and maintain momentum of plans.

- usually includes the required action steps needed to fulfill the vision.

- focuses less on high principles and more on dire business reasons and situations (economic, market, and competitive conditions) to galvanize action and proceed with operations.

Here's an example of a CEO communicating a no-nonsense, Pragmatic Vision (PV) that focuses more on direction, priorities, and strategy than on a "feel-good" conceptual "grand" vision with a broader, deeper philosophical view:

> I see our organization dramatically changing over the next five years. No longer will we tolerate turfs and fiefdoms. We're going to cooperate and wear one hat that says XYZ Company and put the good of the company before your department or division. And we will be trimming down some more—flattening our hierarchy and slimming our bureaucracy to speed up our decision making to make us more agile and responsive to each other and our customers. And we're going to be focusing on becoming the absolute technological and innovation leaders in the industry. We'll be the leading-edge company when it comes to bringing new and better products out faster than any of our competitors. Everything we do will be directed to finding and exploiting opportunities as fully and as quickly as we can. We'll become masters of analyzing and exploiting future trends before anyone else does.
>
> Team approach with real employee involvement will be the way we will operate on a daily basis. We can't afford to let ideas rot in our employees' heads. We'll farm those ideas and harvest the benefits together. And instead of trying to be all things to all of our customers, we're going to be slowly divesting ourselves of unprofitable businesses and just focus on the three areas of expertise that give us our unique competitive advantage: microprocessor-driven actuator devices, artificial intelligence voice controlled software interfaces, and total system integration within all our future product ranges. Our vision will remake our organization into a more strategic-focused, productive, innovative, efficient, and customer-driven force to be reckoned with in the industry over the next decade. Here are some details of the plan to make that vision come alive . . . .

Create a Motivating Vision That Really Means Something

Activity without a vision is empty. A vision without a plan is a dream, but planned activity to fulfill a vision is exciting. Business is turning off to executives who just focus on thinking up creative rosy visions of the future without implementing them with hard-core plans. Many see that as today's equivalent of yesteryear's "idea man" who did nothing but stare out the window with feet on the desk thinking of tomorrow's blockbuster ideas. Executives need to be more than just imaginative visioneers, they have got to be detail-oriented "mechanics" who fix problems and methodically make things happen. Therefore, as a toptalker, you need to both articulate a vision of a project or plan and then, in as detailed a fashion as necessary, give the action-oriented, no-nonsense specifics of how to get there; and then do it effectively and efficiently. In essence, you've got to first put on the hat of architect (who creates the rendering), and then switch to builder (who constructs it). You've got to be an organization alchemist weaver who spins straw into gold and turns dreams into reality.

Ideas to Help You Craft Your Vision

There is no "right" or "wrong" vision—only one that works for you and your intentions. Too much altruism can make it vague and wishy-washy; too much pragmatism can make it stainless steel cold and uninspiring. Ideally, your toptalk vision to an executive audience should have elements of both an altruistic vision and a pragmatic one. You can excite them with a vivid picture that caters to their psychological and spiritual needs, while giving them the hard-nosed, bottom-line, real-world strategy to reach that wonderful vision. To help you design and articulate your vision ask yourself these questions:

1. What specific emotions/feelings do I want the audience to experience as a result of my vision? Example: pride, power, indignation, hope, faith, trust, control, excitement, anticipation, "can do."

2. What theme, metaphor, slogan, or speech device (e.g., repetition) can strengthen my vision and help make it concise, poignant, simple, and memorable?

3. How can I use my vision to clearly focus on my mission, goals, strategy, and critical points? How can I get people to feel the same way I do?

4. How can my vision give a deep sense of purpose and value to what I'm proposing for the audience?

5. How can I make my vision personally meaningful for every-one in my audience?

6. How can I articulate my vision in a poetic way that literally paints a scenario of a positive, attractive, "let's-march-toward-it" future?

7. How might my vision help illuminate my strongest beliefs?

8. How can I evaluate the usefulness of my vision and who can help me in its creation?

9. How can my vision create a sense of righteous conflict - to overcome "something bad" that hurts the quality of life for my audience?

10. How can I make my vision demonstrate the force of my intent and commitment?

11. What can I do to make my vision imaginative and unique?

12. How can I creatively design a vision that will grab the very souls of people and provide a sense of purposefulness and ownership into the future?

13. How can my vision challenge the audience to change their attitudes and exceed their goals and performances?

14. What facts, examples, statistics, descriptions will bring a sense of pure realism to the vision?

15. How can the vision be designed and spoken about in ways that will fit within the culture of the organization?

16. What would make my vision truly inspiring and motivational?

17. What can I do to impart a sense of urgency needed to fulfill the vision?

18. How much "passion" should I use when delivering my vision?

19. What paradigm or framework of the world will my vision paint?

20. How can my vision help to maintain momentum of my project or plan?

21. How can I use the technological power of interactive computerized multimedia to help create an "awesome" vision using CD-quality music/sound, video, animation, text, or special effects?

Passion—When a Word from the Heart Goes Straight to the Heart

Displaying passion with purpose during a presentation is *leadership by contagion* and sets up a "Go for it!" climate in the audience. A speech or presentation without any feeling is lifeless, sterile, flat, and barren. A stiff, reserved, unresponsive presenter cools the audience down quickly—takes the fire out of them. Passion, however, is a powerful emotional projection and an honest display of your personality, values, hopes, and commitments. William Jennings Bryan put it aptly, "An orator is a man who says what he thinks and feels what he says." Texaco senior vice-chaiman, Allen Krowe, feels uncomfortable with presenters ("with an absolutely placid face") who show no emotional concern about things. "I like for them to be joyous at victory, saddened about defeat. And I'd like for their adrenaline to rise when a challenge is ahead," he told me.[32]

A display of emotion is appropriate depending upon the dynamics you're seeking from your high-level audience. The more you want them to change or move in a direction, the more your emotion acts as a persuasive catalyst. While executives have bluntly told me that they don't like a *needless* display of emotion during a presentation, which (they feel) weakens a person's credibility or interferes with the rational points being made, they are genuinely moved by a leader whose passion communicates an appropriate sense of commitment, dedication, urgency, energy, optimism, and a zeal to succeed and overcome regardless of the hardships ahead.

Passion is an ardent, soul-stirring, group-seizing, and hormone-stampeding emotion that can energize and motivate an audience into following a leader. The world is moved by highly motivated people who stir themselves up before they stir others—who believe in something to the depths of their soul and who want to make a difference for others. It's a fact: *An audience doesn't care how much you know unless they know how much you care!* Anatole France said, "I prefer the errors of enthusiasm to the indifference of wisdom." I've had executives tell me of numerous presenters who gave a thorough, accurate, and informative presentation, but it was given with no feeling whatsoever. It had no (audience) "moving power."

When painting that inspiring vision, or advocating dramatic change, or when rallying the audience to a cause, passion is the needed explosive fuel to ignite the charge to surge forward. It was

Lord Alfred Tennyson who said, "The happiness of a man in this life does not consist in the absence but in the mastery of his passions." And La Rochefoucauld noted, "If we resist our passions, it is more due to their weakness than to our strength." Zestful strong leaders who are possessed by this 360-degree enthusiasm are masters of their own deep passions . . . *and they show it!*

The most effective leaders have a flair for displaying their intense feelings about their visions, goals, and dreams because they know that intellectual points wrapped in a warm package of sincere emotions is a dynamic elixir for stimulating the hearts and souls of the audience. Master speech writer and executive speech coach John McGrath told me, "I believe that an audience will believe you only to the degree that they believe you believe yourself. That requires more than data. Data never excited anybody. If you want them to be excited, you have to be excited. You can't raise an audience above a level you're at."[33]

Stronger and more long lasting than enthusiasm, passion is a driving emotion that comes from deep within the visceral essence of a person. When communicated by searing words, a voice tone saturated with hope or expectation or righteous anger, and body gestures electrified with fervor and force, it rubs off and *into* people. Each of the world's great leaders in government, commerce, science, and elsewhere publicly displayed their own special firebrand of quiet or volcanic passion.

In his book *Selling the Dream*, author Guy Kawasaki focuses on passion when he details the concept of business "evangelism," which he describes as a process of convincing people to believe in your product or idea *as much as you do.* Evangelism, according to him, is selling your dream by using fervor, zeal, guts, and cunning. And when people believe in your cause, they sustain it during difficult times and against all comers. His concept of an evangelist is not some wide-eyed, ranting and raving megalomaniac proclaiming the miracles of following a particular concept or proposal, but a dedicated, highly rational, well-organized, and articulate professional who uses the dynamic power of passion to help sweep people onto the magic carpet heading toward the vision magnificently painted by the evangelist.[34]

Audiences are more prone to deeply trust a person who displays a sense of *righteous* passion because they know that money, fame, or power are not the primary selfish motivators of that person.

Passion evokes a spiritual type of energetic and unflagging dedication to, for example, a high-principled cause. Soulful passion from the leader shouts to the audience, "I want to make a difference," "I'm dedicated," and "I'll succeed for you because I must!"

Not every toptalk needs or deserves passion. Executives are not recommending that speakers display unchained passion when presenting dry information updates on last quarter's performance, but they do feel that an appropriate display of energizing emotions for a new innovative project, idea, or proposal, for example, will certainly generate excitement for the audience. In times of corporate turmoil, indecision, insecurity, and doubt, one strong passionate leader can emerge and create a path from the darkness of trouble to the light of success for all to begin the journey. The greater the challenge . . . the more minds need to be pried open . . . the more an executive group needs to be shaken or awakened, the more the need to inject passion into the delivery of the presentation.

It's not a matter of "acting" passionate or forcing the dynamics of enthusiastic emotions or faking it, but simply letting your real emotions sculpt the information and ideas you're proposing into a masterpiece of conviction. I believe that often when making a decision, people would rather have one powerful, soul-satisfying emotion than a dozen facts. While executives pride themselves on making analytical decisions, many I've interviewed agreed that they mix the rational with the purely emotional. Blaise Pascal put it: "The heart has its reasons which reason knows nothing of."

A Passionate and Visionary Presentation that Helped Launch a World-Class Car

Robert P. Marcell, general manager of Chrysler's Small-Car Platform Engineering, is the perfect example of a crusader-type of leader using creative communication leadership during his toptalk.[35] His passion-filled persuasive presentation evoked heartfelt visions of what might be and was instrumental in persuading then Chrysler Chairman Lee Iacocca (now retired) to give him the approval to do what many in the auto industry thought impossible: create an inexpensive, top-quality, high-performance world-class subcompact, the Neon, to be built solely by Chrysler (with no partners) in North America at a profit (most subcompacts are not profitable).

He gave his presentation twice—once to his staff and then he showed the videotape (with audience reaction) to Iacocca. Marcell knew his presentation had to dramatically impact his audience, reignite the imagination, and fire up the motivation of his 1,000 employees. His toptalk had to deftly challenge a financial hard-nosed and skeptical Iacocca to support them in proving their detractors wrong—that they, indeed, could build, using American ingenuity and teamwork, a superb small car by breakthrough engineering design and efficient manufacturing.

Instead of a conventional presentation laden with specifications and statistics, design renderings, or financial projections, Marcell's strategy was to grip his audience in an emotional vice and focus on symbolism and dreaded analogy. He began by displaying 35mm slides he recently took of his home town—Iron River, Michigan. A once thriving mining community, the pictures now showed the empty school he attended, the boarded-up church he had been married in, and the abandoned railroad yards that once gave his neighbors a safe, secure living. I watched the videotaped presentation he sent me as his emotion-filled crackling voice sadly narrated the story of a town where two thirds of the population left "because we couldn't compete." His audience later told him they cringed every time he *purposely* repeated that death knell phrase . . . "we just couldn't compete."

His searing point was that if Chrysler didn't break paradigms and be willing to compete head-on with their strongest competitors and beat them at their own game, then their fate might very well be the same as his ramshackled home town. He went on to paint a vision of not only survival, but *yes-we-can-do-it* success. "We can make this happen *only* if we dare to be different." His passionate message was that "the situation is this serious and if we're successful, the consequences could be this great!" Instead of being tired of running and being on the defensive, his stirring vision implored his group to take the high-ground and mount an offensive to win: "We're out to get back what we once had!"

His vision of making an all-out stand to compete *and win* with the world's best poignantly focused everything. And that vision was aimed at lifting them to that higher—rarified—plateau where the soul's engine breathes the fuel of accomplishment and greatness, as he bottom-lined-it, "If we're successful, small cars can be built in America and Chrysler can survive. We could be reason U.S. industry is competitive. We could be the reason our kids won't have to work their adult lives in some fast-food place."

Bob Marcell motivated his team and his superiors to do much more than they originally expected to do. He dramatically raised their level of consciousness about the critical outcomes and ways of reaching them. He got people to transcend their own self-interests for the sake of Chrysler and perhaps the nation and appealed to their righteous higher realm principles.

Epilogue: The Neon went on to rave reviews even before its 1994 sales introduction and was named car of the year by *Automobile* magazine and rated best least-expensive car by the American Automobile Association. A great car might never have seen the light of day had Bob Marcell not used vision and passion to give it a chance for engineering and manufacturing greatness.

HOW TO WIN OVER EXECUTIVES WITH TOPTALK HUMOR

The kind of humor I like is the thing that makes me laugh
for five seconds and think for ten minutes.

—William Davis

Humor is a key part of a leader's vibrant communication strategy to amuse, invigorate, persuade, entertain, sharpen a viewpoint, reduce tension, engage, show the ridiculousness of an idea or situation, and strongly bond with an audience. Contrary to what many people believe, appropriate and well-done humor is appreciated by senior executives who often dread sitting through data-packed, tedious, and seemingly endless meetings. The stereotyped image of a group of serious, stone-faced board members is a wrong one. Many business leaders that I've talked with regarding humor seem to believe what seventeenth century French writer Francis de La Rochefoucauld wrote, "Solemnity is a trick of the body to hide the faults of the mind." There should be some *funny business* going on in the boardroom.

Emerson said, "If you would rule the world quietly, you must keep it amused." When you think of inspiring leaders, you'll find that many of them used humor in their speeches or would display a sense of humor in tough times that would momentarily shift their followers away from paralyzing fear or pain and help lift their sagging spirits to push on against the tide of adversity. Effective leaders believe that the love of truth lies at the root of much humor. Aristotle said it long ago, "Humor is the only test of gravity, and gravity of humor, for a subject which will not bear raillery is suspicious, and a jest which will not bear serious examination is false wit."

Poignant humor can give us a mental and emotional wake-up call with the ferocity of a sonic boom and all of a sudden focus a whole new emphasis or understanding of problems as it illuminates, enlightens, and showcases ideas and information in meaningful new ways. One senior executive who was trying to get board approval for his new creative plan to "reinvent" (as he termed it) his marketing and sales organization, ended his presentation with this conclusion: "There's the story of a chairman of the board who was suddenly stricken with an illness that required surgery. As he was wheeled from the operating room, he was handed a telegram signed by his company's board of directors which read, 'We wish you a speedy recovery—by a vote of nine to five!' As the group's laughter died down (especially the chairman's), the speaker got serious with, 'Well, we need a speedy recovery too, but I need more than a majority vote—I need all your support and commitment. Can I count on it?' He got it!"

Malcolm Kushner, former San Francisco attorney, is one of the country's leading experts on business humor and author of *The Light Touch: How to Use Humor for Business Success*.[36] He told me, "Successful executives use humor to their advantage and that helps them to be among the most admired members of their organizations. Good leaders have a light touch that produces solid results in their communications. They use humor as a powerful magnet to draw people deeper into their presentation. People want to be around them. The value of humor cannot be overestimated in a business environment." Kushner believes that appropriate humor can dramatically help advance your career.

Having a "Scent" of Humor

What is humor anyway? It can be a joke, anecdote, amusing comment or retort, clever quote, creative satire, cartoon, or bizarre fact that makes people laugh, smile, feel amused, or that prompts them to react with a warm, knowing smile of appreciation. It can be planned, but it's usually best when it comes across as natural and spontaneous, which gives it a sense of intimacy. However, the idea that it implies "comedy" resulting in laughter—is a gross misconception. Belly laughs are great, but few of us are capable of bringing them on with others. Besides, being a stand-up comic in the boardroom can, indeed, be a "career-limiting" move. While humor need not be hilarious, it does have to amuse, even if ever so slightly.

A major part of humor is *having and displaying a sense of humor*—being ready to smile, chuckle, and easily laugh at the jokes of others, laugh at yourself or at your mistakes, and to find the absurdity in everyday life. The simple act of just smiling during a presentation gives people the impression that one has a sense of humor. And executives feel that a sense of humor is a nice quality to have. In our executive survey, when we asked executives how they would like to improve *their* presentations, using more appropriate humor in their presentations was placed third in their top list (coming across more polished was first and improving verbal and nonverbal speaking skills ranked second).

Researchers concur that humor stimulates creativity, helps in problem-solving, and is a powerful catalyst in cementing strong interpersonal relationships. *The fact is once you get people laughing, they're listening and then you can tell them almost anything.* People remember points much better when they're smiling.

An Image Booster for Leaders

Boston University history professor Joseph Boskin, who teaches a course on humor in twentieth-century America, says that humorous people are usually wiser, have broader perspectives on situations, and are often better workers.[37] Or perhaps they're just perceived that way. Using humor or displaying a sense of it can elevate your status in the eyes of the audience. As author Romain Gary puts it, "Humor is an affirmation of dignity, a declaration of man's superiority to all that befalls him."

Dealing with humor in any of its forms clearly gives your toptalk audience the impression that you're relaxed, confident, in control, and enjoy what you're doing. And that means enhanced credibility as a leader. Using humor in a natural way implies that you feel very comfortable with yourself and the audience. Good humor helps a business presentation stay light, maneuverable, and open to change.

Tasteful and appropriate self-deprecating humor can make a leader appear much more approachable, "human," and real to his or her followers, and this encourages them to open up to the leader. It endears people to the leader. The right humor tells the audience that you always take your job and responsibility very seriously, but that you don't always take yourself seriously. An ample-girthed chief financial officer of a small San Francisco software company told me that he poked fun at his shape by connecting it to the explosion of database information available today: "I get heavier as I get older because there's a lot more information in my head."

One CEO of a $200 million midwest manufacturing company made some unpopular but (by all accounts) necessary decisions to cut overhead costs, capital improvements, and staff. He described to me a short briefing he gave to a large group of tense plant workers on the reasons for the company's seemingly drastic actions. He began, "With all that's been going on recently, I guess I'm not the most popular guy around. The only person who thinks I'm a 10 is my shoe salesman. I'd like to explain exactly why we absolutely had to do what we had to do . . . " It broke the ice and made him appear just a bit more empathic and caring. G. K. Chesterton put it nicely: "Angels can fly because they take themselves lightly."

Will Your Humor Pass the "Test"?

For humor to be effective in your toptalk, it should pass these tests:

Is It Relevant? It's one thing to tell a great gut-wrenching joke at a party and another to tell one at a board meeting that has nothing to do with the discussion at hand. *Business humor is meaningful.* It makes a well-intentioned point and adds strength to the business message. It has an objective, is specific to the audience's interests, and is message-oriented!

Is It Appropriate and Tasteful? Humor that is hurtful, sarcastic, ill-mannered, or in otherwise poor taste can wreck a presentation. Gender, racial, ethnic, sexual, coarse, or "gross" humor is a turnoff and plain unprofessional. It shatters credibility immediately. If you insult your audience or even just make them uncomfortable, you've lost them. One bawdy New York City regional sales manager for an electronic parts manufacturer gave a presentation to his peers in a rather conservative southern city during the Christmas holiday season. He thought he was being witty and amusing answering one of his colleagues who challenged him on one of his ideas by saying, "You've noticed that I placed a sprig of mistletoe just under the tail of my coat." What might have otherwise worked in anything-goes New York bombed there. As business humor consultant Malcolm Kusher advised me, "If in doubt, leave it out."

Is It Well-timed? A sales vice-president from a major retail chain told me, "At just the point when my audience seems to suppress a yawn, I try to spark a somewhat dry business talk with a quick, humorous pick-me-up." Use planned or spontaneous humor to punch through tension, apathy or misunderstanding.

Develop Your Own Humor Style

Effective leaders can become "humoricators"—people who use humor to communicate in a dynamic fashion. While some people can't tell a joke to save their lives, everyone can learn to use humor more effectively, most experts tell us. The secret is to develop your own style, learn a few tricks, and take the time to practice. Joke books are fine for a start to give you ideas for brainstorming, but you're better off looking for material from your own experiences. Placing cartoons on your visual aids from such publications as *The Wall Street Journal*, *The New Yorker*, and other magazines or newspapers is an easy and effective way to add humor and lightness to an otherwise dry presentation. And more and more computer clip art is available for you to customize your own cartoons and captions; it's safer than using your own delivery because the cartoon is making the point. Finally, forget that outdated rule that a presentation must open and close with a joke. Unless you have material that has consistently proven itself, why risk starting off with your important group with an attempted slam dunk that's more slam than dunk? And never "force humor." You can pretend to be serious; you can't pretend to be humorous.

Creating Stunning Visuals

The two words 'information' and 'communication' are often used interchangeably, but they signify quite different things. Information is giving out; communication is getting through.

—SYDNEY J. HARRIS

One of the biggest challenges in creative communication leadership, as we've constantly stressed, is to convey ideas, messages, thoughts, and feelings concisely (but completely), accurately, persuasively, and with *dynamic impact.* That's a tall order by itself but even more difficult when portraying abstract, conceptual, or highly technical ideas and thoughts. How do you keep a presentation perfectly understandable, informative, interesting, and even thought provoking—all at the *same time?* How do you rivet the audience to their seats when you have what may be initially perceived as dry information by the audience? It's not easy!

Presenting everyday information in an emotionally enticing way (to inspire and motivate the audience to action) requires very careful planning and creative delivery. That's where effective visual aids (overhead transparencies, 35mm slides, multimedia/computerized slide shows, videotapes, and flipcharts) can make an enormous difference between a presentation that's "acceptable" and one that stirs the audience to immediate rousing action in the boardroom. Communication is getting through to people, and visuals are a superb tool to assist in that critical and oftentimes difficult process.

213

Throughout, I'll use the terms "visual aids" or "visuals" inter-changeably to cover media such as flipcharts, 35mm slides, overhead transparencies, large charts, and even those formats such as video-tapes, audiocassettes, film, or computerized multimedia or slide shows that have a sound content (e.g., voice, music, audio special effects, computer synthesized voice).

This chapter will cover some important ways to strategize, design, and use visuals that will help make your toptalk as effective and efficient as possible. This chapter will not cover the detailed specifics or show illustrations of the correct or incorrect design of visuals but, instead, will focus on strategic ways to use visuals to help meet your toptalk objectives.

HOW VISUALS WILL HELP YOUR TOPTALK

Visual aids have the capability of creating an *arresting* presenta-tion—one that quickly grabs attention and holds the audience as "prisoners of interest." Their power to change attitudes, compare and contrast, to sell products and services, and, in some cases, to weave an emotional tapestry of feelings in the audience is an accept-ed fact inside the boardroom and out. The "show-and-tell" aspect of visuals boosts communication efficiency and information retention. For example, various studies over the last 30 years demonstrate that while we remember approximately 20 percent of what we *hear* and 30 percent of what we *see*, we retain 50 percent of what we *see and hear*. If your presentation involves a lot of visual information critical to learning and understanding (e.g., showing an operational process or explaining complex patterns, trends, connections, or relationships or demonstrating how to perform a skill behavior), learning in these situations will be achieved approximately 85 percent through the eyes, 12 percent through the ears, and 3 percent through other sens-es.

A study by the Wharton Center for Applied Research done for the 3M Corporation concluded, "People are more likely to say 'yes' and act on your recommendations when you use visuals, particular-ly overheads. According to their research, you'll be perceived as being more professional, persuasive, credible, interesting, and better prepared. The probability of the audience reaching consensus is 79 percent versus 58 percent without visuals.[1] Another study done in 1986 by the University of Minnesota found that presentations using visual aids were found to be 43 percent more persuasive than were unaided presentations.[2]

These studies and others simply prove that visual aids can dramatically enhance creative communication leadership. Visual aids are such an imbedded part of business presentations that, without them, people feel like Paderewski trying to give a concert without a piano. When Ross Perot was running for President in 1992, he made extensive use of his color (pie, bar, and line) charts and retractable pointer to clearly describe the details and vividly highlight the implications of the national debt and budget deficit. While impersonators latched onto his strong trademark business presenting style (developed during his years as an IBM supersalesman), Perot probably did more for widespread acceptance of visual aids than many before him and this, no doubt, prompted President Clinton to make use of computer-generated visuals for his presentations. And Larry Speakes, a former aide of President Reagan, tells of the remarkable influence that his budget director, David Stockman, was able to achieve with Ronald Reagan by using "simplistic charts and graphs to illustrate his points." To slam home a point concerning relative U.S. and Soviet troop strength, Stockman used red and blue silhouettes of soldiers in proportionate size to his projections of U.S. military needs.[3]

Visual aids have gone through major technological transitions over the last 100 years: from a simple chalkboard to flipcharts to "film media" such as filmstrips, overhead transparencies, 35mm slides, 16mm film, and then the ever-popular video and audiocassettes. And now an exciting emerging technology called "interactive computerized multimedia" (explained in the following chapter), will revolutionize the way we communicate.

More sophisticated and useful tools were progressively developed to help a communicator to deliver impressive, "send-the-audience-forth-marching" presentations. Unfortunately, improperly designed and incorrectly used visuals often fogged the situation; the very tools that were supposed to help, often hindered. Too many speakers forget that effective visual aids are designed to *support* their talk, not *replace* it or *dominate* it. Visuals might dilute the presence and power of a boardroom communicator by stealing attention away from him or her. That's why it's critical that a toptalker should be the best "audiovisual" via a strong and polished voice delivery (audio) and through confident and dynamic use of body language and movement (visual).

Executives Want and Like Visual Aids

In our executive survey, we asked executives several questions about the visual aids used in presentations given to them. Conclusion: executives *strongly* prefer that a speaker use some sort of visual aid in helping to get his or her points across: 89 percent said that visual aids were either important or very important to use; while only 11 percent said they were "somewhat" important. Executives had comments such as these that supported their enthusiasm about visual aids:

- Helps make the point stronger and clearer; tells a story.
- Adds impact and retention if designed well.
- Your mind gets flat unless you look at something. The added dimension of sight keeps the audience alert and helps in understanding subject matter covered.
- Makes the presentation appear more factual.

More than half, 57 percent of the executives preferred that a speaker use overhead transparencies, while the second favorite choice, listed by 26 percent of them, was 35mm slides. Only 12 percent preferred flipcharts (no data on multimedia was available due to the lack of widespread knowledge of this new technology at the time of our survey). Executives especially liked overhead transparencies for their informal, easy-to-use characteristics and the fact that they're considered more flexible to use than other media. If the audience needs to review information from a previous transparency, the speaker can refer to it quickly. They also liked the fact that overheads can be shown in a lighted room and there is no need to worry about slide jams as with 35mm media. Plus, professional-looking overheads can now be created by practically anyone very quickly, easily, and inexpensively on today's laser printers, color printers, or service bureaus.

MediaNet, a New York City Computer graphics company, performed a three-year research study of over 1,500 business presentations as they relate to a number of important factors. According to Tom Mucciolo, one finding showed that different age groups preferred different types of visuals. Those under 30 mostly preferred electronic images (e.g., computerized slide shows and multimedia), and those over 60 preferred overhead transparencies.[4]

Jack Grayson, president of the *American Productivity and Quality Center (APQC)* in Houston, emphasized to me that it's important to use the right tool for the right job: "I use all kinds of visuals—overheads, slides, flipcharts. I don't think you should say I'm a 'slide person' or an 'overhead person' or a 'flipchart person.' Be flexible and use what's good for that group and situation. Visuals supplementing words are very valuable to make presentations more interesting."[5]

Surprisingly, the quality of visual aids used in executive presentations are NOT up to the quality standards desired by the boardroom occupants. In our survey, the majority (53 percent) of executives said visual aids used in presentations to them were of only "moderate" quality; 42 percent rated them as "good" quality, and zero percent said that visual aids used by most people were usually of excellent quality. It's apparent that presenters are not adequately availing themselves of IBM-compatible and Apple Macintosh computer presentation software programs that could create relatively low-cost, fast, easy-to-use, and stunningly attractive 35mm slides, overhead transparencies, and computerized slide shows. Unfortunately, in spite of these excellent computer presentation programs and supporting tools, many presenters are still in the technological dark-age mode of creating low-tech, dull, and incorrectly designed visuals for their important audiences. Executives definitely want visual aids used, but not abused.

Visuals . . . the Good, the Bad, and the Ugly

In a lot of respects, visual aids such as 35mm or electronic slides, overhead transparencies, flipcharts, videotape segments, and the emerging multimedia programs can be a double-edged sword. Designed and used effectively, they can work wonders in helping to organize and make a speaker's messages clear, concise, and persuasive; poorly designed and used incorrectly, visual aids can damage a person's otherwise acceptable briefing. While our written survey did not specifically ask questions related to problems with a speaker using visual aids in an executive presentation, my discussions with numerous high-level decision makers about this topic brought to light the following mistakes (not in priority order) that presenters typically make:

- Too much detail and information on visual aids

- Too many visual aids—"eye and brain overload" (e.g., a stack of 40 overheads used for a 15-minute briefing!) used in a frenzied "got-to-get-through-it" way

- Design of visual aids is distracting and speaker doesn't properly lead the audience through relevant parts of the visual image

- Speaker reads visuals word-for-word (uses them as a presentation script)

- Speaker misuses visuals (blocks view of audience, leaves projector with slide on long after visual is needed, etc.)

Frank Sonnenberg, president of RMI, a New Jersey marketing and advertising firm and author of the book, *Marketing to Win*, is an authority on persuasive presentations. He mentioned to me that presenters must diligently avoid the common deadly sins of designing visuals that are too verbal, too dull, too complex/comprehensive, too crowded, or too vague (or otherwise confusing).[6]

Audiovisuals take time to design and create and, depending upon their complexity and depending upon who creates them (you, a member of your staff, or an outside vendor), they can be expensive. If they're designed wrong or they're used improperly, they can imprison and limit a speaker's flexibility. As Dr. Harry Andrews, senior vice-president at 3M Corporation noted to me, "The more an overly structured presentation depends upon the sequence of slides or charts or video, the more it becomes an encumbrance rather than a useful tool because if someone wants to back up and revisit a specific issue, that's usually a pretty awkward process to do. Random access process is needed. That's one of the design concepts for our future electronic systems."[7] And finally, there's always the chance of malfunction of equipment—a burned-out bulb, a slide jam, a computer or multimedia projector going down, or equipment that was supposed to be there but that never showed up.

DEVELOPING A TOPTALK VISUAL AID STRATEGY

While executives *expect and want* the toptalker to use visual aids to support his or her main points during the presentation, they expect effectively designed ones that are properly used for *effect.* Too many people take the use of visual aids for granted. For example, the first thing most people, unfortunately, do is to think "tactically" by asking themselves, "What (words, graphs, tables, clip art, etc.) do I put on my visual aids?" Instead, presenters should be first thinking *strategically* in terms of the *intended effect* that their visuals should have. They need to answer these types of important questions:

- How can I use visuals to help me reach my presentation objectives?

- How can I use visual aids to greatly improve my overall communication effectiveness and efficiency for this presentation?

- How can my visuals help the audience understand and focus on the critical points I want to make?

- In what ways can I use them to enhance the professionality of my briefing and add to my credibility?

Executive speechwriter and coach John McGrath makes an important point often missed by many executive speakers, "Visual aids should create an *impression,* not just give data. Instead of showing static data, show change over time and do it with color, charts, or other graphic forms that stick in their minds. If you show columns and columns of data, for example, the impression people get is that you had a lot of data up there. The impression you want to give them, for example, is that sales are growing, our market is shifting, competitors are changing, or the consumer is evolving. The valuable visual message is more than data."[8]

When planning the design and use of your visual aids for maximum impact, here are some specific strategic questions to help you make optimum use of your visuals by determining what you want to accomplish, not just what you want to show on them.

1. How can visual aids save time?

Time in front of executives is precious. One of the major benefits of using visual aids is to help your high-level group comprehend your information and overall conclusions as quickly as possible. Think about ways of designing and using visuals to get your messages across faster. How can your visuals reduce unnecessary detail while increasing understanding of the "big picture" and overall key themes? How can you best use pictures, illustrations, diagrams, graphs, tables, process or flow charts, symbols, or cartoons to reduce the need for extended examples, explanations, or descriptions? How can your visuals reduce interruptions from your audience? How can you use them to quickly summarize key points?

2. How can they create or enhance a desired audience mood?

If you're desiring to evoke emotions (e.g., pride, anger, shock, fear, anticipation, envy, impatience, or if you want to challenge the audience) ask how visuals can help. How can music, still pictures, video clips, color, animation, cartoons, illustrations, or other visual images and sounds add action, dramatics, theatrics, humor, or passion to your messages? How can you design and use your visual aids to help entertain your audience while you're giving them information? How can you use visuals to tell an emotional story that can't be told by words alone?

3. What can they do to help your audience remember your key points?

Visuals can help people retain ideas and information long after the speaker has said, "in conclusion . . ." Audiences remember that which is important to them or that which is unusual, interesting, shocking, fascinating, curiosity-evoking, or otherwise mentally and emotionally stimulating. How can your visuals focus on and intensify themes, symbols, metaphors, highly creative slogans, product demonstrations, poignant personal stories/testimonies, visually "amazing" comparisons/contrasts, or anything else that tickles the senses to cause people to retain that information or feeling long afterwards. How can you use your visuals to strongly repeat your key points in ways that are not "obviously repetitious," but have variation built in (after all, repetition is a proven strong technique to get people to remember).

4. In what ways can you project realism and credibility with your visuals?

Theories, ideas, thoughts, stories, operations, events, and descriptions can be amplified, crystallized, and brought to stark reality by properly designed visuals that "translate" general concepts into meaningful, pragmatic, and easy-to-grasp everyday notions or situations. As one executive in our survey said, "Well designed visuals can definitely help the audience wrap their hands around a slippery concept." With today's advanced computer modeling, animation, and image manipulation, for example, we're introduced to a three-dimensional moving world that gives incredible support for explaining and describing complex topics.

Ask yourself how you can use video sequences, sound, photographs/pictures, illustrations, animations, or solid models to give believability and authenticity to information by showing patterns, sequences, relationships, cause-and-effect situations, scenarios, and interactions. Ask yourself how you can design your visuals to prove a point, justify your statement, or give much added weight to your recommendations or how you can use them to remove doubt, skepticism, confusion, ambiguity, or apathy from the minds and hearts of the audience.

5. How can visual aids organize your presentation?

Properly designed visuals can help you deliver your briefing in an orderly, logical way that creates an easy flow of thought from idea to idea. They can keep your presentation on track rather than going off on tangents. Determine how your visuals can help to simplify your message and condense it in a way that will reduce unnecessary questions or discussion. Use

*your visuals to creatively organize your thoughts and infor-
mation into meaningful "bottom line" messages. Ask yourself
how you can sequence your information on visuals in a way
that is easy for the audience to follow. Picture using your
visuals as steps on a staircase leading the audience up to your
natural "undeniable" conclusion.*

6. How can they help you in speaking?

*Some executives have complained that speakers use visual
aids in place of cumbersome and impersonal speaker's
notes—that the visuals are so detailed and comprehensive
that many speakers don't "talk with the audience," they read
from their visuals at the audience instead. If a speaker uses
visuals as "crutches," he or she won't be able to flexibly move
in the direction the audience wants the toptalker to go. A balance is needed. You need to decide how to design your visuals with just enough text and graphics (illustrations, pictures,
etc.) to logically help you guide your presentation along by
"jogging your memory" with transitional points.*

*Effective visuals should enable you to conversationally
cover your material, instead of forcing you to read it word for
word. This can be accomplished if they're general enough
(with just the key words and illustrations) that you can talk
in a more natural, unrestrained, and conversational way.
Ask yourself how your visuals can best help you to be smooth
and remember the material while enabling you to be flexible
enough to deviate from the material if the audience requests
it.*

7. How can audiovisuals attract attention and hold audi-
ence interest?

*Executives have told me that the average attention span dur-
ing executive presentations peaks after about 20 minutes.
They concur that first impressions often set the tone for acceptance or rejection of the toptalker's proposal. Putting life into
presentations from the very beginning is critical. That's why
it's very important to determine how your visual aids can
immediately get your audience to sit up and listen and then
continue to give you their full concentration on your points.*

One manufacturer of an LCD (Liquid Crystal Display) projection system advertises that it will, ". . . Make Your Ideas Scream Out and Wake Up the Dead!" Perhaps that's a bit much, but your visuals definitely need to tightly hold your audience's interest. Susan Gillette, a talented creative director and now president of DDB Needham Chicago, a noted advertising agency, believes in the importance of being visually bold, " . . . to do something that goes beyond the ordinary and capture attention. To turn the prospect's head, to pay attention to what's being said. Then, if you're saying the right thing, and saying it well, your odds of succeeding are vastly improved."[9]

Ask yourself how your visuals can help your presentation to focus on financial, operational, and career and personal benefits to the audience. How can they fire up the group's intellect and emotions? How can you use cartoons, music, video interviews, computer animation, video clips from movies or news shows, photographs, caricatures, illustrations, and other visual "enticements" to entertain your group while you're making solid points? How can you use color, illustrations, sound, and so forth to give energy and life to your oral briefing?

To keep audience interest, a presenter must interact with his group. There's an old saying in sales: "If the customers don't share [in the sales conversation], they don't care." So ask yourself how you can design your visuals in such a flexible manner that the audience has the full capability (and encouragement) to interact with you in a discussion mode rather than in a tightly structured, one-way-only "monologue." Executives have stressed how important it is to have a toptalk that enables everyone in a small group to participate in questions, comments, and so forth.

8. How might you emphasize and focus on your critical points?

One of the biggest problems executives face today is information overload. There's so much "raw data" available. It needs to be collected, sifted, refined, translated and put into an effective form for the executives to digest and use, and make

sense of what it all means. That's why graphs, charts, flow dia-
grams, illustrations, and computer modeling can take data and
present them in a much more understandable, meaningful, and
impacting way. What would you prefer to look at—rows and
columns of seemingly endless numbers or easy-to-decipher bar
graphs with different colors, sizes, and shapes to make for imme-
diate visual impact of the meaning and significance of the num-
bers represented? Ask yourself how you can use visual aids to
slam your points across. Consider using stark comparisons and
stunning contrasts to help the audience see relative changes
much better? How can you design your visuals to make critical
or important points just "jump out" at the audience?

Developing a "Class Act" with Visuals

I've sat through many high-level management and boardroom presentations in my career. I've found that practically everyone can
improve in the realm of good design and handling of visual aids.
When you see a toptalker who masters the design, strategy, and proficient use of any type of visual, there's something almost inordinate-
ly impressive about it. It can significantly add to the effectiveness of
the toptalk. When a presenter uses visual aids in an impacting, highly polished, and supremely competent way, his or her image as a creative communication leader is greatly boosted. Becoming proficient
means understanding how to conceptually design them (even if you
have someone else actually create them) from a communication message standpoint and how to use them in such a way that the visuals
don't stand out—YOU and your focused information do.

Effective and Efficient: Two Basic Design Goals to Aim for

The best designed visual aids have only two goals: (1) to make the
communication process more *effective* and (2) more *efficient*. Visuals
that achieve these goals are ones that ideally are:

- *Simple and clear* . . . they almost immediately (within 5–8 seconds) enable the audience to grasp the major point and sup-

porting ideas that the visual aid is making. The ideal visual gets your ideas across clearly, yet does not draw attention to itself. Walter Kiechel, assistant managing editor of *Fortune* magazine, told me that, "visuals should be 'startlingly compressed' in the information they provide."[10]

- *Visible* . . . smallest details on the visual can be seen by everyone in the audience and the visual is designed in a "neat," easy-to- view way.

- *Legible* . . . typefaces, text, illustrations, pictures can be read quickly and easily.

- *Focused and interesting* . . . draws audience's attention on the main points being supported and visually captures and holds them.

- *Entertaining* . . . can "showcase" a point in an amusing, humorous, witty, or clever way.

- *Appropriate and relevant* . . . contains only critical information or illustrations, pictures, graphs, and other elements needed to help the audience to understand and agree with the points being made.

- *Consistent and customized* . . . there needs to be a sameness in terms of design (uniform colors, graphic style, text, headings (e.g., doesn't look as if random slides from many sources were haphazardly put together).

TEN TIPS TOWARD DESIGNING BETTER VISUALS

Let's examine some specifics to help you in effectively designing visuals that help make your points as opposed to distracting from them:

1. Design each visual to make just *one* major point (with all visuals supporting *one* theme). The dominant idea or concept should jump out at the audience immediately, and there should be supporting information for it. Maybe the idea is that "Sales are exploding," or "Productivity is hurting in plants A and B and the reason is . . . "

2. Keep your visual simple, neat, and uncluttered. Make sure it is not complex or "busy." Don't squeeze all the text or graphics into a small area in the center. Spread everything out and make everything as large as possible for easy viewing.

3. Use large, clear BOLD letters. General guideline is to limit a visual to between 35 and 45 words. Have 6 to 8 words per line and 5 to 7 lines per visual. Use a single type style with upper- and lowercase letters. I use sans serif faces such as Helvetica because they are most readable when projected. According to the book *How to Make Type Readable,* the authors note that lowercase letters are 13.4 percent faster to read and are more legible and pleasant than all capital letters. They note that too much mixing of type faces (using italic, bold-faced, various fonts) creates excessive contrast that can slow reading by 11 percent.[11] One of the most amusing excuses for bad design was this one told to me by a client who used lots of words on his visual with *very* small type size, "I use small lettering so people can't see what I'm talking about since only I can read it up close to the screen."

   Use as few words (use active, dynamic ones) as possible to create a complete idea, but not so concise as to make it at the expense of comprehension. People are accustomed to reading or looking at something from left to right and top to bottom—keep that in mind when you design your visual. Don't use vertical printing (i.e., horizontal letters stacked on top of each other)—it's hard to see. Round numbers off ($6,800 is easier to read than $6,798.45). Finally, look at everything on your visual and ask if you absolutely need it or it is better just to talk about it.

4. Copyedit and proofread. Use all noun phrases or all verb phrases and consistent tense for text lines and title. Check spelling and consistent punctuation and verify accuracy, especially names of people and organizations. Tom Mucciolo of MediaNet notes that other than a quoted statement or a question mark or exclamation point you should never see a "period" on a visual. Double-check data. Frank Sonnenberg, president of RMI, notes that, "typographical errors, misspellings, and factual errors loom larger than life. One mis-

take can make people suspicious of the entire presentation."[12]

5. Have short titles that creatively communicate something. They should encapsulate your idea or point, grab attention, and titillate interest. Determine the feeling and impression you want to portray via the title. Be creative when called for. A straightforward title, "Quality in Plant #2" is informational, while "Plant #2: Superb Quality Boost!" is dynamic in character.

6. Highlight words or graphic elements by using color, different size text or fonts, bolding, underlining, italicizing (or combinations). However, italics are hardest to read from a distance. Use arrows, asterisks (usually indicates what presenter needs to clarify or explain), or enclose items in rectangles, ovals, or use screens. Use emphasis for just that reason; overdoing it defeats its purpose.

7. Don't mix horizontal and vertical formats for your visuals. Stick with one or the other. A horizontal format is preferred because it appears larger and conforms to images shown on television and movie screens, which people are accustomed to.

8. Don't "overdesign" your visual (to overwhelm your audience) with lots of colors, text fonts, clip art, and borders. Today's computer presentation software and desktop publishing programs give lots of design choices and one might be tempted to create a wonderful work of art that, unfortunately, detracts and distracts rather than helps to communicate. An attractive, "elegantly simple" design is best.

9. Avoid stark contrasts (in color, size, or style of design) from one visual to another. Avoid mixing very serious visuals with humorous ones—they should fit the audience situation and mood.

10. Use colors sparingly. Overdoing and mixing too many colors will detract from the main points or viewing focus. Frank Sonnenberg recommends sticking to no more than three basic colors per visual. Use colors to contrast, highlight, differentiate categories, separate groups of data, or call attention to something. Here are some complementary colors pleasant to the viewer's eyes and legible and easily viewable:

Light Colors on Dark Backgrounds:

- WHITE on dark shades of blue, black, green, red, or purple
- YELLOW on black or dark shades of blue or green
- GOLD on dark shades of blue, green, or black

The research done by MediaNet shows that yellow/white on a dark blue background to be the most visible from a distance.[13]

Dark Colors on Light Backgrounds:

- BLACK on yellow, white, orange, or pink
- BLUE on yellow, white, or orange
- RED on yellow or white
- GREEN on white or yellow

Dark colors on light backgrounds may be appropriate for large charts or other display visuals, but, according to studies done by MediaNet, visuals with light backgrounds have an abundance of reflective light and are distracting to the eye.

WAYS YOU CAN EFFECTIVELY PRESENT YOUR TOPTALK VISUALS

Once you've created well-designed visuals, the next step is to make sure you use them in a polished, dynamic, and effective way. Here are some techniques and tips to help you do that:

1. Don't block the audience's view of your visual. I've found that a lot of presenters repeat this mistake during their briefing. Place your projector and screen in an optimum position that reduces the chances of your blocking their view and, if necessary, stand next to the screen and point to areas of the visual while you are speaking. Always be aware of the viewing effect of where you stand or the effect of moving around the audience. Tom Mucciolo of MediaNet recommends that the presenter stand on the audience's left, which is the natural reading pattern of the audience (left to right).

2. Speak with extra volume (*project* your voice) when using visual aids—especially if the room is darkened. Although you want the audience to view the visual, you still want them to focus on what *you* are saying.

3. Don't read the text on your visuals word for word (we can safely assume that executives can read); instead, point to a line of text, let the group read it for a moment, and then speak about the information in a general conversational way.

4. Have your body face your audience and use your arm closest to the screen or flipchart to point to a specific section; avoid twisting your body around to point to an area and don't face the screen while looking at the visual (with your back to the audience). When you need to look at the next point on the visual in order to speak about it, glance at it for a moment and collect your thoughts and then focus your eye contact right back on the audience.

5. Change slides or overheads yourself. You have more control, and it's less distracting to the audience if you avoid repeatedly saying, "Next slide, please!"

6. Have a designated assistant standing by to handle any equipment problems (burned-out bulbs, jammed slides, computer/projector glitches, etc.) while you recover to continue your talk without having to disrupt it by fixing the equipment yourself.

7. Have your equipment fully set up and the first visual aid placed and ready to go before you get up to speak. Your overhead or slide projector, for example, should be properly positioned, focused, and ready to be turned on with your first visual in place. This especially applies to computerized slide shows where the complexity demands good preparation upfront.

8. If need be, ask someone to switch the lights on and off, adjust the sound system, or handle other equipment needs while you're speaking. Decide on simple and subtle "signals" beforehand to indicate your needs. Know how to adjust all lighting in the room. Shut off lights directly over your projection screen to prevent "image washout."

9. Clean your projection equipment lens, mirror, or surface beforehand. Have spare bulbs and fuses available in case of problems.

10. If your presentation's objectives are critically based on your using visuals, have backup equipment (e.g., projector or computer and peripherals) standing by fully set up to use *immediately* in case of failure.

11. After you've set up your screen and projection equipment or flipchart, walk around the room to check for visibility from all the seating positions. Remember that people may need to see over someone's head, so adjust the screen and position the equipment, flipchart, or writing boards appropriately.

12. If you're setting up your meeting room, consider using vinyl adhesive tape to tape cords from equipment to the flooring where you are speaking or in audience "traffic areas." This will prevent you or someone else from tripping over, disconnecting, or knocking over equipment (or all three at once). When possible, run cords along a wall far away from the audience and make sure long extension cords are available.

13. Fully check out *all* aspects of the functioning of your visual aid equipment before you begin and make any adjustments or fixes needed.

14. While you are changing your overheads or slides, keep talking. You want to stay about five seconds ahead of your next visual to keep your transitions and flow smooth. Abrupt silence as you change visuals can be distracting, especially if your presentation requires lots of visuals. If you use notes, mark down transitional points going to your next slide or on overheads. A great technique is to use the cardboard borders on your overhead transparency not only to write down memory-jogging notes about the information on the visual, but to tell you what the *next* visual is so you smoothly transition your talk into it even before you show it.

15. If you plan to use a slide or overhead transparency several times, have it duplicated and placed in the correct sequence of use, instead of stopping your presentation to relocate it and use it.

16. Position your (slide, overhead, or multimedia) projector in a way that enables you to fill the entire area of the projection screen to ensure maximum viewing size for your audience. Adjust the screen up or down to perfectly "frame" the image, giving it a professional, crisp look. If using a tripod screen, consider using a "keystone corrector" (most come with one). It's a thin metal arm that you pull out from the top of your projection stand and use the notches in it to attach the top of the screen, which points the whole screen forward. This makes certain that your projected image is perpendicular to the screen to reduce distortion called "keystoning."

17. If you're using a retractable pointer avoid "playing with it"—repeatedly extending and retracting it, or using it in any other distracting manner. Extend it only when necessary, use it to point, and then retract it when finished or hold it stationary at your side. If using a laser pointer, remember not to accidently flash it on audience members as you gesture. While its low-intensity beam is supposed to be harmless, it's very disconcerting to the "human target" and those surrounding them, especially if it hits their eyes.

18. Avoid wearing out the audience by repeating such phases after each visual as: "In this slide, we see . . . " or "Here we have a picture of . . . ," or "What we're basically trying to say here is . . . " Instead use *varying* transitional or explanatory phrases such as these examples: "Now we'll see how this all ties together," or "Here's how the plan is implemented . . . ," or "The main point being shown here is...," or "Now you'll fully see the impact."

19. Make sure the "O" ring on your 35mm slide tray is securely fastened to prevent your slides from falling out. It's a good idea to number your slides in the upper corner to help you load them in correct sequence or quickly reload them if you somehow accidently drop them.

20. Bring an extension cord for your slide remote control unit if you have to position your projector any extended distance from you. For convenience, consider taping the remote control to the podium if you are using one. Or consider using a wireless remote control to change slides.

21. Make sure your slide projector is placed high enough to project its images over the heads of the audience. Don't tilt the slide projector at an extreme angle by putting large books, ash trays, and the like, under it. This not only creates a distortion of images—keystoning—but, since the slides are gravity-fed, it greatly increases the likelihood of jamming. Use a correct-height projector stand instead.

22. If using a podium in a well-equipped audiovisual meeting room, become familiar with the controls for room lights, P.A. system, projection screen lowering/raising switch, and so forth. Have a pitcher of water and glass on the lower shelf not conspicuous to audience and away from any of your gestures that might accidently knock it over (I came very close several times).

23. Move away from the podium after you feel comfortable with the audience. Buck Rogers, well-known author, popular lecturer, and highly successful former vice-president of world-wide marketing for IBM, is a big proponent of getting close to his audience. "I have four basic rules I follow," he told me. "One, I don't use a podium for my speeches. I want to move around the stage and develop rapport with my audience. Two, lights up—no spotlights on me. I want to see the audience and I want them to see me in the same light. Three, I use a hand-held cordless mike to enable me to move around into the audience. Four, I focus on various individuals in different places in the audience (to give everyone equal eye contact)." Buck told me that he has received lots of compliments from people who told him, "I thought you were talking just to me!" And Buck's reply was . . . "I was!"[15]

    My belief, though, is if you're super nervous and a podium "shields you" and reduces your high anxiety, stay there! However, if you feel comfortable venturing away from it later on, it will enable you to develop more rapport with your group, as Buck does so well.

24. When using a flipchart, make sure the legs of the easel are locked firmly into position. Position it close to the group and make sure everyone can comfortably see it (walk around the room prior to the meeting and check various optimum posi-

tions for the flipchart). And be careful not to back into it as you move around—I've knocked one over several times as I moved close to it. If you do knock it down, don't draw attention to yourself or make a big deal out of it. Just pick it up and continue as nothing happened.

25. Write only short sentences or draw small sections of illustrations on your flipchart at a time, then step back so the audience can see it. Occasionally, talk while you write to prevent repeated long uncomfortable silences. Don't try to write too much on one page.

26. For flipcharts, use several color markers for titles, to highlight key points, or to emphasize certain parts of an illustration. Staple two to three pages together to prevent the marker's ink from seeping through, and since this makes the page thicker, turning the page over will be a lot easier.

27. Flipcharts are more appropriate for "brainstorming" or other interactive discussion or facilitation-type sessions in the boardroom to capture ideas and thoughts. You can create a flipchart with some prepared questions, discussion items, or pieces of information and then leave blank spaces on the page and/or include several blank pages afterward to fill in items as they are discussed. You can then rip pages off the pad and temporarily tape them to the wall for frequent reference or updating.

Feed Your Audience a "Visual Bite" at a Time

One of the biggest mistakes a majority of presenters make when it comes to using visual aids is their unfocused display of information—not feeding information to the audience in planned, digestible bites. The important goal is to precisely control *what* you show the audience and *when*. For example, the typical presenter will show an entire overhead transparency or slide with numerous bulleted lines of text on it or columns of data. Instinctively, the audience feels compelled to read all the lines of text sequentially (curiosity does it) or to read the data in all the columns. After an overall scan of everything on the visual, some audience members may be thinking about the information on line four, for example, while others are wondering about the information in line five . . . while the speaker is still referring to the ideas in the first bulleted line. The audience can miss the speaker's important points because he or she did not *direct* and *control* their attention to a specific part of the visual. This not only applies to text or data-oriented visuals, but also relates to elements of an illustration, for example, such as an organization chart, a flow-chart, or an "exploding view" of a product design.

Whenever the audience is given an opportunity to see something, they take ALL of it in, instead of fully concentrating on what the speaker is saying. The more "busy" a visual aid is, the more the audience neglects the toptalker to soak in the displayed information or images, trying to read it or view it and make sense of it, not waiting for the speaker to get to it. A speaker must control exactly what the audience sees and should display or otherwise highlight and direct the audience's attention to specific pieces of information, text, or illustration elements.

What the speaker needs to do is subtly direct or "force" the audience to concentrate on only those parts of the visual that he or she is speaking about. Like a waiter delivering a seven-course meal, the speaker is giving the diners the next portion only after they have finished with the previous one. The technique of doing this with visual aids is called "revelation" or "selective (or progressive) disclosure" or "visual focusing." Here are some effective techniques for your audience to focus on exactly what you want them to:

Show/No Show Technique. When a speaker leaves a visual up for display, the audience is tempted to "blindly stare" at it, especially when they're getting bored. This especially happens with overhead transparencies. The presenter will leave the projector light on with the visual showing long after he or she is finished referring to it. Or the presenter will take the transparency off and forget to turn the projector light off, distracting the audience with the projector fan buzzing and the bright light blazing on the screen. As soon as you're finished showing an overhead, for example, turn the projector off or use a piece of cardboard to cover the transparency if you plan to talk about the next point on it later on. If using a slide projector, leave the next slide slot empty and use the remote control to advance to the next slide (empty slot) which (with newer projectors) will produce a blank (no light) screen image. If you're using a flipchart and have finished referring to a page on it, turn it over to a blank page or turn the flipchart stand away from the view of the audience to avoid distracting them.

This concept applies to any type of projection or computerized visual equipment or even large-scale printed charts. When you're finished making your point and want the audience to pay attention to you, turn the machine off (or blank out the projected image) and all eyes and ears will "snap back" to focus on you. When you want the audience to refer to the visual, place another transparency on the machine and turn it on (or advance to the next 35mm slide or advance to the next computer image) and they will automatically—as if on cue—look at the visual. This show/no show (or "on/off") technique—the purposeful alternating focus between the projection screen and yourself—is a subtle, natural, but very powerful way of telling your audience where to focus their attention.

Pointer Technique. To direct the audience's attention to any portion of a visual (could be a number, line of text, part of an illustration, etc.) you want to point to that which you are speaking about at the time. There are several ways to do this. You can stand next to the screen and use a retractable pointer to point to a specific part of the projected image. You can also lay a retractable pointer, a pencil, a pen, or any number of other specially designed pointers on the plate of the overhead projector pointing to an area of the transparency that you want to highlight. This gives a very bold and clear image of the area you're focusing on. However, if you stand next to your projector and point directly on it, you need to position your projector and screen in such a way that your standing there does not block anyone's vision.

Finally, you can choose to use a laser pointer (which flashes a brilliant red dot several hundred feet away) or a flashlight pointer (less intense light, but useful at close range) to direct your audience's attention to specific parts of the visual on the screen. Make sure you have new batteries in your pointers and bring extra batteries (they usually last 2 to 8 hours continuous use, depending on the pointer).

Overlays. Overlays consist of several transparencies mounted on the same cardboard or plastic frame. They are fastened with adhesive tape or hinges to either the same or to different sides of the frame. The base transparency shows the basic information and you then flip over the overlay sheets to build text items or show parts of illustrations (or other graphics) sections at a time. They are great to show contrasts/comparisons (e.g., last year's versus this year's financial figures) and to build a concept from scratch one piece at a time. Overlays are easy to make using today's presentation software programs and laser printers.

Some very creative people even use "masks" made out of cardboard that fit over their transparency. The masks have different size and shape holes cut in them to let selective information show through on various parts of the overhead transparency.

The most effective "overlays" are those that are created on computer slide shows or multimedia programs where images (pictures, photos, etc.), data, words, illustrations, or animated sequences build and dissolve on the screen when the toptalker uses a wireless mouse, for example. This technique of feeding elements of the visual to the audience is superior to all others. But it requires preparation and practice to do it smoothly and effectively.

Write-on Technique. You can create overhead transparencies and use marking pens of various colors (green, red, blue, orange, etc.) to highlight information (underline, circle, check-off, cross out, draw arrows) for the audience to focus on. You can also have a transparency that is partially created and you can use the color pens to fill-in information or complete an illustration (e.g., a pie chart that you write in numbers for each of the sectors). If you want to reuse your original base transparency, you can use water soluble ink pens and wipe the markings off with a damp tissue. Or you can temporarily tape a blank, clear transparency over the base transparency to write on and then discard the one written on.

Computer-Generated Visuals: Inexpensive, High-Quality Power

I strongly recommend using today's Macintosh or IBM-compatible computers to create extremely professional slides, overheads, or a computerized slide show quickly and relatively inexpensively. Presentation software packages take the guesswork out of designing visuals by creating formats and templates that the user easily follows (see resource list at the end of book for vendors). While there are options built in for background designs and colors, type fonts, and styles, these programs enable you to use designs *already* created for you—you don't even have to have any slide or graphic design experience. These programs also have outlining capabilities and enable you to create very professional looking speaker notes with encapsulated printouts of each visual if you wish. Finally, most of them have basic drawing and graph-generating (bar, pie, line, area) capabilities.

Using inexpensive, commercially available color *clip art* (illustrations of people, objects, symbols, equipment, diagrams, cartoons, buildings, etc.), you can add that extra polished touch to ensure high-quality visuals. Also, with today's high-resolution color flatbed (or even hand-held) scanners, you can "capture" any images—photos, pictures, illustrations, diagrams from magazines, newspapers, annual reports—any published materials. If it can be photocopied, the scanner will be able to take that image and have your presentation software program put in your 35mm or electronic slide or transparency (depending on use, check for copyrights and get permission to use).

After designing your visuals on your computer, you can get your overheads or slides made in a number of ways: (1) black and white or color ink-jet or laser printers will create transparencies; (2) you can deliver your diskette to a service bureau (see resource section for names) for them to image your work and create mounted 35mm slides or color overheads; (3) if you have a computer modem, you can even transmit your files over phone lines to the service bureau for super-quick processing; or (4) you can buy a high-resolution film recorder and create 35mm slides on the spot.

If you have an outside vendor custom design your slides, it typically costs $10 to $80+ per slide (average is about $30) depending upon how much custom graphic design is needed. And it might take a day to several days or longer for turnaround. With your creating black-and-white overheads on your laser printer, it'll cost less than a dollar a copy; if you create your own slides and have them processed by a bureau, it will typically cost less than $10 each. And you can have them much quicker (some imaging bureaus have your visuals to you the next day). Doing it yourself gives you flexibility and can save you money.

The Future Is Excitingly Computerized ...And It's Here Now

Another capability of many presentation software packages is that of creating *electronic computerized slide shows*. You design the visuals basically the same way you might do for slides or overhead transparencies, but instead of creating film, you store the "slides" on your computer's hard disk and you use an LCD or CRT projection device (Chapter 9, Using New Multimedia Technology to Develop a State-of-the-Art Toptalk explains more about these devices) to project your image from the computer (which is connected to the projection device) onto a screen.

There are many advantages to creating electronic slide shows: (1) It costs virtually nothing to design other than electricity and your time, assuming you have the equipment and software—you don't pay for any imaging service or film you would ordinarily use in a laser printer; (2) it's quick—as soon as you finish typing the data and creating the illustrations, within the software program, you can show it; also, making modifications is a snap—it's done electronically on your computer, even minutes before your presentation; (3) finally, you can use effective build/transitional effects to feed any parts of the image you want one piece at a time to your audience. For example, if you have a six lines of text on your slide, you can show them one line at a time in a "build" type of way. And the distinction between multimedia programs and electronic slide shows is blurring as some electronic slide shows can show animation and video and audio.

Handouts for Your Toptalk

Handout materials are a form of visual aid used to supplement the oral portion of a presentation. We were curious about how executives viewed the materials used as reference handouts at a presentation. In our survey questionnaire, we asked the respondents to list "the *most common and pressing problem* associated with handouts (e.g.. proposals, notes, literature, etc.) used by the speaker at an executive group presentation." We asked them to pick just one of the following eight statements to choose from. There was also an "other" category for them to write down other choices not listed. The following numbers represent the percentages of people who selected what they considered to be the *main problem* with a toptalker using handouts. Here are the responses (in order of importance):

33% Handouts were distracting (e.g., distributed at inappropriate times during the presentation)

24% Handouts were too lengthy or detailed in nature

14% Speaker spent too much time going over information in the handouts

10% Handouts were too technical or full of meaningless jargon or contained unnecessary product information

7% Handouts were not relevant to the presentation being given or did not otherwise support the points that the speaker was making

5% Speaker did not lead audience through relevant parts of the handouts or explain nature of handouts

4% Handouts were not professionally (or attractively) created (e.g., sloppy, inaccurate, incomplete, etc.)

2% No handouts for reference were available

1% Other: Some typical responses were:

> If someone gives me a handout, I don't want them to read it to me.

> Not enough handouts for the audience.

> Handouts were not focused on speaker's main points as they should have been—handled side points instead.

When It Comes to Handouts . . .

Here are some suggestions for designing and using handouts for your toptalk:

- Distribute handouts before or during your presentation *only* if you cannot orally (or with the support of visual aids) cover your points. You want to maintain control of the presentation rather than have audience members read your handout instead of listening to you. Lead the group through the handout and point out specifically what you want them to read or view and what the main points are. Give them enough time, but when you're ready to have the audience focus on you tactfully ask those lingering readers to put the materials aside.

- Like any visual aid, ask yourself if you really need a handout, what the purpose of it is, and how it should be designed to help reach your presentation objectives.

- Like your toptalk, keep your handouts brief and simple. Cover only the main points and critical information needed by your group to make a decision regarding your proposal. Executives hate reading thick, detailed-laden proposals (I call them "litterature"). Peter Goldman, editor of *Boardroom Reports*, advises that presenters keep reference handouts to a *maximum* of 10 pages with a 1–2 page executive summary and the remainder consisting of illustrations and strategic highlights of the presentation. He recommends that large, double-spaced type be used to make it visually appealing to read.[16] For those executives who require very detailed information about your proposal, inform them that you have a more comprehensive writeup available for their later study.

- Consider using computer desktop publishing to create very visually appealing handouts. Rule: lots of white space, use graphs, illustrations, and other graphic elements to replace tiring text whenever possible and to quickly encapsulate key ideas in a persuasive way. Design each page to enable the reader to quickly and easily focus on the priority messages and information. Many computer presentation software packages have quick and effective ways to make handout copies of your visuals with accompanying notes. These might serve as primary or supplementary handouts.

IMPORTANT: See the Resource Section at the back of the book for a listing of audiovisual products and services that can help you.

Using New Multimedia Technology to Develop a State of the Art Toptalk

Language is the most imperfect and expensive means yet discovered for communicating thought.

—WILLIAM JAMES

We have definitely been spoiled by having the best movies, radio and television programs, best training videos, and yes—whether we like to admit it or not—the best television commercials ever. We love heart-pounding, gut-tugging, and mind-blowing adventure, suspense, humor, and romance. We're held spellbound by vicariously experiencing the "thrill of victory and the agony of defeat" of today's modern-day sports gladiators. Booming crystal-shattering Dolby-surround sound, eye-popping bewildering special effects, and nonstop, die-hard action are the entry fees to grab our attention and lock in our interest in our microsecond-attention-span, I-want-it-now, sound-bite, channel-surfing world. We're even becoming amateur producers, directors, and entertainers (look at all those national television programs featuring creative home videos).

LEARNING ALL ABOUT THIS EXCITING COMMUNICATION DIMENSION OF SIGHT AND SOUND

Like it or not, we're now addicted to snazzy forms of sight and sound media. After more than a decade of video games, MTV, and fantastic computerized special effects in the movies, we're used to a barrage of interesting visual stimuli (tech lingo is calling it "eye candy"), and that's changing the way we are being communicated to. The fast-paced, jumpy, visually packed style of music videos and MTV has crossed into advertising where some are cramming more than 1,600 images into a 60-second commercial.[1] Once our senses become bombarded and saturated by lustrous sights and ear-perking sounds, anything less, for an extended period of time, tosses us into a dark pit of *sensory deprivation.*

Business communicators can now take advantage of a large dose of that same type of visual and audio excitement to develop "Oh my gosh!" presentations. Computer-powered tools and techniques are helping business people to create innovative and dramatic ways to distinguish and showcase their products and hold their customers spellbound. There is now available a computerized technology commonly called MULTIMEDIA that is significantly improving the way we put together and communicate information, ideas, concepts, visions, goals, solutions, and feelings. With its elements of video, photography, speech, sound, and animation, it enables the fullest and most creative range of human expression.

This chapter will give an overview of multimedia covering its definitions, applications, components, and its strengths and weaknesses. We'll describe and show the connection between left-brain/right-brain functioning and multimedia and how this can give the toptalker a decided advantage in the arena of persuasion.

Get on the Multimedia Bandwagon Now!

Because it's developing into such an important total communications medium, organizations need to quickly learn how to put multimedia to effective use. Keep in mind that even though we repeatedly refer to this technology platform of communication, it's *not* the technology that's important—it's what it *does*. There are computer industry pundits who predict that within 5 to 10 years (many say sooner) of the onslaught of multimedia, traditional 35mm slides and overhead trans-parencies will go the way of auto tail fins, computer punch cards, and eight-track stereo.

Many innovative organizations are right now using some form of multimedia while exploring a myriad of additional and advanced uses for it. A caution is in the air though. While multimedia is available right now and is useful in several key ways, it is going through growing pains and a maturation process and its widespread use is probably years away.

Many smaller companies, for example, are finding, that multime-dia can give them a commanding lead over much larger competitors right now. President Clinton had jumped on the bandwagon in the beginning of his administration by installing multimedia PCs for use in White House briefings. And the CIA has struck a deal with Analysis Corp., a Washington-based company, to commercialize language courses the agency developed for its covert operatives and other employees. The courses combine full-motion video with recorded native-speakers' voices, text, graphics, animation, and user audio play-back. According to George Conrad of Analysis, "This is going to revo-lutionize language learning."[2]

Executives or other professionals should *not* spend their valuable work time becoming multimedia presentation designers. But they should understand the capability and features of it and be knowl-edgeable enough about it to tell an experienced multimedia designer the types of effects and impact that they want to make on their audi-ence. And they should learn the basics of operating a multimedia pro-gram (on a personal computer) that was created by a multimedia development expert. But as multimedia software programs become much easier to use, the *average person*, though, including executives, can learn to quickly create *basic* multimedia programs (e.g., electron-ic slide shows) right at his or her desk.

With Multimedia, You're No Longer a Member of the Bored

Dazzling . . . Awesome . . . Captivating. Those are just some superla-tives being used by multimedia users to describe the reactions people get when seeing (or should I say *feeling* and *experiencing*) a full-blown multimedia creation. Imagine that you've just spent three months getting an exciting project proposal ready. Now you have to take it to the board for approval and funding. Instead of dull black-and-white overheads packed with reams of text and tables of numbers, your multimedia presentation features brilliantly colored, three-dimensional financial bar and pie charts that grow and explode off the screen, eye-catching titles that move or change shape and color, explanatory text that is fed to the audience in digestible bites—one line at a time—briskly building onto and dissolving from the screen.

There's more! Your project implementation team is personally "introduced" to the group by cleverly showing the team chart. A photo and accompanying voice narrative profiles each member—one person at at time—right before the audience's eyes. And to top it off, you show poignant video segments of internal company advocates, enthusiastic customers, and respected consultants extolling the virtues of your proposed project—each cementing it with ever stronger justifying reasons. Portions of this are backgrounded with CD-quality music by Mozart and other sound effects in a moving storyboard fashion designed to weave a wonderfully vibrant "tapestry" of a visually persuasive message that begs action from the audience. It's the difference between presenting the facts and telling a great story. Multimedia at its best supremely engages, informs, cajoles, entertains, and convinces.

What Is Multimedia?

Don't confuse the term "multimedia" with *multiimage* presentations. The latter is generally defined as any audiovisual presentation in which at times there are several projected images held on a screen simultaneously, either as a superimposition, or as side-by-side projection, or as some combination of these two possibilities. Chances are you've seen those impressive multi-image (big screen) presentations given to large audiences. The complex set-up consisted of perhaps 20 to 40 (or more) 35mm slide projectors and one or more 16mm film projectors all precisely synchronized by a programmed controller. Those productions could take months to shoot the pictures and photos, create slides, edit, and debug. They typically cost $40,000–$100,000+ depending upon the sophistication of design and execution. They were physically unwieldy and universally complex.

Multimedia refers to the ability of a personal computer or workstation to manipulate and direct *multi*ple *media* elements such as text, graphic illustrations, pictures, photographs, animation, sound, and video. Hence the term "multimedia." It can be used to create live (interactive) or videotaped presentations, training programs, video brochures, kiosk functions, and many other business and broadcast applications.

Multimedia goes by different names for different applications. It's also known as "desktop video," "desktop media," or "desktop video publishing." The term that most communication and computer industry people tend to advocate is, "computer-based interactive multimedia." For our purposes though, we'll just call it multimedia. It is *not* a set of products. Rather, it's a convergence of many new and not so new (hardware and software) technologies that work together in new and ultra-meaningful ways to bring multi-sensory, nonlinear approaches to our communication and learning situations.

Macromedia, a major multimedia software company says, "multimedia involves using a computer to generate and combine media into a dynamic production with motion and sound." Apple computer prefers the term *interactive multimedia* and describes it as "multiple forms of communications media, controlled, coordinated, and integrated by the microcomputer." IBM says this about multimedia: "Multimedia is the integration of sound, graphics, animation, still images, full-motion video, new user interfaces such as touch and voice recognition into information systems technologies."

It's Really "Hollywood in a Box"

Once you strip multimedia bare of its considerable pretensions and technical jargon, it's essentially one thing: computer applications that aspire to communicate in an enlightening and entertaining way—just as good television programs or movies do. Multimedia is a powerful *fusion* of the computer and video worlds—it's "Hollywood in a Box," as some people are metaphorically referring to it. At its base level, everything is converted into digital form—strings of zeros and ones—and this enables precise and almost unlimited creation and manipulation of sound, pictures, and graphic images as never before possible or even imagined years ago.

Practically everything being done in a television studio editing room can be done on multimedia computers: video and audio editing and manipulation, creation of fancy titles and moving logo animations, text special effects, and broadcast-quality 3-D animations. Just as desktop publishing puts the equivalent of a page layout and print shop on your desk, multimedia computing is doing the job of racks of specialized professional studio equipment such as special effects and character generators, animation equipment, edit controllers, and audio mixers that totaled $150,000–$200,000 years ago. Multimedia can now give you the equivalent of a video studio at your fingertips for about one tenth the cost.

Even highly sophisticated still and moving special effects (such as those in science-fiction and adventure movies) can be done on a multimedia system. If you think the movies *The Abyss, Terminator 2, Lawnmower Man,* or *Jurassic Park,* with their incredibly realistic computer-created creatures and other special effects were fantastic, wait till you see the future where Hollywood and Silicon Valley merge to form "Gollywood." Thresholds are being broken every day with all the computer pixel power transforming Tinseltown into Digitown. Long-dead actors and actresses—ones that exist only in the neurons of a creative designer's mind and are stored in a computer—will look and speak in such ways that you won't be able to tell that it's all digitized bits of data that have sprung to life in re-created "synthesbian" form. Nothing is out of bounds as it relates to multimedia and it's not far-fetched to say that entire movies will be made in a single room packed with only computers and a team of writers, cinematographers, artists, and special-effects experts. *If you can imagine it, someone can do it.* As the saying goes, "A hologram is worth a billion words! While this may seem far removed from the boardroom, it may not be, simply because we have not yet begun to understand how to tap the immense power of multimedia to change the way we communicate and relate with audiences.

The Wave of the Future: A Digital Revolution Is on the Way

When it came to computer applications, the 1960s was the decade of data processing; the 1970s focused on word processing; the 1980s was the decade of desktop publishing, and the 1990s will be the time of exciting multimedia. Just as desktop publishing has exploded in terms of its use and importance, multimedia is promising to be even bigger in scope and relevance during the next 10 years. Market Intelligence, a market research firm in Mountain View, California, noted that sales have been quickly increasing and predicts multimedia hardware and software sales will reach about $24 billion by 1999. That figure might be very conservative. Forecasts from industry pundits vary widely and many have predicted an explosive growth in the $40–$70 billion dollar range by the year 2000. While analysts may defend their own crystal-ball projection figures, one thing everyone agrees upon—multimedia is going to be big . . . VERY BIG business over the next 10 years.

Major companies such as Apple, IBM, Hitachi, Sony, Toshiba, AT&T, Hewlett-Packard, Microsoft, and many others are devoting huge resources to the further development of multimedia. Strategic alliances to promote multimedia are growing quickly. Former fierce rivals Apple Computer, Inc., and IBM were among the first to create a joint venture called Kaleida Labs to develop standardized multimedia software. Then the baby bells and cable companies started their multi-billion dollar merges in the hope of creating massive media empires.

The potential uses of multimedia go well beyond presentation support. It involves an entire mainstream business market including sales and marketing communication, education, professional training, entertainment, information retrieval, and general business management. Multimedia will move into business, home, and school environments via "electronic rivers"—networks—using ultra high-speed fiber optic cables. Estimates vary, but the *information superhighway*—the huge interactive digital network—is expected to cost nearly nearly $100–$200 billion dollars over the next 10 years and will fuel the further growth of multimedia and other "information appliances" (as the yet undefined, not-yet-created information and media-related devices are being generically called).

John Manzo, corporate manager of Advanced Technology Marketing for Digital Equipment Corporation (DEC), highlighted to be the universal business communications potential for multimedia: "Via networking, multimedia will reach anyone in the world with a personal computer connected into a distributed network. Imagine someone being able to receive or transmit video pictures, animation, photos, music, sound effects, and voice as opposed to just text and numbers flashing on your computer monitor. Instead of bland electronic memos, people right at their desks will see videos of newly promoted executives, for example, describing their jobs and plans, exciting previews of new products to be shortly announced, or the company CEO giving a multimedia presentation about quarterly results.

Current electronic mail will seem like the dark ages of black-and-white silent pictures of the early century compared to today's sophisticated movies!"[3] While it can be done today, Manzo acknowledged that further advances in digital video transmission technology are needed before *distributed multimedia* becomes commonplace. If electronic mail gives one-dimensional information, multimedia can become a kind of electronic story-telling medium: It can reach to the higher plane of what I would call the "electronic tale."

Multimedia is a big part of the massive transformation toward "convergence" into a digital future that will have immense implications for *everyone* in business, home, school, and elsewhere. Computers, consumer electronics, publishing, telecommunications, and entertainment will converge and overlap into a mega-industry based on digital technology. All the pieces are falling into place. Michael P. Schulhof, vice-chairman of Sony Corporation of America, said that the digital future is simply "computing plus entertainment."[4]

It was former Apple Computer Inc. chairman John Sculley who estimated the size of the digital market at more than $3 trillion by the year 2000! Then *Newsweek* magazine, on their May 23, 1993 cover devoted to *interactive*, noted a "zillion dollar industry (maybe)." *Newsweek* also said it would become the first general interest magazine to publishing ongoing versions on multimedia compact disks. To tell the story, the CDs will mix text with still photography, video, animation, and even *Newsweek* correspondents doing voice-overs. They'll even feature interactive advertising that, could, for example, let the viewer test-drive a new car.

The catalyst for this incredible metamorphosis will be *digitization.* Just as vinyl records were replaced by digital compact disks in the 1980s, information and images will be converted to digital bits—the strings of 0s and 1s that are the language of computers. Everything from the analog signals of television, radio, and telephone to the images of movies, photos, books, pictures, magazines, paintings, documents, and fingerprints is going digital. Digitization will enable limitless design and creative manipulation of sound, images, and information, thus thrusting us into a rich information and multimedia world unlike anything imagined even by the most visionary prognosticators 20 years ago.

And those individuals and companies that start thinking about and planning for these tidal-wave "digital lifestyle" products and services will be able to better control their destiny. But the implications should be clear to perceptive organization leaders: Since critical information availability and transformation is at the heart and soul of this change, examining the immediate roles of multimedia in your organization should be an important short-term goal; examining the impact of upcoming significant convergence technologies should be the longer-term goal.

Physicist Fred Dyer, codirector of the Multimedia Technology Laboratory at the Georgia Institute of Technology, agrees that it's important for organizations to "seize the moment"—to grab and reap opportunities multimedia offers *right now*, rather than waiting for it to become well-known among all those in the business community. "I don't see any limits to multimedia," says Dyer whose organization is bent on evangelizing on how to use multimedia tools.[5]

WHAT YOU WILL NEED TO PUT TOGETHER A SUCCESSFUL MULTIMEDIA TOPTALK

A computer-based interactive multimedia system can range from a basic primary computer configuration (i.e., CPU, monitor, keyboard, high-capacity disk drive) where the program is played on the computer screen to a more comprehensive layout involving numerous pieces of audio and video equipment and sophisticated projection devices connected to a personal computer or workstation. However, if you think you need to lug around a bulky personal computer with you every time you give a multimedia presentation, that's *not* the case. Powerful (video-capable) laptop computers used with small, lightweight projectors and compact high-capacity disk drives make for a very convenient *portable* and *powerful* package.

Technology, product innovation, and investment costs are changing so rapidly in this booming application area that I'm not going to get into specifics as to what models or configurations to use. Rather, I'll list the general computer components plus the input and output devices that can comprise a multimedia system as follows:

Illustration 9-1
Multimedia System Components

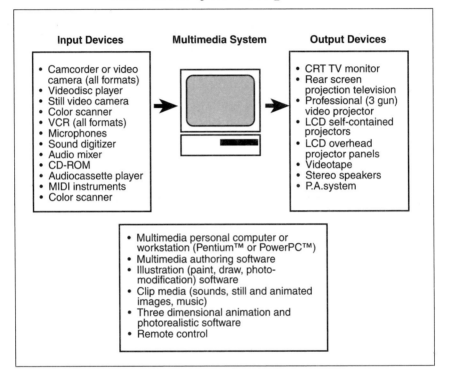

Input Devices	Multimedia System	Output Devices
• Camcorder or video camera (all formats) • Videodisc player • Still video camera • Color scanner • VCR (all formats) • Microphones • Sound digitizer • Audio mixer • CD-ROM • Audiocassette player • MIDI instruments • Color scanner		• CRT TV monitor • Rear screen projection television • Professional (3 gun) video projector • LCD self-contained projectors • LCD overhead projector panels • Videotape • Stereo speakers • P.A.system

• Multimedia personal computer or workstation (Pentium™ or PowerPC™)
• Multimedia authoring software
• Illustration (paint, draw, photo-modification) software
• Clip media (sounds, still and animated images, music)
• Three dimensional animation and photorealistic software
• Remote control

Input Functioning. Using any video device such as a VCR, videodisc player, CD-ROM, or camcorder, you can select any portions of video you want to input into your program "as is" or for possible editing and modification later on. The same applies for audio. You can speak into a microphone or use other sounds that are then converted into digital signals (by a sound digitizer) for input or editing by the computer. Music, sound effects, and other audio input can be taken from a CD-ROM, audiocassette player, stereo receiver, the sound track of a videotape, or any other common audio device and stored or manipulated. MIDI (Musical Instrument Digital Interface) instruments such as keyboards, saxophones, drums, and other instruments can be connected to the computer to provide music and synthesized sound effects.

You can also use a *still* video camera (that records 50 or more full-color images as single frames at a resolution of 400 horizontal lines or more on a video floppy disk) to input still pictures. Color scanners can take any illustration, photo, picture, drawing—*anything* that you might photocopy—and capture the image to input and later edit for your multimedia presentation. This gives you extraordinary power and flexibility. As a general guideline, almost any video or audio device can be connected to a multimedia computer to give it a video or audio material to use.

The Computer and Software. A personal computer is the "producer" of the multimedia program and the master controller of all the input and output devices. Video, audio, and other related equipment are connected to the computer, which accepts all the signals and data from the input devices and converts them into digital data, processes them, and then stores or displays the finished product. The multimedia software program is called an "authoring system" because you are writing a "script" for your presentation. It performs all the synchronizing, editing, compiling and processing, and input and output functions of the program. The multimedia program has the capability of importing illustrations from all types of paint, draw, and photo-manipulation software programs, animation programs, clipart and clipmedia (which is software that has predrawn *animated* illustrations and prerecorded sounds that you can easily transfer directly into your multimedia program).

Contact computer vendors to find out the best models and configuration (RAM memory and hard-disk capacity, monitor size, video cards, other peripherals) to run the types of multimedia programs you'll need. Several excellent authoring programs exist today for Macintosh- and Windows™-based personal computers. They range from simple integration programs designed for multimedia business presentations to powerful authoring programs designed to create high-impact presentations. Since multimedia is such a fast-paced, dynamic industry, great software programs and tools are coming onto the market every day. Contact the companies listed in the resources section at the back of the book to find out what's available and check for other sources as well.

Output Functioning. Once you've created a simple or dazzling production, you have several options for showing it. You might want to narrate an interactive multimedia slide show complete with video, animation, text slides, graphic illustrations, and elements of sound and music that is projected onto a large screen. In that case, you are the primary focus, and the multimedia program, like any other visual aid, is a support tool for you. Or you can print your presentation to videotape using an RGB-to-NTSC video converter to be seen by others at their convenience. In this case, your system functions as a desktop video publishing system.

If you're using interactive multimedia for a toptalk, your audience can view your program in several ways. You can use the following types of projection devices that directly connect to a multimedia-capable laptop computer or conventional personal computer:

- One or more large-size television (CRT) monitors such as those ranging in size from 25" to 40" made by Barco or Sony. These are like consumer television sets with the exception that they are commercial models that handle video and computer inputs.

- Rear-screen projection systems typically ranging from 40" to 60" in size that accept both video and computer signals. These are like consumer models, but they are designed for commercial use such as multimedia.

- Flat Panel (LCD) projectors are notebook size and weigh about 7 to 12 pounds. They require that you place them on top of an overhead projector to use its light source for projection. They can show video and computer graphics and typically are the lowest-cost and lowest-resolution projection device for multimedia. Their greatest advantage is portability and relative cost.

- Portable video projectors are Liquid Crystal Display (LCD) projectors that use the same basic technology as flat panel projectors, but they have their own powerful built-in (metal halide lamp) light source for projection. Various models weigh between 5 and 30 pounds, and some can project an image up to 25 feet (diagonal), which is 176 times larger than a 25" television screen. They provide quick and easy setup, are portable, and have acceptable resolution quality for small meeting rooms such as most boardrooms. Some have built-in audio amplifiers and speakers. With a multimedia-capable laptop computer, you can easily carry and quickly set up a multimedia presentation for smaller groups.

- Cathode Ray Tube (CRT) projectors consist of three (green, red, and blue color) tubes that come in 7-,8,- or 9-inch lengths (the longer the tubes, the brighter and sharper the image). CRT projectors can deliver a wide range of colors for demanding multimedia applications, especially video projection. They weigh over 150 pounds and give good quality resolution, brightness, and contrast. Many boardrooms in larger companies use these types of devices.

- Light-valve projectors made by General Electric and Hughes-JVC are the latest technology premium projection devices for multimedia and are used only in very large and demanding audience situations. They offer the brightest and highest quality image projection at sizes up to about 35 feet (diagonal). They are said to be about 10 times brighter than CRT projectors and are very expensive—costing from about $30,000 to $50,000 or more.

Your multimedia system can also supply high-quality audio output by being connected to speakers or into a powerful public-address system as well.

DESIGNING A TWENTY-FIRST-CENTURY INFORMATION CENTER IN THE BOARDROOM

Multimedia environments are increasingly being designed into the nation's leading boardrooms. Progressive organizations are upgrading their executive meeting rooms. These presentation palaces reflect an image and sense of power, taste, comfort, and sophistication. They represent leading-edge technology that will enable any toptalker to display the latest in multimedia, teleconferencing, and to access and display information from local or distant networks or even live satellite feeds from numerous sources. As we get fully drawn into the thick of the information age, many companies are making their executive meeting environment *sensory-rich and information packed* using state-of-the-art computer, audio, and video technology. And that has made them ever more versatile and sophisticated, and (most important) *productive* when it comes to presentation, problem-solving, or idea-generation activities.

According to *Presentation Products Magazine*, which highlighted 12 very impressively designed and well-equipped "Executive Briefing Centers" (as boardrooms are also being called these days), many are brighter, warmer, less stoical, but still on the conservative side. Such companies as Metropolitan Life Insurance Company, Perkin Elmer, MCI Telecommunications, Mobil Oil Company, and Nu Skin International share several characteristics: All have large-screen projection, easy-to-use audiovisual control systems, and very functional audio and lighting setups, and all achieved the goal of cleverly and tastefully integrating that technology within these hallowed business chambers by hiding or disguising the equipment when not in use.[6]

THE SEVEN KEY CHARACTERISTICS OF MULTIMEDIA

Let's now take a closer, more detailed look at how and why multimedia can dramatically help a toptalker to be his or her best—to give concise, creative, clear, vivid, persuasive, humorous, and results-oriented presentations. There are seven key ways and reasons:

One: Animation. The human eye is drawn to movement—ACTION! Animation, whether it's showing a video clip or whether it's generated by today's incredibly realistic computer animation programs, grabs and holds interest. Animation energizes static graphics and text. Video portrays reality as no text, chart, or table packed with dry data can do. And three-dimensional (photorealistic) modeling software (especially in an animated mode) can go beyond the reality of videotape and illustrate surreal fantasy and objects and scenes that are limited only by the imagination.

Two: Flexibility. Most visual aids chain the toptalker to a rigid sequential structure—a series of slides or overheads, for example, that one must follow. A well-designed multimedia program, however, has an effective structure for the presenter to follow, but it also enables him or her to easily and flexibly deviate from the planned outline of topics into other related areas of interest to the audience.

Multimedia accomplishes this by enabling a toptalker to create and randomly access any number of modules (with different topics, subtopics, and levels of detail associated with each). It's almost like instantaneously delving into an electronic file cabinet with all types of information filed by major category, types of information, and levels of detail.

For example, suppose an executive in the boardroom asks the toptalker, "Could you give me more detail and an illustration of how you calculated that return-on-investment figure you just mentioned?" Since the speaker anticipated that such a question *might* be asked, she included information about it "just in case" in one of her multimedia modules. By typing in a command from the computer keyboard, or by using a wireless mouse or other remote control device, the presenter goes to that part of the multimedia script she has created and quickly shows an example of how the financial calculations were created step by step. This flexibility and level of preparation enables the presenter to be *fully interactive* with the audience and to satisfy all anticipated questions.

With multimedia, the audience becomes involved—they are engaged in what is happening. And our survey and my personal interviews with executives repeatedly stressed the need for interaction (not monologue) between presenter and audience. This critical concept of accessing information (via many paths in multimedia) enables high levels of interaction between speaker and audience. This is called the "navigation" feature of multimedia. It's the ability of the speakers to effortlessly move around—randomly jump to any part of their multimedia program quickly and easily–thus enabling them to dynamically respond to the needs and wants of the audience.

Three: Attention-grabbing and Interesting. Many business people regard meetings as the black holes in their otherwise stellar calendars. I've had numerous executives complain about speakers with monotone delivery who bombarded them with lifeless visuals of endless charts, tables, and text-laden slides to the extent that they were drowning in a sea of confusing or boring data. One senior manager told me of his colleague, "Finally, he's putting some fire into his talks. Now if we could just get him to put more of his talks into the fire!"

You obviously don't want to overstimulate your audience to distraction, but the more you can perk them up, the more you can make the content enjoyable to listen to and watch, the greater the chance of your message being focused on 100 percent and being retained a long time afterward. And multimedia with all its dynamic elements of sight and sound can cut through the clutter to deliver crystal-clear, easy-to-understand information in a most interesting way.

Four: Easy and quick changes. Let's say you have a standardized sales presentation that you give to various executive customers to introduce them to your company and its products (i.e., an overview "orientation" presentation versus a solutions-oriented one) But, as all competent toptalkers know, you don't want to give an impersonal "canned" briefing; you need to customize it for each group. It might involve changing perhaps 5 to 15 percent of your content, and therefore your visual aid content as well. With a multimedia program, if you want to change text or illustrations, you simply type in your changes or modify your illustrations or tables right on your computer. Changes in video and audio are relatively easy too. The changes are *immediate* and as easy as typing in a command, redrawing an illustration, or using your computer mouse to give directions to your multimedia program. As such, you don't have to wait several days until your graphic designer or slide-processing company makes those changes to overheads or slides. Armed with a camcorder, for example, you can even shoot some video and put it into your multimedia program minutes before your presentation.

Another advantage is cost. High-resolution color overheads and 35mm slides need to be designed and processed. For example, slides created by an outside vendor can typically cost $10 to $100+ for each one depending upon its complexity. If your company uses 1,000 slides or more per year, that's expensive. You don't incur that cost if you use multimedia or presentation software programs running electronic slides. I'm not suggesting that executives making $250,000 per year and up should be creating multimedia programs to save their company money. That's NOT a good use of their expertise and time. I am suggesting that a company should look into getting their in-house production staff to add multimedia and electronic slide show capability to their traditional ways of creating visuals. However, executive presenters *can* easily learn to run their electronic programs.

Five: Visual control. Great toptalkers are audience "control freaks," and you'd never know it because they're so effective and subtle about it. They want to make sure the audience sees and hears *only* what they want them to view and listen to regarding the audiovisual aid they display. Flash a slide with six lines of text on the screen and guess what? The audience will read *every word* before their attention eventually comes back to you. Or they may continue to ponder something long after they read it on the visual. Obviously, that's not good for the speaker. People can think three to five times faster than a speaker can talk, and that leaves lots of time for pondering other thoughts that might crop up.

Loss of control means loss of attention, which means some important points will be missed by the audience . . . which ultimately means the speaker might not be able to reach his or her objectives. Multimedia has the capability to *build* and show images one word, one line, one illustration component at a time. You therefore methodically and precisely "feed" the audience only that which you are talking about, so it's impossible for them to get ahead of you. This is great for illustrating flow charts, organization structures, exploded parts of a product, or lines of text one at a time.

Six: Integration. What other form of audiovisual can "seamlessly" combine high-quality text, pictures, photographs, still and motion video, music, sound effects, photorealistic animation, and detailed illustrations in one combined media format? No other medium can put it all together as quickly, easily, and relatively inexpensively as multimedia does.

Seven: Ability to take abstract or complex concepts and ideas and translate them into concrete and clear thoughts. The video and three-dimensional animation capability of multimedia means that highly complex, abstract, or scientific techniques can be explained in more simple terms by visually illustrating the idea. Houston Area Research Center (HARC) in The Woodlands, Texas, fosters advanced scientific research on lasers, materials, science, space technology, astroparticle physics, DNA research and other leading-edge exotic research devoted to addressing major problems in society. They use multimedia, for example, to conceptualize and help communicate the immense complexity of decoding genetic information in human DNA structures (which is estimated to take 15 years and $3 billion to complete.). They are also involved in maglev technology (wheelless trains) and use multimedia to explain how linear induction motors operate. They find that multimedia is a superb communication tool to disseminate (in conferences) the results of their far-reaching work. As the president, Dr. W. Arthur Porter, told me, "Multimedia is effective when seeing is critical—when you can't take an audience to see a facility, when a subject is very, very complex and all you can hope to do is lay some groundwork for understanding it. Multimedia can give you an overview of a complex situation from which you can then begin to tackle the smaller pieces."[7]

SOME REAL-LIFE WAYS TO USE MULTIMEDIA AS A POWERFUL COMMUNICATIONS TOOL

The number of ways of using multimedia as a powerful communication tool in your toptalk is limited only by your imagination. The more experienced an organization becomes with multimedia, the more myriad uses and applications they discover for it. Here are just a few sample ideas:

- *Your company story for high-level customer visits.* A 10–15 minute impressive "personalized" overview of your company with video clips of your offices and modern plants, recorded greetings from senior staff, an animated historical overview of your company's financial history, and a rolling picture of the evolution of your products and current research and development can create a positive impression of your organization. It can be quickly personalized for your customers using their logos, interconnecting themes, customized text, and their names in the program. This program will help set the mood for a good beginning relationship.

- *A vivid financial or engineering overview.* Using the power of animation, you can take "sterile" financial, engineering, or other data and create three-dimensional illustrations that clearly bring the numbers to life. Bar and pie charts, trend or area charts, or other diagrams can be made to grow in segments and create a moving storyboard that takes data and visually pieces it together in ultra-comprehensible ways. Animation is perfect for quickly evaluating or comparing "what-if" scenarios used in strategic planning sessions, engineering design evaluations, or other types of change situations.

Via clear illustrations of the data represented, you can immediately see how changing one financial or engineering/design variable will affect others or how it compares to other options. Allow your audience to call out their own numbers as you enter them into your multimedia computer and then watch as the animated results are *immediately* projected onto the screen. This is an especially persuasive way of convincing them since they've taken part and have seen the results of *their* inputs. When an audience can see and understand the whole by constructing it in pieces, view the relative changes, sharply understand comparisons/contrasts, cause-and-effect relationships, and other connections taking shape before their eyes, it gives a new perspective and a better analysis of the meaning and implications of the numbers.

- *Real life renderings.* Architects or engineers can use multimedia to show photorealistic simulations of a new building, or plant being designed and how it looks from the exterior or interior. Multimedia can actually take the audience on a complete tour of the planned building, and this is a very cost-effective way to preview a proposed design for acceptance or changes. Several years ago, NASA used a realistic multimedia rendering of their proposed space station *Freedom* and, from a viewing standpoint, you would actually feel you were inside a real mockup seeing—and almost touching—every inch of the proposed orbital structure. Also, product designers can show any three-dimensional external and internal view of new products (tools, cars, clothes—anything) being designed. They can preview several alternative designs for thorough evaluation by the audience. Finally, marketing executives can judge concepts for new advertising campaigns that are done in a preliminary fashion on a multimedia system.

- *Executive sales presentations.* Salespeople can use short video vignettes of satisfied customers endorsing their product (or service) within their toptalk to help strengthen their points. They can also put the customer clearly in the picture by creating a simulation of a product's use within the future customer's organization and a precise lay out the functions and benefits of it. For example, a salesperson, selling a total computer network configuration, can show (via animation) how each network component is connected and would function within each department of the client's organization. In addition, video can provide an "almost live" sales demonstration of a product. Salespeople can also use a camcorder to shoot video of current customer situations for vivid comparison with a video segment of the new proposed solution (e.g., present plant machinery versus the salesperson's new equipment).

An "electronic champion" triumphed in a major sale several years ago. Multimedia played a pivotal role in convincing the International Olympic Committee in Tokyo in September 1990 to pick dark horse Atlanta over sites in six international cities. Georgia Tech created an informative and glitzy interactive multimedia presentation that took the viewer on a journey through Atlanta's proposed Olympic Village. The presentation combined graphics merged with video images of Atlanta and was projected on three six-foot diagonal screens. It enabled Olympic officials to "walk" through a village that existed only as computer images.

Fred Dyer, co-director of the Multimedia Center at Georgia Tech told me that multimedia is a superb vehicle to present a sparkling vision or exciting dream of something, and in this case it portrayed what the Olympics would look like in Atlanta in 1996. Dyer said, "We targeted the whole thing to answer questions that the committee might have and then used the technology to answer them in a short-story format." Besides being extremely visually informative, the multimedia program apparently accomplished the planned challenge of creating a visceral experience that led to a decision to select Atlanta.[8] Multimedia apparently gave Atlanta a strong competitive advantage since no other sites in contention used the technology to promote themselves.

- *Entertainment presentations.* Meeting kick-offs, award banquets, product introductions, media publicity events, and other entertainment-oriented situations are perfect for the creative blasting power of multimedia. For example, at an annual week-long sales award meeting of an East Coast electronic controls company, the theme was strong leadership and new strategies. Multimedia was used to show old movie clips of both serious and funny war movies. Some were purposely edited to simulate "silent movies" with humorous captions about the new strategy. Also, the multimedia program was used to take the faces of several sales executives and impose them with the bodies of several of the movie characters—as if they were the "generals" in the still picture. Funny sound effects were used to complement the captions. This multimedia presentation nicely mixed themes, metaphors, and humor with a serious motivational message to create a smash hit.

- *Promotion.* On a visit to offices of the E.P.I.C. Group in The Woodlands, Texas, president Vic Cherubini demonstrated to me a "Catalog-on-a-Disk" they recently produced for Shell Oil. On a single 3.5 inch high-density disk, E.P.I.C. crammed over 300 pages of technical information, animation, full-motion video clips, graphics, and sound. The program was designed for use by adhesive chemists and includes an interactive formulation guide. An engineer can use it to do "what if" formulations on the computer monitor (instead of in the lab).

  It even contains an interactive trivia game that pits the knowledge of the chemist against the computer. Cherubini said, "Although it was designed as a direct mail piece, the program could be uploaded on electronic bulletin boards (such as Compu-serve™ or Prodigy™) and transmitted anywhere in the world for the price of a long distance phone call." It's common for a chemist who receives the program to spend 45 minutes to an hour with it. It is unlikely that he or she would have spent as long with a printed catalog. Cherubini calls this the "Nintendo Syndrome." When you involve the viewers in the media, it's easy to lose track of how much time they have actually spent with it.[9]

  These examples of multimedia applications barely scratch the surface of communications, marketing, training, and other opportunities awaiting multimedia's magic touch. The technological power has never been as cost-effective and easy to use as now. Multimedia is limited only by your imagination to use it.

LEFT BRAIN, RIGHT BRAIN: USING MULTIMEDIA TO FEED INFORMATION TO BOTH SIDES OF OUR BRAIN

To fully understand and greatly appreciate exactly how multimedia can dramatically improve the way we communicate, learn, make decisions, and creatively express ourselves, you need to understand how our brain basically processes data from our senses. Most important, though, knowing about fundamental brain activity can help you in all forms of persuasive and informational toptalk design and delivery.

Exciting scientific discoveries over the last 20 years have shown that we actually have two separate cerebral hemispheres—a "right" brain and a "left" brain. They are connected by the *corpus callosum* (whose name means the "hard body," although it is not really hard)—a thick nerve cable containing millions of fibers that transmits continuous important information between these two hemispheres. The two halves of the brain's cerebral cortex look something like the sliced halves of a melon that have not quite been put back together again. Each hemisphere takes in and processes information in a very different way and getting to *use* both sides of your brain is a critical step in making much better decisions and unleashing your inherent creative potential. This means that each of us perceives and processes information and expresses the results differently.

The implications of using multimedia as a presentation tool are far-reaching: Multimedia is the *most powerful* communication tool to feed lots of rich information to *both* sides of our brain. And that ability translates into presentations that are both more *effective* and more *efficient*—much easier to understand, more memorable, more persuasive, more motivational/inspirational, more impacting, and more productive.

Our senses (sight, hearing, touch, taste, smell) provide information that goes to the left brain or the right brain or (in varying degrees) to both. Working together in a holistic fashion and communicating via the corpus callosum, the two brains analyze the data from each of these sources and enable us to reach a conclusion, generate ideas, prompt us to react in a certain way, or cause us to retain information and emotions in a specific manner. The less input from our senses, the less information the two halves of the brain have to evaluate situations and advise us accordingly. However, the more our senses feed our mind with "nutritious input," the easier it is for us to make decisions and feel more conclusive about something and the greater the quantity and quality of ideas we can come up with. That's exactly why multimedia (with its diversity of text, illustrations, charts and graphs, still pictures, video, sound, and animations) is ideal for quickly and fully loading *both* the right and left brains. Multimedia can enable a toptalker to have the audience experience much more impacting information and feelings.

Do You Know Your Right from Your Left Brain?

An understanding that we have two separate brains with different functions began to come to light in the 1940s when split-brain surgery, or commissurotomy (surgically cutting the corpus callosum) was performed to relieve epilepsy symptoms. In California research laboratories in the early 1970s, studies about the the human brain were eventually to win Roger W. Sperry of the California Institute of Technology a Nobel Prize and gain worldwide recognition for Robert Ornstein of the University of California for his work on brain waves and specialization of function. These and other studies have led to new insights about human knowledge, creativity, consciousness, learning, decision making, and intelligence. Armed with an understanding of how left brain/right brain processing works, a toptalker can use multimedia as an information filter, synthesizer, amplifier, analyzer, and idea generator.

In his breakthrough research, Professor Ornstein performed measurements of people's brain waves as they were performing specific mental functions such as adding numbers, arranging colored blocks, logically analyzing problems, daydreaming, and writing letters. He measured the mental "processing" activity coming from the two halves of each person's brain as each task was progressing. He discovered that the left brain most efficiently handled such areas as mathematics, language, logic and analysis, writing, and other structured-type activities involving sequence and linearity while the brain's right hemisphere was primarily responsible for tasks involving imagination, fantasizing, color, music, rhythm, images, dimension, and other spatial skills. The following table details the *prima-ry* functions of each side of the brain (although activities are some-times shared by both sides to various degrees):

Illustration 9-2
Thinking Styles and Hemisphere Functions

LEFT-BRAIN THINKING
(also known as Western, focused, logical, hard thinking)
* *Sharply focused "laser thinking"*

• Intellectual	• Analytical	• Sequential/linear
• Routinization	• Deductive	• Critical/evaluative
• Convergent	• Temporal	• Pragmatic
• Reality-based	• Digital	• Precise
• Logical	• Consistent	• Mathematical
• Specific	• Concrete	• Serious
• Focused	• Goal-oriented	• Objective
• Controlled	• Systematic	• Conventional
• Orthodox	• Traditional	• Evaluative

RIGHT-BRAIN THINKING
(also known as Eastern, diffused, creative, soft thinking)
* *Widely dispersed "spotlight thinking"*

• Intuitive	• Nonrational	• Emotional
• Divergent	• Holistic	• Gestalten
• Playful	• Improvising	• Imaginative
• Dreamy	• Fantasy-based	• Subjective
• Experiential	• Symbolic	• Visio-spatial
• Nonlinear	• Experimental	• Metaphorical
• Surreal	• Paradoxical	• Impulsive
• Fuzzy	• Artistic	• Visionary
• Mystical	• Nonverbal	• Simultaneous

Holistic—Balanced—Brain Activity Is Needed

Professor Ornstein found that people developed "dominant" sides of their brain by *favoring* use of one side over the other more frequently. As a result, they were unable to use the other side as effectively. You'll hear people in various careers and job functions actually flaunt their presumed "hemispherical superiority." Financial executives or engineers, for example, might pride themselves on being "left-brained"—highly organized, pragmatic, numbers-oriented, no-nonsense *bottom-line* achievers. They prefer detailed analysis, written instructions, and lists. Marketing, advertising and entertainment executives, as a group, might boast that they are the "right-brained imagineers"—creative, clever, intuitive, visionary, artistic, and innovative trendsetters. They respond to visuals, charts, and maps. You'll find left-brainers following instructions *exactly*—step-by-step; right-brainers generally visualize the final result and are more prone to combine, skip, or substitute steps in a seemingly random or intuitive way to meet changing needs.

Numerous research studies prove that when the weaker (less dominant) of the two brain hemispheres cooperates with the stronger side, there is a dramatic increase in mental effectiveness. In his landmark book, *The Psychology of Consciousness*, Ornstein highlighted the fact that Western-cultured people have been using only half of their brains and hence only half of their true mental capacity.[10] He said that in Western societies the left hemisphere is generally more active because of our emphasis on language, logical problem solving, rationality, and our push for technological innovation. In the holistic, mystic, intuitive, and opportunity-seeking cultures and religions of the East (such as Japan, China, Korea, etc.), the right brain is accorded high prestige and, therefore, more use.

Carl Sagan, the famous astronomer and biologist, in his Pulitzer-Prize winning book *The Dragons of Eden* notes that the most significant creative abilities of a culture are the joint work between the brain's left and right halves.[11] Tony Buzan, an authority on creativity and learning, in his book, *Make the Most of Your Mind*, said that famous painters such as Cezanne and Picasso used both sides of their brain to produce stunning works—they were highly mathematical and geometric in their artistic achievements.[12]

Brilliant achievers are often mistakenly labeled, "artistic" (right brain) or "scientific" (left brain) when, in fact, they are both.

Leonardo da Vinci was considered one of history's most "complete-ly balanced" men because he not only excelled in linguistic, logical, and mathematical areas, but made marvelous use of imagination, color, and form. Einstein's greatest discoveries took advantage of wild imagination in addition to ultra-complex physics and mathematics. And flamboyant and eccentric Nikola Tesla, who many claim to be the greatest inventor the world has known, was almost supernaturally gifted with left- and right-brain dynamos. Churning at breakneck speed and synchronized together in a bewildering display of astonishing creative visualization combined with fevered intellectual activity, his balanced mental strengths made him one of sciencedom's amazements even to this day.

Unfortunately, years ago few people claimed being "whole-brained"—that they balanced the use of both hemispheres. Using both sides of the brain is like using two hands to do a job—it's a lot faster, easier, and better. Today left-brain worship in business is quickly on the wane; right-brain intuition, creative problem solving, and imaginative idea generation are respected as complementary thinking functions and is taking on great importance as we approach the challenges of the twenty-first century. We need to grasp the relationship of parts to the whole—and that's precisely what multimedia can help us to do.

Our Brain Is Steeped in Visual Imagery

Our brain thinks and remembers in vivid pictures and sounds and images, symbols, and experiences—not words. Feed it a picture . . . give it sounds, let an emotion mark it, and our brain will make us understand it and remember it *immensely* better than a bunch of words or numbers strung together. Because multimedia appeals to *both* our logical left and the imaginative/emotional right side our brain, it covers all bases. When your multimedia toptalk shows text, numbers, sequences, outlines, flow or process charts, engineering animations, tables, lists, or spoken segments from videotapes or synthesized speech, the left brain is functioning and quickly absorbs that directed information. The incredible power of multimedia to plan, organize, define, clarify, verify, question, and show how information is gathered and manipulated sharply satisfies the information craving of the left brain.

Now, when multimedia uses music, sound, color, symbols, video sequences (involving emotional interchange) and when it shows realistic or even surreal fantasy-type animations, cartoon sequences, art forms, and other visualizations of ideas, the right brain is fed its creative nourishment. The three-dimensional aspect of multimedia especially appeals to the spatial qualities of the right brain. Multimedia is, indeed, the best visual and audio tool today to quickly illustrate thought patterns and show complex relationships (that cannot be easily defined verbally) and idea connections that the right brain processes so efficiently. This dramatic power that multimedia has in effectively and efficiently catering to both sides of the brain enables profound learning, creative discovery, and quick realization of solutions to take place.

Multimedia Is Great, but It Has Its Drawbacks

You've obviously gathered that I'm a great fan of multimedia since I've spoken so glowingly of it and highlighted the many benefits associated with using multimedia in your presentations. Indeed I am! I have a friend who jokingly calls me the "Patron Saint of Toptalk Multimedia." I firmly believe that it will be the creative electronic communication equivalent of the genie in a magic lamp. But I need to balance my fervor for multimedia by telling you that it's not for everyone and it has drawbacks. Here are some to consider:

> *You can overdo it.* Some executive presentations don't require the audiovisual firepower of multimedia. While I generally recommend using color visuals whenever possible (for maximum impact and retention), simple black-and-white computer-designed overheads printed on a laser printer will often do just fine. The very strength of multimedia can be its biggest weakness as well. Because multimedia has such awesome creative and technical power on tap, many people (especially newcomers enthralled with its whiz-bang features) are tempted to show off if they can. Perhaps a few Walter Mitty types are aspiring to be the George Lucas or Steven Spielberg of the boardroom by using every glitzy, flashy feature and special effect available. That *can* and *will* overwhelm the audience. "The message is hopelessly lost in all the pyrotechnics" one computer-literate CEO of a medium-sized service company told me.

Dr. Arthur Porter, president of HARC, stressed, "Sometimes the glamor of the presentation exceeds the needed substance. Problems occur when the presenter is infatuated with the (multimedia) technology and attempts to demonstrate his proficiency in the depth and breath of all the 'wizardry' while losing sight of his communication points."[13] The technology must be used to *enhance* the content, not bury it. Jonathan Swift, eighteenth-century English satirist, said, "In oratory the greatest art is to hide art." That same concept of hiding the technology and creativity and letting the communication content shine through is critical in using multimedia.

A study conducted for the 3M corporation by Douglas Vogel a leading computer-based presentations researcher, identifies which technology tools help audience retention and understanding and which reduce effectiveness. The research project found that a fancy multimedia presentation won't help an unprepared speaker impress the audience, but an effective speaker can use relevant and simple animation (such as bar charts that grow or text revealed line by line) to boost audience retention. *Meeting Management News*, a publication of 3M Corporation's Meeting Management Institute said this about the study's findings regarding presentation special effects, "Using just transitions (such as wipes, fades, etc.) between graphics detracted significantly from the audience's perception and retention. When consistent transitions (using the same transition effect between each image) were combined with animation, audiences responded much better than to transitions alone and slightly better than they did to animation alone."[14]

An important point to realize is that with any technology you don't want to come across as a special-effects technician, computer expert, or graphics designer. You do want to come across as a leader, communicator, and problem solver—a toptalker! Finally, if you use "overkill" visual aids for a simple presentation, whether it's multimedia or richly designed color overheads or slides, the impression the audience might get is that you're spending your time or the company's money in unwise ways.

The "complicated stuff" requires experts and is costly. A complex and highly sophisticated multimedia program with video, illustrations, animation, 3D rendering, music, sound effects, and pictures requires someone who is both technically competent and artistic—someone who has well-rounded personal computer, graphic design, scripting, audiovisual production and editing, illustration, music, authoring system expertise, and perhaps photography skills. And being creative is a must! A 20 to 30 minute comprehensive multimedia program might cost $30,000–$60,000 or more depending upon the level of sophistication.

At a trade show, I overheard one talented multimedia designer telling a potential client, "I can make Hollywood caliber presentations for the price of electricity." Sure, but it certainly costs the customer a whole lot more! An impressive multimedia program for important customer visits, trade-show programs, heavy traffic kiosk applications, or repeat, large-audience presentations might justify the cost of these highly elaborate productions.

Technical problems and growing pains. Like any new technology, multimedia is evolving and being molded into different forms as it matures. There are numerous technical hurtles that must be addressed before widespread use of multimedia explodes throughout the business world. One of the biggest problems now is storing full-motion video images in digital form on computer storage devices. *Digitized video and audio take up an incredible amount of space with today's storage media.* For example, an ordinary CD can hold over 70 minutes of music and about 600 millions of characters of digital storage. That seems a lot, but to digitally store all the frames and audio from an entire motion picture, for example, would require approximately 360 CDs (where one analog videotape would do it).

However, new and ingenious digital compression technology, called Moving Picture Experts Group (MPEG), among others, will enable a feature film to be stored on just two CDs. That's a dramatic improvement. Still, new higher-density storage devices and yet more efficient compression schemes and semiconductor chips that enable computers to more efficiently handle video are being created to make video storage and display easier and cheaper. Also, multimedia authoring and other software programs are going through a continuous period of maturation. They are being enhanced to make their use much easier and quicker for the novice. Just as desktop publishing was initially used by commercial graphic artists and is now in widespread use by nonartists, multimedia programs will mature and gain popularity—likewise.

Equipment problems and expertise. Multimedia systems are the most complex of all audiovisual aids, and hence there is a greater possibility that something might go wrong (e.g., compared to using an overhead projector). If your computer hardware, software, video projection, or television (CRT) monitor experiences problems, your whole presentation might collapse unless you have either a backup multimedia system standing by (ready for immediate switchover) or have backup overhead transparencies and a projector to use in its place.

Anyone who uses a multimedia system needs to be proficient in the use of a personal computer as well as minimally understanding how to activate and navigate through the multimedia program (even though it's been designed by another). Also, while the average "computer literate" person can learn to design basic multimedia programs, the fancy stuff is definitely not for the faint of heart. One multimedia designer told me, "We sometimes get calls from marketing and sales people who don't realize that producing a highly complex interactive presentation is not just a matter of buying the right tools. Usually, after a few months, they give up and call us. They find out the hard way that it often requires a team of experienced graphic artists, programmers and technical people. You don't want to 'slit your throat on the cutting edge of technology.'"

Improved resolution needed. If you show a multimedia presentation on a large TV monitor (such as a 35 inch CRT), or use a larger rear projection TV system (e.g., 60 inch) viewing clarity is perfectly fine in a small meeting room such as a boardroom. But, for ultra-crisp demanding viewing applications in lighted rooms, the projection resolution needs to improve in overall quality. The problem is not multimedia, it's the state of current video projection technology. While recent technical improvements have made video projection devices (especially LCD projectors) *much* better than ever, film media such as 35mm slides and film and overheads still have much crisper resolution, better brightness, deeper color saturation, and superior contrast compared to large-screen video projected images.

Industrial use light-valve projection systems (they're called *light amplifier projectors*) from General Electric and JVC/Hughes Aircraft, for example, are capable of providing the highest level of impressive video projection quality right now, but they're very expensive to rent or buy. Further advances in projection devices and the future commercialization of flat screen High-Definition Television (HDTV) monitors (that will be wall size and even larger) being developed in worldwide laboratories right now will match the quality of high-output slide or over-head projectors.

Start Your Multimedia Exploration and Implementation Now

Getting started now by using some form and application of multi-media will pay big dividends in much more effective presentations at all levels. You'll also find myriad other valuable uses for this ultra-powerful communication amplifier. Vic Cherubini, president of E.P.I.C. Software, advises, "You can lead or follow, but you should-n't ignore the revolution taking place on your desktop." He counsels his clients to be on the leading (not "bleeding") edge of technology by starting small to "test the water."[16] One way to begin is to con-tact the suppliers in the resource section (at the back of the book) and get them to tell you who in your area can give you a demon-stration of multimedia and explore some immediate uses of it in your organization. Some companies supply demonstration video-tapes that can explain multimedia and give you examples of appli-cations. Actually seeing and hearing a sample of multimedia, how-ever, will convince you of its potential to change your organization's communication environment. Consider having the vendors run sev-eral in-house presentations for people in various functional areas of your organization.

Encourage people to start with the "easy stuff." Instead of try-ing to create full-blown multimedia presentations, people should get acquainted with it by starting off with the most basic application—a computerized slide show. It's very easy for anyone who operates a personal computer to use the multimedia authoring software to cre-ate visuals that consist of text, graphics, simple illustrations, and some static or animated clip art. Later, as people become more confident and proficient, they can begin to use more functionality of the program including adding some video (from clips or from shooting video from a camcorder), adding some audio clip art or digitized sound, and putting in touches of music within the program.

Identify high-priority areas of use for multimedia in your organization. Analyze the types of organizational communication situations that would best lend themselves to each level of multimedia sophistication. Establish some ideal criteria for use and determine which applications might benefit from immediate use of multimedia and which ones are longer-term in use. Determine how you might use multimedia for internal communications, with customers, suppliers, strategic partners, or with the community. Examine every important presentation and communication problem you're experiencing and see if multimedia can help. And think about opportunities, not just problems. Look for innovative ways of using multimedia to grab opportunities—to do things you've never done before. Experiment and be bold!

You'll find that once multimedia is "seeded," resourceful people will quickly find many additional useful applications for multimedia once they're aware of its powerful functionality. People from sales, marketing, employee training, engineering, research and development, public relations, and communications might be typical first-draft benefactors. Multimedia can give your organization a powerful competitive edge in lots of areas. Don't wait. Rather than be swept away by the digital age, begin riding the wave now!

IMPORTANT: See the Resource Section at the back of the book for a listing of multimedia products and services that can help you.

Chapter
TEN

Creative
Communication
Leadership

*By logic and reason, we die hourly; by
imagination we live.*

—J.B. YEATS

I've enjoyed watching perhaps hundreds of highly accomplished
speakers from all walks of life. I've found that while each followed
certain traditional rules of great "public oratory" or boardroom communication, the exceptional ones added a unique aspect to their presentations. Something magical. Something special called "creativity."
When you have the three Ps—Poise, Polish, and Passion—in your
presentation and then add doses of rich imagination into your executive talk, you can't help but WOW the audience into enthusiastic
acceptance of your idea or proposal.

Lots of people who attend my various presentation skills-build-
ing workshops often ask me how they can add interest, pizazz, and
sheer excitement to their presentations. They want the secret elixir on
how to make their performance outshine all others. One super-moti-
vated fellow in my advanced presentation workshop, asked, "How
can I get my presentations to *sizzle*?" Invariably, my answer is: "Use
as much creativity as you can in the design and delivery of your presentation!" In response, I often get these dejected looks from them as
if to say, "Me creative? . . . are you kidding? I'm delighted if I can just
develop a 'regular' presentation that's acceptable. I just want to get
through it." How unfortunate that "I-can't-do-it" attitude is!

273

Creative Communication Leadership means using your imagination in wondrous ways that will get your executive audience to understand, agree, and act upon your recommendations. Dial "C" for creativity and connect with your audience in ways you never dreamed possible. And for yourself? It's entertainment for your soul.

USING CREATIVITY TO FIRE UP YOUR AUDIENCE

Ask someone to define creativity and most people will have a tough time wrapping their arms around this oftentimes ethereal thought process and behavior form. One brilliant physicist from Lawrence Livermore Laboratory in Berkeley, California, describes the creative moment as "all the bells and whistles going off in my head." Most of us can instinctively see something that's creative; we can *hear* it, *feel* it, and *judge* it more easily than we can precisely explain what that elusive quality is. When asked to define jazz, the great Louis Armstrong replied, "Man, if you gotta ask, you'll never know." Creativity is like that. The famous psychologist Carl Rogers echoed that sentiment when he said, "The very essence of the creative is its novelty, and hence we have no standard by which to judge it." E. M. Forster said, "In the creative state, a man is taken out of himself. He lets down as it were a bucket into his subconscious, and draws up something which is normally beyond his reach. He mixes this thing with his normal experiences and out of the mixture he makes a work of art."

Creativity Is . . . Some Definitions

But here are some accepted guideline definitions to help give you more perspective on the topic:

Creativity . . .

- is an original act that produces surprises.
- is a daring journey beyond the familiar into the unknown.

- is the generation of the "new" or the rearranging of the "old" in a new way.

- is the process of integrating facts, feelings, and impressions (from all prior experiences) into a new form.

- is imaginative, free-wheeling thinking that ventures outside the usual route, recipe, pattern, or formula and that leads to fresh insights and even revolutionary ideas.

William James touched on out-the-rut-thinking when he offered, "Genius, in truth, means little more than the faculty of perceiving in an unhabitual way." When it comes to using creativity to enhance your presentations, the definition I use is:

> Creativity is the act of coming up with novel and useful ideas that can be used in the planning, development, and delivery of every aspect of your presentation. The goal of creativity is to improve your chances of reaching into the minds and touching the hearts of your audience to achieve your toptalk objectives.

Any time you can make your presentation more interesting, you significantly increase the chances of riveting your audience's attention. Any time you use a creative approach to making an unpopular view suddenly seem more sensible, acceptable, and palatable, you're closer to your objectives. Any time you use your imagination to translate a tough-to-understand concept into something that's now remarkably "obvious" to your audience, you're stacking the cards of success in your favor. *Creative communication leadership works!* What it does is elevate your thinking and action to a much *higher plane,* way above the ordinary, the mediocre, the "average." Creativity puts your presentation in the ivy league of excellence.

Creativity, however, is not an all-or-nothing trait. Each of us has the capability of being creative—almost always to a larger degree than we realize. Sure there are those very creative people we truly envy—people who seem to be able to exhibit strokes of brilliance without any sweat at all. But as Ralph Waldo Emerson put it, "We boil at different degrees." Imaginative thinking IS hard work. When confronted with a problem, it's natural for us to grasp at the first lifeline of hope that pops into view.

Our Brain Is That Marvelous Organ of Creative Thought

Napoleon once said, "Imagination rules the world," and in a way, the power of imagination can help us rule our own world. Creativity, properly channeled, enables us to be absolute masters of our universe—to be creators of our destiny. To appreciate creativity, though, you have to appreciate the *creative engine*—our amazing (God-given) brain. We take for granted the complexity and inherent power of our mind—the power to solve seemingly "unsolvable" problems and to come up with ideas ranging from clever to downright brilliant. While an enormous amount of discovery has taken place about the working of our brain over the last ten years, so much remains a shrouded mystery, yet to be unraveled. While some researchers are telling us we are using less than 1 percent of our brain capacity, others are shockingly estimating that we are using perhaps one-hundredth to one-thousandth of its true potential. Yet, for all the educated guesses (and pure speculation), it's absolutely certain that human beings have not cracked the code to tap into the mystical mainstream of the power of thought, emotion, and imagination. As one of the participants in my workshop on corporate innovation aptly put it, "I wish my brain came with operating instructions!"

Upon physical examination, our brain looks deceptively simple: a lumpy gray mass (that resembles a bunch of cauliflower with a thick hairy rope hanging down underneath) of deep ridges weighing about 3 pounds and averaging about 82 cubic inches in size. You wouldn't think it is (as far as we know) the universe's *most complex* piece of "equipment." Our brain can store over 100 billion bits of information in a lifetime–500 times the information contained in a complete set of encyclopedias. Over 100,000 different chemical reactions occur in our brain *each second*. As a result of this firestorm of activity, our brain soaks up almost a third of the energy consumed by our entire body. Its electrochemical process produces the equivalent electricity of a 20-watt bulb. The brain has an estimated 100 billion nerve cells called neurons (a cell, *each* of which acts as a powerful computer). Each neuron is able to interact with all others in an ultra-dense communication web of complex circuitry. It's estimated that the number of these interconnections is more than 10 followed by 800 zeroes!

Our brain is often compared to the working of a computer. One speaker at a recent creativity symposium I attended said that in using today's technology of microprocessors, memory chips, and other circuitry, the human brain (in computer form) would fill a densely packed ten-story building occupying the entire land size of the state of Texas. While this analogy is eye-opening, our brain is so efficient, so different, so complex, so powerful, and so elegantly engineered that any comparison with computers (or anything else) is essentially meaningless.

In describing the miracle of our marvelous brains, I hope to encourage you to use even an extra one-tenth percent of that "miraculous machinery" to imagine novel ways of adding creativity to not just your toptalk, but to everything you do. French political philosopher Baron de Montesquieu, perhaps cynically, noted that "when God endowed human beings with brains, He did not intend to guarantee them." His fellow philosopher Rene Descartes added, "It is not enough to have a good mind. The main thing is to use it well."

HOW TO AVOID MAKING THE BOARDROOM INTO THE "BORED ROOM"

Creative communication leadership is one that adds a whole new daring dimension and exciting perspective to a topic. Call it imaginative depth and breadth, clever positioning, business showmanship, or a brilliant and ingenious display of energy, the point is this: creativity WILL transform your presentation from being like an average meal into a sumptuous feast. A brilliant idea deserves a brilliant presentation. Even average ideas can be beautified and strengthened with creativity.

But *having* an idea and creatively *communicating* an idea are two entirely different things. The problem with most executive presentations is that they are stodgy, dry, and devoid of anything that tickles the senses and emotions and that challenges the intellect of the audience. They need more *"Infotainment"*—giving information in an (appropriately) entertaining way. Too many people believe that executives are somehow overly conservative, nonfeeling, "no-nonsense" people who only want straight facts and data presented in a sterile fashion. *Nonsense!* In our survey, 64 percent of executives said that the use of creativity in designing and delivering a presentation was important, while 22 percent said it was very important.

Executives and a lot of lower-level managers sit through *lots* of meetings and presentations. It's tiring and difficult to concentrate after a while. Anything that can break up the monotony is greatly appreciated—fresh new styles and approaches are welcome respites after some yawn-filled briefings. What executives don't want, though, is a form of unwarranted, useless creativity (I call it "flash that's trash") or, worse yet, a tribute to mondo bizarro at their expense. Executives disapprove of anything that adds little value (unnecessary window dressing) and, instead, proves distracting and extraneous to the main points being presented.

Six Reasons to Use Creativity for Grappling Effect

To help reach your overall communication goals faster and better by grabbing your audience, consider using creativity in your presentation or speech when:

1. You want to transform a complex (e.g., abstract, intangible, technical) topic into one that is highly understandable to the audience.

2. You've analyzed that your audience's attitude toward your topic is unfavorable. You decide that a radically new persuasive strategy is needed.

3. You want to slam home some points in a way that sticks in the hearts and minds of your group.

4. You want to shed a whole new light on a topic in such a way the audience has never thought about before–perhaps even creating a *paradigm shift* ("paradigm" being a mental model of our views about something).

5. You want to outshine other speakers (e.g., your sales competitors) in a fashion that makes your presentation more impressive and memorable (as George Bernard Shaw put it, "One man who has a mind and knows it can always beat ten men who haven't and don't".)

6. You want to either subtly or directly "entertain" your audience while doling out information.

A speaker's imagination can be the explosive fuel that blows apart the entrenched, outdated ideas of the audience. Look at anyone who has sold a challenging vision to a group. Examine any successful innovator, trend setter, entrepreneur, corporate "mover 'n' shaker," and you'll see someone who has fired up an audience with the sizzling flames of ideas, hopes, and dreams all fueled with hot-blooded imagination.

Yes, *You* Can Be More Creative

Moving an executive audience from "status quo to get-up-and-go" requires more than the usual dull, strait-laced presentation. Presenters who want to be *change agents* (in their organization) have to add zestful, creative communication leadership to their talk. But, erroneously, most people feel that they are incapable of being creative. To many, creativity has a Casablanca mystique to it. They often mistakenly feel that only "special" people—only a select few artists or otherwise exceptional people—have this elusive trait. Others connect creativity with genius. *Don't believe it!* While most of us are not highly creative (in the artistic sense), we're all capable of tapping into our reservoir of innate creativity.

Each of us CAN generate lots of good ideas for our speaking situations—whether it's in the executive boardroom, on the lecture circuit, or sitting at our desks communicating with a colleague. "Imagination is more important than knowledge," Albert Einstein once said. Sure, it's true that both are needed, but as you know, solid information delivered in dull, unimaginative ways will quickly fall on deaf ears. Why can't we present knowledge and ideas in a truly imaginative way—a way that gets the audience to move at warp speed in the direction we want them to? The answer is we can, if we make the effort.

Another reason creativity has been underutilized is that people are generally afraid of leaving the safe sanctuary of a traditional presentation format to try something new and perhaps unproven. Don Blohowiak, author of *Mavericks . . . How to Lead Your Staff to Think Like Einstein, Create Like DaVinci, and Invent Like Edison*[1] told me that, "If we want to inspire our audiences to break *their* bonds of old habits and perceptions, we must first break our own." And Emerson wisely notes, "It is a lesson which all history teaches wise men to put trust in ideas, and not in circumstances."

Remember that creativity is essentially defined as the power to be more advanced and exploratory in your thinking. We can learn to redesign old presentation ideas and discover clever solutions to vexing problems or take advantage of seemingly out-of-reach toptalk opportunities.

SEVEN EXAMPLES OF PRESENTATION CREATIVITY IN ACTION

Remember that the end product of exercising creativity is IDEAS— any and every idea to make your toptalk sparkle in the eyes of the audience. The ideas can be small or large, evolutionary or revolutionary, brilliant or just clever. Here are a few examples of how some creative people enriched both their presentations and their professional image:

ONE: One manager at a New England electronic components company did a great job memorizing and naturally speaking (with a poker face) an entire paragraph backwards! The audience of senior managers had no idea what she was saying until she explained her action and repeated the paragraph (which contained her key points) correctly. This unorthodox gutsy approach dramatically helped her illustrate to her audience that the marketing campaign being considered was a big step backwards and that the company's customers would not understand the real value of the new products being introduced (just as the executive audience could not understand her). This little touch of creative symbolism not only got their attention but their promise to modify the marketing messages.

TWO: As a timely theme, one sales vice-president of a sporting goods company used the Olympic games to highlight the concepts of (1) winning; (2) excellence; (3) training and preparation; and (4) ability to recover from defeat. He imaginatively used stunning (still and video) pictures of performances and post interviews with the athletes, excerpts from commentaries, and clever connecting themes and slogans. He presented his new sales-development program (with those four concepts in mind) by communicating to the board of directors that his long-term plan would produce sales champions that are "world-class" in effectiveness. He compared less expensive and shorter-term plans used by the company's competitors as the equivalent of trying to transform a novice athlete into a superb one within a six-week period of time. In spite of the board's initial apprehension to fund a longer-term sales-development effort, they were sufficiently impressed and convinced it was the "common sense" thing to do. As the speaker later said, "They [the executive committee] were moved and as a result they moved [on my proposal]."

THREE: Creative showmanship can blossom in small ways. I attended a motivational keynote speech several years ago and sat in the back of the room, among about 400 people. I clearly remember the speaker using this large (about 3-foot-long) arrow to point to the screen where his overhead transparencies were being projected. Each time he pointed, it immediately drew my attention to the visual messages he referenced because he used his big arrow-shaped pointer so well (it didn't seem heavy or unwieldy) and you could vividly see this oversized prop and what he was pointing to. I had a chance to ask him about his pointer and he told me he prided himself on his low-budget resourcefulness. He went to an art store and bought a thick foam-core board and traced the image of a wide, three-foot arrow and then cut it out with a razor knife. He then painted it a two-tone color to stand out. He uses his arrow only to dramatize key points during strategic parts of the presentation because he doesn't want to dilute the effectiveness of that creative prop.

FOUR: Several years ago, at a convention of managers in the pharmaceutical industry, a consultant and author was speaking about leadership versus management. About five minutes into his luncheon talk, a telephone rang on the podium next to him. The telephone's ring was amplified by the microphone so the entire audience's attention was drawn to it. He abruptly stopped talking and let the program chairman answer it saying, "It's for you!" Looking puzzled, the speaker shot back, "Tell them to call back later. I'm talking to a group of 350 people now!" Moments of dramatic silence were broken when the chairman replied, "The caller insists he can help you in your speech right now!" He picked up the phone and held about a four minute conversation with the caller (whose voice was also amplified), who was a respected senior vice-president of one of the well-known companies in the industry. He proceeded to tell the speaker six ways that the audience can focus on visionary leadership. Of course this "sudden surprise advice" was well planned out and rehearsed. The little bit of theatrics by the program chairman and speaker kept the audience's attention riveted on this "interruption," which helped to reinforce the speaker's points.

FIVE: At a recent association gathering of regional meeting planners, I heard one speaker being introduced in a creative and wonderfully humorous fashion. At the end of her speech, she told me that her friend, an expert impersonator, mimicked the voices of Dr. Ruth Westheimer, Bill Cosby, Clint Eastwood, and President Clinton for each "personality" to say a little bit about her qualifications. It was recorded (relatively inexpensively) in a broadcast studio to give it high-quality sound. Prior to each of her presentations she has her cassette player (with her introduction tape) connected into the public-address system of the meeting room. Her topic is lighthearted, and that imaginative introduction sets a great tone for the rest of her talk.

SIX: Like me, a sales friend from a major computer company used to give lots of slide presentations to executives about computer networking solutions to major banks. He had a warm, infectious personality with a bit of lovable mischief in him. Before his big presentations, he used to purposely put a particular slide in the carousel tray *upside down* with a duplicate slide correctly inserted in the following tray slot. When he showed the upside-down slide during his sales presentation, he'd say something like, "Oops . . . sorry about that. Let me fix it [the slide]." He'd then push the slide projector remote control button to advance to the following (duplicate) slide that was positioned properly. People in the audience would wonder how he could possibly "fix" an incorrectly inserted slide without stopping the presentation to pull the slide out of the carousel slot to arrange it properly in the tray. Clever! And he'd follow that stunt with something like, "If you think that's amazing, you ought to see how quickly we can get your electronic funds transfer system up and running without a hitch!" According to him, his audiences loved it!

SEVEN: A combined team of research engineers and fabrication specialists from an automotive parts manufacturer had the goal of convincing their senior management that manufacturing processes in several plants needed a major overhaul. Their study pointed out a needless loss of quality and the high cost of rework due to poor processes, not worker dedication. Other managers broached this topic with little success. The executive committee had responded with "deafening silence," as one plant manager described it. "A little waste is to be expected" was their justification for not disrupting present operations and spending more money.

The new team felt that a creative presentation approach was definitely needed to "shake up management." Their goal was to dramatically point out the obvious absurdity of material waste and the inefficiency of human activity in this outdated assembly process. Being creative with their own costs, the presentation team asked the film department of a nearby university if they'd like to produce a video as a student team project. One of the company engineers (who was an amateur mime) volunteered to get dressed up and play the assembly worker. They filmed just one (representative) area and caught on tape all the excessive movement and extraneous machine activity needed to fabricate and assemble one component of the car and to perform rework. They then filmed the flow of the proposed new operation (with the number of assembly steps decreased and with new machinery placement and operation).

When the operation was shown speeded up, the (mime) assembly worker looked frantic and exhausted. It was embarrassingly amusing. The new proposed operation was then shown speeded up as well. But the mime's movement was now like an elegant ballet with smooth, graceful motions, and the new machine placements and modified operations also made it evident that this enhancement (which could be replicated elsewhere on a larger basis) was superior. This impressive creative comparison showed visually convincing evidence that there was a ridiculous amount of unnecessary human and machine activity. The presentation team then carefully supported the video example with eye-opening operating and financial cost comparisons that dealt the coup de grace to the old way. A perfect combination of emotion and logical argument!

Sure, creativity requires extra thinking, extra work, and extra risk, but it's almost always worth the effort, even if you consider starting out with mini-creative ideas and then adding increasingly more imaginative ingredients to your presentation recipe. It also takes a measure of courage to go outside the boundaries of convention to try a fresh and interesting approach. As author of *Mavericks*, Don Blohowiak, puts it, "No guts, no impact!"

To use creativity successfully, you need to understand how much and what types of creativity will appeal to your executive or other audiences and then determine whether the risk of trying something new and clever is worth the intended results. You accomplish that by doing an effective job of analyzing your audience. Finally, know your own ability and confidence to pull off a creative coup.

DEVELOPING THE TRAITS OF "CREATIVE PEOPLE"

You may be a frustrated creative type longing to unleash your full imagination on the job or you may be someone who doesn't particularly feel creative, but who really is. To give more creative toptalks, you need to start off right now firmly believing yourself capable of generating *more* imaginative ideas than you realize and you'll start to increasingly ignite a firestorm of creativity within yourself. Which singular trait do practically all creative people have? While ingenious people are generally considered to be more adventurous, curious, independent, flexible, observant, and more willing to experiment, the major overriding trait shared by ALL creative people is that *they actually believe they are creative*. Simple as that!

So, feeling that you can stimulate your natural (but perhaps dormant) creativity is the critical first step toward illuminating your presentations like a fancy marquee. Also, by knowing the other typical behaviors and attitudes that most creative people usually share, you can begin to emulate those positive traits and also work to eliminate those personal and professional idiosyncrasies that snuff out the creative fire in you. Following are some specific characteristics typically associated with highly imaginative types:

Persevere in spite of criticism. Creative people are extremely persistent in achieving success in spite of obstacles and opposition to their ideas. Creativity expert Don Blohowiak notes that "if you advance a novel idea, expect someone to criticize it. Novelty, by its nature, rubs against the grain of convention. The key is to muster confidence in your ideas and prepare to stand up to the harsh winds of criticism."

Creativity is not for the faint of heart. I call these irrepressible types "Idea Gladiators" because they bravely go back into different arenas to continually fight the (sometimes "bloody" mental and emotional) battles to sell their ideas or proposed ventures. Humor often helps these visionary types to defuse anger. A vice-president of sales of an automobile parts manufacturer winked at me when he said, "People accept my idea much more readily when I tell them Benjamin Franklin (or Einstein, Aristotle, etc . . .) alluded to it first!"

Are prudent risk takers. The stereotype of successful creative people as blatant—even reckless—risk takers is false. Creative toptalkers realize that to be out on the cutting edge of change and innovation, one must take calculated, well-thought-out, and "acceptable" risks (acceptable to them and to those in the audience). They believe that if you risk nothing, you risk everything. These people also have a positive attitude toward making mistakes that lead to creative breakthroughs. They treat failures as "practice shoots." Most of them intimately know that "if at first you don't succeed, you're running about average." Their attitude is, don't build safety nets under me . . . give me more rungs on the ladder to climb.

They can't seem to take "No!" for an answer when problems develop. And they live by what the famous inventor and innovator Charles F. Kettering wisely said: "Virtually nothing comes out right the first time. Failures, repeated failures, are finger posts on the road to achievement. The only time you don't fail is the last time you try something. One fails forward to success. "Creative people seem to be inoculated against failure. The only sure way to fail is not to try. As Gaspara Stampa, a twelfth-century Italian poet, talked of playing it safe: "He loses not, nor wins who never jousts."

Aren't afraid of outrageous ideas. When most people suddenly get a wild (but potentially magnificent) idea in their head, they inevitably play devil's advocate to it (judge it prematurely and harshly) before giving it a chance to digest and blossom. Barbed self-thoughts such as these tend to immediately squelch any idea that is too novel:

Too risky—people won't buy it.

It'll never work. It's not feasible.

Let me forget that idea and be practical.

People will think I'm off the wall.

There are probably a dozen reasons why it won't work.

What a weird and bizarre idea. Forget it . . . No way!

Creative people have no problem stretching their imaginations to their uppermost limits to toy with silly, wacky, far-out, crazy, or otherwise outrageous ideas (although creative ideas need not be bizarre). They're people who have both feet planted firmly in the air. Those in the leading computer hardware and software companies in Silicon Valley call the concept of big thinking "Wide Bandwidth Thinking," from the electronics term that means range of frequencies within a band. This metaphorical caption means someone who can think in a very broad manner.

Innovative types know that nothing great was ever accomplished by mediocre, practical, sensible thinking. Instead of playing devil's advocate, they play "angel's advocate" with themselves by focusing on all the positive aspects of a potentially good idea first, before they carefully evaluate the limitations and problems with their ideas. Successful creative people are not starry-eyed dreamers—they are pragmatic as well; they carefully examine both the pros and cons of their ideas. They also know that selective parts of unusual ideas can be great. They may be salvaged and later brilliantly pieced together to come up with an "insanely great idea" (as Steve Jobs, one of the founders of Apple Computer used to call idea breakthroughs).

Creative thinkers often realize that the best solution may involve starting with a clean slate—that incrementally improving something might work, but that in order to get a dramatic improvement, one must be highly original and break some rules, and go way beyond what is deemed "conventional wisdom." As Picasso said, "Every act of creation is first of all an act of destruction."

Are improvers and visionaries. The phrases, "Leave well enough alone" and "status quo" wax painful to these folks who live and breathe the rich air of continuous innovation. Creative people are *always* looking for a better way of doing just about everything. Just because there are (actually)-over 3,500 patents for a mousetrap, doesn't mean that there is no room for a clever leap forward in design and function. There are creative people out there right now thinking about a new "catch-a-mouse-device" (with patent number 3554?). Imaginative types are also very visionary—seeing way into the future—anticipating long-term needs of people and businesses.

Sometimes very ingenious people are *too* far ahead of their time and have to "detune" their ideas so as not to appear too radical . . . too progressive . . . too bold . . . too soon.

Are intrinsically motivated by their work. Creative people are almost deeply spiritual in their dedication to fulfilling their life's vision and mission via their work. For example, they are enthralled by the sheer rapture and sense of accomplishment of working on a challenging venture—a project that entices them to push their creativity to the limit. This childlike joy of working on something they absolutely love is the *primary* (intrinsic) motivator for them, and they'll often work 90 to 100 hours a week—sometimes to the point of exhaustion—without being asked to. They are *totally* committed and passionate about their creative work. *Extrinsic* motivators such as extra money do practically nothing as long as creative types are being compensated in an amount they believe is fair. However, recognition from peers and their managers are a welcome validation gesture for their dedication and creative talent. Thomas Edison more than any other inventor believed that "the value of an idea lies in the using of it." Creative people are great "Idea People," but *successful* creative people are superb implementers of their ideas—they are *doers* as well as thinkers.

See things differently. Creative people are highly observant. They have an extraordinary sense of visual, auditory, or kinesthetic mental imagery. Many of their best ideas come from "seeing the obvious" (ideas and solutions easily missed by most people because it is *not* obvious to them). Instinctively, they often come up with radically different ways of viewing situations and solving problems. Imaginative people might be seen as mavericks and can usually be at odds with the rest of their (more cautious and traditional-thinking) team who, more times than not, see their creative colleague's ideas as impractical, far-fetched, often intimidating. These out-of-the-box thinkers don't actively try to be different, they just ARE. They march to a different drummer drumming a different beat. They realize that there are much superior solutions to situations if people would just try to break habits and expand their thinking—just be open-minded to all sorts of other incredible possibilities. Just like "a great ship asks deep water," a great thinker asks for much open mental latitude.

Creative people are *"possibility thinkers."* They're highly curious people by nature. They tinker with lots of "what if" possibilities and options before selecting the best idea or approach. They do not automatically accept conventional rules, assumptions, theories, or facts—many can be "giant defiants" of the status quo. While some pride themselves on being rule breakers, others simply believe that "conventional wisdom," may be conventional, but it's certainly not wisdom. Often, creative people are looking for the Holy Grail of Innovation—the quantum leap, the breakthrough, or the mega idea. When renowned architect Frank Lloyd Wright was asked, "What do you consider your greatest achievement," he shot back, "The next one!"

Are "different," playful, and humorous. Highly imaginative people often see themselves as unintentional "noncomformists." They may complain that they feel they don't belong or fit in with the group at work. They often feel misunderstood and almost always feel undervalued for what they can contribute. If they were given a chance to prove their imaginative ways, this may translate into tangible and valuable accomplishments. They oftentimes know firsthand Ralph Waldo Emerson's insight: "To be great is to be misunderstood." Creative people are often uninhibited in their behavior as well as their thinking (for some types, when they're in a state of "creative flux," it can border on eccentric).

A sense of carefree spontaneity contributes to their sense of playfulness. Many enjoy quick banter, sharp wit, and good-natured heckling of their friends and associates. These imaginative people can be "cut-ups" and practical jokers. They enjoy an open playfulness at work and can become even "silly" at times. Many have an active dislike for what they perceive as counterproductive office politics and unspoken uptight conservative codes of conduct. After all, they feel, "Who has the right to imprison creative souls yearning to fully express themselves?" And they love to poke fun at people who are actually anticreative. At one meeting of industrial design engineers, a very conservative-thinking project manager boasted, "I'm a mature business thinker!" to which one maverick engineer immediately retorted,"We know you are—all your ideas are 50 years old!"

Creativity and humor *do* go hand in hand. Playfulness, humor, fun, or a work atmosphere that is sometimes entertaining (or at least pleasant) in nature—whether by design or not—stimulates creative thinking in a very powerful way because laughter and fun activities release powerful stress-reducing chemicals in the brain that stimulate the thought process. A formal, stress-filled, and judgment/punishment based atmosphere at work snuffs out even smoking embers of the creative flame.

WAYS TO TAP INTO A MORE CREATIVE YOU

Regardless of what degree of creativity you possess or use, there's still a lot more available if you further develop your imagination. Here are some proven recommendations to help you generate and channel the power of creativity in your presentations and other activities:

1. Flex Your Mental Muscles

Believe it or not, the brain needs "exercise" to help build a torrent of good ideas from a trickle. So the more you get in the habit of coming up with ideas (the process is called "ideation"), the easier and faster the flow of ideas will come. It's proven that practice actually builds the idea muscle in your brain. W. Somerset Maugham endorsed that concept: "Imagination grows by exercise, and contrary to common belief, is more powerful in the mature than in the young." In the past, researchers believed that it was the number of neuron cells in the brain that determined the horsepower for generating ideas and for overall intelligence. Today, it's believed that the "circuitry"—or the complex connections—between the billions of neurons is what boosts creativity, learning, memory development, and intellectual growth. And, these *neural pathways* are built up the more we think, study, visualize, dream, imagine, and do. As our minds in creative wonderment search for highly novel ways to solve problems or take advantage of opportunities, the more these brain connections build in number and complexity, thus making our mind power stronger and more efficient.

Also remember that coming up with good ideas is a statistics game, as in gambling. The more ideas you think of, the greater your chance of hitting a jackpot. Granted, only a fraction of all your ideas will be usable and valuable, but that's still more ideas than you'd have if you didn't try. Linus Pauling, a two-time Nobel Prize winner, put it ever so simply when he confirmed that the trick in coming up with good ideas is to think up a great many ideas and just get rid of the bad ones.

Brainstorm by yourself or with others and watch the ideas spurt out. Always keep a pad and pencil handy to capture ideas. Or better yet, carry one of those microcassette recorders with you to get a more detailed record of that blockbuster idea. It's amazing how quickly you can forget several good ideas. A thought unrecorded is an idea lost, creativity author Don Blohowiak stressed to me. It's a known fact that we often get our best ideas when we're doing "mindless" activities (that's when our solution-generating subconscious mind is especially free to communicate with our conscious mind) such as taking a shower or bath, exercising, washing the dishes, painting the house, or when first waking up from sleeping. Plato said, "When the mind is thinking, it is talking to itself." When you least expect it, the solution to the problem you've been struggling to find, suddenly leaps out of your head. It's called the sudden "Eureka!" moment or "Aha!"—the point of creative illumination. That's why it's important to be able to record your ideas anywhere and anytime. Begin being creative now. "As James Russell Lowell, suggests, "In creating, the only hard thing's to begin; A grass-blade's no easier to make than an oak."

2. Be a Sponge

You can get the greatest ideas for your toptalks from places, people, and things that seemingly have nothing to do with your topic. The key is to look for the unexpected. I'm a sponge for all sorts of unusual and diverse sources of information and experiences. I get great ideas by browsing in the library looking at the titles and tables of content of all kinds of magazines and books. I also generate great ideas for props to use in my presentations and training workshops from exploring toy, hobby, or high-tech "gadget" stores. Catalogs of both ordinary and unusual products (including joke and gag items) is another great source of inspiration. I'll see something and suddenly get a "connection" for a different idea to use. And the "aha!" answer startles me with its oftentimes obvious usefulness. Charles Peguy said, "It is the essence of genius to make use of the simplest ideas."

Your mind can use only the material you supply it with. In other words, to be more creative, it helps to stimulate your mind with a barrage of wide-ranging information and auditory and visual experiences, not knowing where or when a connection can be made. You can, indeed, "piggyback" on something you've seen, read, or heard—to translate that into something you can use in your presentation.

It greatly helps to be a divergent reader. Read all kinds of different publications: *Mad* magazine, *National Geographic, Architectural Digest, Scientific American, Cosmopolitan, The Wall Street Journal, Aviation Week* and *Space Technology, Business Week, Ladies Home Journal, Harvard Business Review,* and *Reader's Digest,* among others. Scanning through each magazine, you'll almost always find something interesting that you can cut out or copy and file by category or maybe use immediately. You can quickly spot business, social, political, and technology trends by doing a lot of reading from these various sources.

I may never live down telling my readers this, but I even read the so-called gossip magazines such as the *National Enquirer* sold in supermarkets (I jokingly call them my "literary gazettes"). Besides being mindless, entertaining reading to relax myself after some serious, taxing reading, I find that looking at silly or unusual article titles, clever "trendy" phrases in the text, and some of the outrageous stories can spark ideas. Don't be a snob—anything that can give you a new slant on something old or tickle your imagination in new directions is worth the effort.

Ask yourself how you can use ideas from the world of religion, philosophy, architecture, art, sports, science, or entertainment to bring new life to your toptalk. Always be vigilant to see how you can meld, borrow, or modify ideas, principles, and concepts from one field into another. Remember that creative people—via their curiosity and patient experimentation—piece together clever combinations from out-of-the-way sources (of objects, words, ideas, processes, etc.) rearranging the old or different into something interesting and novel.

Another way to get ideas is to visit museums, attend different seminars (outside your field of work), enjoy comedy clubs, watch all kinds of movies and television programs and—important—socialize with highly creative people. While enjoying yourself, you'll be delighted at the wealth of sources for presentation ideas, themes, metaphors, process models, raw information, and real-life stories you find. Finally, get involved in some artistic recreation such as painting, drawing, sculpture, music, dance, acting—anything that helps to stimulate new untapped areas of creativity.

Prior to trying to solve a problem or search for new opportunities, the goal is to brainload—flood your mind and senses with diverse, well-rounded visual, auditory, and sensory experiences. Your subconscious will take that store of information, digest it, work on it, and then suddenly pop out some great ideas. Keep your mind open to all possibilities and expect the unexpected! Alexander Hamilton said, "Men give me credit for genius; but all the genius I have lies in this: When I have a subject on hand I study it profoundly."

3. Open Your Mind to All Possibilities and Don't "Kill" Your Ideas

I think one of the greatest challenges we must overcome is the "closed-mind" syndrome. Education and life experiences have taught us many things that are simply difficult to give up or think around. In school, at work, and in society, we've learned so many rules, so many procedures, so many "known facts," that it's often difficult to escape what has been deeply entrenched into our heads over the years. We take for granted what we've been told is *right and wrong, correct and incorrect, practical and impractical,* that we simply don't question or challenge ideas that may now be hopelessly outdated or inferior. Children are marvelously open-minded and imaginative in the wildest ways. As Aldous Huxley, English novelist and critic, pointed out, "We are all geniuses up to the age of ten."

We need to periodically challenge assumptions, break some rules, overcome rusty mental habits, and take an almost childlike naive approach to asking why something can't be done in a totally different way. Thomas Dewar, British distiller and raconteur, said it aptly, "Minds are like parachutes: they only function when open."

To help channel your creativity, do some brainstorming by yourself or with respected colleagues or friends. First try to come up with the greatest number of ideas in a relatively short period of time (start with 30 minutes), and don't discount ideas that appear silly or crazy (let them "ferment"). The goal is to open your mind's *idea faucet* and let everything flow out full force. Write everything down. Once the ideas start to dry up, you can begin to judge and select several workable ideas. Remember that you can piggyback on some outrageous ideas that later can be converted into something suitable for your presentation.

Most presenters are eager to quickly design the content of their presentation and to get it over with. So, in the planning stage, they typically settle for the first set of ideas and solutions they come up with. Creative toptalkers, however, are more daring and patient, and they venture beyond the obvious pieces of information or methods of presenting it. When designing their content and strategy, they brainstorm their ideas from several different approaches, angles, perspectives, and outlooks. After they've exhausted every possible option, they then carefully choose the best one. The guideline is: don't settle for the first thoughts that pop into your head—try to get at least three to five different ideas, solutions, or approaches.

4. Think Sizzle, Pizazz, Electrifying, Enlightening, Mind-blowing

If you wish to add some "sparkle and color" to a typically bland presentation landscape of desert-dry data, rolling spreadsheet visuals, and hackneyed themes and if you want your audience to vividly remember some of your key points, then you've got to experiment with some potentially outrageous conceptions. You can't do that by being conservative and "playing it safe." You need to mentally toy with highly imaginative approaches that tickle, massage, or hug the audience's beliefs, desires, principles, values, fears, and motivations. People pay close attention to that which is out of the ordinary. You're certainly not trying to turn your presentation into a boardroom "Ripley's Believe It Or Not" show, but you need to make your points as attention-getting, interesting, and thought-provoking as possible—to make your points leap out at the audience.

Senior executive audiences are not receptive to "shock therapy" from a speaker and usually frown upon overblown theatrics or inappropriate showmanship that is distracting, time-wasting, or otherwise unprofessional. But there are definitely those times when you need to shake up decision makers—when you have to use some creative technique or strategy to shift their thinking 180 degrees; when you need to hit their sensitivities with some dramatic prop, example, story, audiovisual, or other unusual idea. One of the ways to add that sizzle, pizazz, and electrifying impact to your presentation is to brainstorm using superlatives.

To be highly creative, you need to develop a sense of exaggeration and aggressiveness in coming up with dramatically novel ideas. By being cautious and conservative in your imaginative attempts, you'll only develop mildly improved ideas. To be a Steven

Spielberg of the boardroom—where a presentation is more an adventure and experience—brainstorm ideas using "superlatives," those excessive and exaggerated words that "force" you to think in a much more imaginative fashion.

Look at each of the following descriptive words and think about how you might develop relevant ideas around each one. Don't be afraid to come up with several wild and tempestuous ideas. You can then examine those ideas and spin off more realistic and down-to-earth ideas from them. But, why not use these words to "prime the imagination pump"—to stretch your mind into new and exciting directions?

Focus on each word below. Spend a minute or two on those that catch your attention. Ask yourself: "How can I add the following characteristic to my toptalk?" For example, "How can I use stunning analogies to really dramatize my main points of . . . ? or "What are some startling ways that I can use these financial figures to slam home the idea that we need to make some innovative changes right now?"

• surprising	• shocking	• curiosity
• outrageous	• fascinating	• bizarre
• exceptional	• amazing	• stimulating
• fantastic	• mind-boggling	• eye-opening
• titillating	• ridiculous	• stunning
• hilarious	• ingenious	• disgusting
• senseless	• absurd	• startling
• dramatic	• unusual	• idiotic
• sensational	• enlightening	• inspiring
• stimulating	• dreamy	• spiritual
• incredible	• embarrassing	• awakening
• greatest	• monumental	• perfection

5. Use the Power of Metaphors

From the time of ancient Greek and Roman philosophers to today's authorities on brain research and creative thinking, it's been said that powerful metaphorical thinking is one of the direct signs of creative genius. Yet, you don't have to be a cerebral sorcerer to come up with metaphors that can add incredible clarity, persuasion, and overall power to your executive communication messages. Metaphors are one of the best (but also one of the most underutilized) creative communication tools at a presenter's disposal.

A metaphor is the linguistic application of a word or phrase to an object or concept (it does not literally denote) to suggest a comparison with another object or concept. Metaphors are like analogies or similes (a figure of speech in which two unlike things are explicitly compared). The real power of using creative metaphors in your presentation is that they can (1) take a difficult-to-grasp abstract concept and make it understandable and clear by comparing it to something we are already very familiar with; (2) enable the audience to accurately *visualize a complete mental picture* of a presenter's thoughts very efficiently—obviating the need to go into a lengthy explanation of a concept or idea; (3) make language very colorful, dramatic, and picturesque to get the audience's attention; and (4) help to make a presenter's points very convincing.

"Life is a journey" is a well-known metaphor. Journey (e.g., by car) as metaphor brings to mind all the possible elements and characteristics associated with a journey: a beginning and end; it can be smooth or rough; there can be good planning and direction or we could get lost or delayed several times with detours, dead ends, and traffic jams; we might have several small accidents or maybe a big one; we could meet a lot of people along our route. You could go on and on to fill in the life-as-a-journey metaphor. Former Soviet president Mikhail Gorbachev, in response to the Russian crisis threatening to impeach Boris Yeltsin in March 1993, used this visual metaphor, saying that Yeltsin appears to be guided by advisers ready to "set the house on fire in order to fry themselves an egg."

Actress Lauren Bacall used this clever metaphor for creativity: "Imagination is the highest kite one can fly." "Empty nest" is a metaphor for the situation (new feelings and lifestyle changes) for parents when children grow up and leave the house to lead their own lives. When people refer to the "carrot and stick" method of motivating employees, that's a metaphor for reward and punishment (or as as others might more gently say, "encouragement and discouragement"). When President Ronald Reagan wanted to give a big picture of what the former Soviet Union was all about, and to make it stick like glue in our minds, he used the metaphor "Evil Empire," extracted from the popular movie *Star Wars*. If you've seen the movie (and chances are, you have), it enabled you to fully understand exactly what President Reagan meant without his having to explain any of it. In 1946, Winston Churchill coined the brilliant metaphor "Iron Curtain," for the communist division taking place in eastern Europe.

When NASA originally conceived of the space shuttle over 20 years ago, the metaphor of "space truck" was born. That term helped to crystallize the function, design, and operation of a new-concept space vehicle. After all, a truck (relative to a traditional rocket) is quick and easy to load and unload, easy and inexpensive to "drive" and maintain; can serve many materials transportation purposes, and could be driven or parked anywhere.

"Computer virus" (a program created by a "hacker" malcontent that creates mass sabotage of computer software) is another popular powerful metaphor that enables people to understand how computers get *infected* by a *dormant bug* and how it *quickly spreads* to others as a result of *close contact* between computers.

Princeton professor of computer science Richard J. Lipton, in explaining the difference between a traditional supercomputer and his "massive memory machine" uses a metaphor of a sports car versus a bus to let nontechnical audiences easily understand his complex design. Lipton explains that a supercomputer is like a Ferrari, for example, that can whisk a couple of people rapidly from point to point, like data being transported within the supercomputer. His computer is like a bus. It drives slower, but carries more people, so for carrying around lots of data, the "bus" design is better.

Finally, in a past magazine advertisement, the Japanese automobile company Infiniti used a metaphor to tell people what it was like to own and drive their new J30 personal luxury sedan. Their headline read: "It's not a car. It's an aphrodisiac." What a metaphor!

Metaphors are a great creative tool to help executives make decisions concerning change and to help in the design, for example, of new programs for marketing, sales, employee development, advertising, customer improvement, new product or service development, or any other number of purposes. Metaphors are also great for high-level planning and competitive strategizing or creation of vision and mission statements. When used with complementary visual aids (especially computerized multimedia) to further amplify the effect of metaphors, they can "burn" ideas, feelings, or principles deep into the collective psyche of the audience.

Metaphors can run the gamut from being humorous to straight-forward to downright bizarre. The more colorful, poignant, and understandable the metaphor, the more impact and memorable it will be. You can brainstorm a metaphor with the characteristics you want. See how the following examples of differently phrased metaphors paint a "picture" of a point without the need to go into any lengthy explanation. Create your own descriptive metaphors in your executive presentation and see how they can enhance your objectives.

Examples of Metaphorical Phrases

- Antibiotic for morale
- Administrative chain gang
- Capitalist missionary
- Straightjacket for the mind
- Competitive mousetrap
- Fat-free advertising diet
- Mental aerobics
- Vampire boss
- Paid unemployed
- Microwave advertising
- Fertilizer for the mind
- Corporate slumlord
- Cafeteria of resources
- Smoke and mirrors
- Cat-eating sparrow
- Recruiting marathon
- Political dynamite
- Financial alarm clock
- Media junk food
- Pitbull politics
- Sales olympics
- Boomerang strategy
- Merger magician
- Solution pollution
- Stealth leadership
- Information superhighway
- Voodoo economics
- A spreadsheet Michaelangelo
- Executive cheerleader
- Gift-wrapped garbage
- Stainless-steel spine
- Innovation junkie
- Heimlich maneuver for the economy
- Severing our financial artery
- Writing a plan in invisible ink
- Using a nuclear weapon to kill a fly

- Merger between lion and lamb
- Corporate greenhouse for budding ideas
- Rocket-propelled turtle (to beat the hare)
- Mary Poppins plan of action
- Putting on dirty laundry after you've taken a shower
- The David and Goliath of competitors
- Evangelist of technological change
- Asking a crippled elephant to dance
- Bandaid solution to a problem needing an operation

Ideas-Spurring Questions

Remember that creativity involves doing things *differently*. But, the concept of "original" is a difficult one to grab hold of because everything new is really an outgrowth or mutation of something that already exists. Auguste Rodin, sculptor of the famous statue the *Thinker*, proudly stated, "I invent nothing. I rediscover." You can rediscover by rearranging or otherwise modifying something about your toptalk.

Examine *every aspect* of your executive talk (as some of the following examples show). Don't try to be practical. Instead, give yourself full permission to be "outrageous." And don't set your ideas in concrete right away. Ask these following categories of questions based upon the work of Alex Osborn, who was a well-known advertising executive, author, and the prime originator of the brainstorming process. Additional related (but subtly different) words are included in each question to help spark ideas, perhaps from a slightly different perspective.

1. What can I COMBINE?

What seemingly unrelated topics, ideas, elements, or parts could I put together that would create a fascinating synthesis? Experts agree that one of the strengths of highly creative people (traditionally artists, chefs, fashion designers, architects) is to combine things that were initially seen as unrelated. Picture what might happen if you combined the elements of entertainment plus infor-

mation giving ("Infotainment").
Others: *blend, fuse, integrate, join, unite, centralize.*

2. What can I REVERSE?

Sometimes being a contrarian thinker can enable you to come up with ideas that would otherwise have been out of view previously. Suppose you started with your presentation summary and asked the group for funding before you gave the details of your proposal?
Others: *alternate, 180 degrees, opposite, exchange, invert, recycle, turn inside out/upside down, hold back.*

3. What can I ADD?

Asking yourself what additional things you can add to what you already have is a way to enhance the quality and effectiveness of your toptalk. For example, suppose you added a videotaped testimonial (from an outside "expert") to your written documentation?
Others: *build up, deepen, repeat, exaggerate, expand, magnify, multiply, stretch, complement.*

4. What can I ELIMINATE or DIMINISH?

Omitting or minifying something from your executive talk can make it different and better. For example, who said you need to include voluminous handouts with your executive talk; why not a one-page "detailed" summary?
Others: *abbreviate, decrease, shrink, squeeze, streamline, understate, divide, purge.*

5. What can I REARRANGE?

Changing the sequence, assembly, or setup of things can give a new look, feel, and impact to something. How could rearranging the seating in the meeting room make your presentation more effective?
Others: *interchange, jump ahead, reclassify, shuffle, sort, vary, transpose, break up.*

6. What can I SUBSTITUTE?

Experimenting by replacing one (or more) things with another can give you a tremendous number of different options to your original. Instead of the usual structured "presenting" of information, why not pose ten key questions (that you know the audience would want answers to) and simply go on to answer them?

Others: alternate, exchange, instead of, what else, how else, where else, who else, different approach.

7. What NEW USES can I find for unrelated things?

Stretch your imagination far and wide to find uses in your toptalk for other products, technologies, services, situations, ideas, or processes. For example, how can you "plant" a professional magician (and pose him or her as an outside consultant) as part of your project team that is presenting to the executive board? What magic tricks could he or she do in a very professional, tasteful way that would vividly dramatize your key messages?

MORE CREATIVE IDEAS!

Here are some other examples to stimulate your thinking of (general and specific) questions that you can pose to yourself to think through this creative generation and rearranging process.

Audiovisual Aids and Props

- How can I use visual aids with no text—just illustrations, pictures, and other graphics?

- How might I use music, sound effects, computer-generated sound to enhance my presentation? How can I use more clip art or more color to make my visuals more impacting?

- How can I mix visual aids (e.g., use flipcharts with overhead transparencies) in a way that gives me great flexibility to get my ideas across quickly and interestingly?

- How can I cleverly use my audiovisuals to highlight my presentation theme and other key messages?

- How can I add subtle humor and other characteristics to my visual aids to break up the monotony of my technical or financial talk?

- What can I do with audiovisuals to grab the audience's attention from the moment I begin my presentation?

- What *relevant* and clever props (e.g., paper airplanes, guitar, fire extinguisher, horn, roulette table, football, miniature guillotine, blow torch, plastic model of boat, can of spray paint . . .) can I use to dramatize or help prove my points?

- Can I use costumes (T-shirt, hats, gloves) in any way?

- What novelty aids, magic tricks, or other interesting effects might get the audience to vividly remember my points?

- How can I demonstrate a piece of equipment or operation that would be an effective "show-and-tell" technique?

- How can customized posters, banners, or other artwork help me out?

- What pictures, illustrations, or other graphics can I get enlarged (e.g., blow up life-size "statue" of the CEO doing or saying something related to your key point; enlarged newspaper articles)?

- Suppose I have a "fake" magazine or newspaper article made with the headlines of my project and a brief writeup explaining it exactly as if our company went ahead with the "successful" project?

Presentation Organization, Content, and Delivery

- How could my presentation team put on an entertaining "skit" that would communicate our points better than a traditional stand-up-and-speak presentation?

- What type of ingenious presentation introduction can I use to set the tone of my great proposal and really get the audience's attention?

- What ideas can I borrow from television and radio programs (drama, comedy, news, educational, sports, variety, etc.) to enhance the format and messages of my presentation?

- What creative (but always audience-appropriate) activities, questions, "games," stunts, exercises, demonstrations can I use to get my audience directly involved in my presentation?

- What fascinating and relevant statistics, facts, quotations, contrasts, comparisons, examples, anecdotes, or stories can I use to slam home my points?

- How can I imaginatively use psychology and persuasion to get the audience quickly on my side? Suppose I start out by telling my audience not to give me funding for my project; give them "weak" excuses followed by a "devil's advocate" approach that happens to give strong reasons for funding my project?

- How can I use imaginative and powerful emotional appeals (using metaphors, themes, visions, inspiring stories) to touch the hearts and souls of my group?

- What kind of out-of-the-ordinary presentation conclusion can I use to get them to vividly remember my presentation until the next time I speak to them?

Handout Materials

- How can I make my handouts more readable, interesting, attractive, and impressive? How can my handouts better support my oral points?

- What if the presentation handouts consisted mainly of easy-to-understand illustrations and other graphics that take the place of all that tiring text?

- What if my handouts had interesting cartoons that made some important points in a humorous way? How can I put other entertainment value in?

- How can I change the size, style, color, shape, texture, design, or other characteristics of the handout (e.g., a "papyrus" scroll instead of pages)?

- How can I use pictures of the audience in my handouts to give it a real personal touch?

- Suppose we didn't give people any handout reference materials?

- Why can't we use audiocasettes, videocassettes, computer diskettes as "handouts?"

Room Layout

- In what ways can I "decorate" the boardroom or other meeting room (e.g., posters, banners, props, other signage, handouts on table, etc.)?
- How can I change the "atmosphere" in the room to create a certain mood (e.g., lighting, music, etc.)?
- In what other good places (perhaps nonbusiness locations) can we meet for my toptalk that might give fresh perspectives on the topic?
- What about giving a presentation on the golf course?

To help you in brainstorming your creative presentation, consider buying two powerful, easy-to-use software programs (for both Macintosh and IBM compatible computers). The first is Ideafisher.™ It contains over 700,000 associative connections to help you generate innovative ideas.[2] The other software program is Inspiration,™ which is a comprehensive brainstorming, diagraming, and writing tool.[3]

RESOURCES

Audiovisual Products/Services Catalogs, Magazines, Newsletters

Presentation Products Magazine
23410 Civic Center Way, Suite E-10
Malibu, CA 90265
310-456-2283

Visual Horizons
Powerful Presentations Buyers Guide
180 Metro Park
Rochester, NY 14623
716-424-5300

Highsmith Audio Equipment and Supplies
W5527 Highway 106
P.O. Box 800
Fort Atkinson, WI 53538-0800
1-800-558-2110

3M Meeting Management Institute
3M Austin Center
6801 River Place Boulevard
Austin, TX 78726
Fax: 512:-984-7169

Computer Presentation Software Programs

Aldus Corporation
411 First Avenue South
Seattle, WA 98104
206-622-5500

Borland International
1800 Green Hills Road
Scotts Valley, CA 95066
1-800-437-4329

Computer Associates International, Inc.
10505 Sorrento Valley Road
San Diego, CA 92121
1-800-531-5236

Microsoft Corporation
One Microsoft Way
Redmond, WA 98052
206-882-8080

Symantec
10201 Torre Avenue
Cupertino, CA 95014
408-253-9600

Software Publishing Corporation
3165 Kifer Road
Santa Clara, CA 95951
408-986-8000

Lotus Development Corporation
55 Cambridge Parkway
Cambridge, MA 02146
617-577-8500

Letraset
40 Eisenhower Drive
Paramus, NJ 07653
201-845-6100

Image Processing Services

Genigraphics Corporation
Two Corporate Drive
Suite 340
Shelton, CT 06484
1-800-638-7348

Autographix, Inc.
63 Third Avenue
Burlington, MA 01803
617-272-9000

Multimedia Software

Macromedia Inc.
600 Townsend Street
San Francisco, CA 94103
1-800-288-8108
415-252-2000

Asymetrix
110-110th Avenue N.E.
Bellevue, WA 98004
206-462-0501

Lotus Development Corporation
Graphics Products Group
161 First Street
Cambridge, MA 02142
617-577-8500

Microsoft Corp.
One Microsoft Way
Redmond, WA 98052
206-882-8080

Media Sorcery
1055 Joaquin Road
Mountain View, CA 94043
800-228-8584

Adobe Systems, Inc.
1585 Charleston Road
Mountain View, CA 94039
415-961-4400

Video Projection Equipment

Proxima Corporation
6610 Nancy Ridge Drive
San Diego, CA 92121
1-800-447-7694

Barco, Inc.
1000 Cobb Place Boulevard
Kennesaw, GA 30144
404-590-7900

Telex Communications, Inc.
9600 Aldrich Avenue South
Minneapolis, MN 55420
612-887-5531

Eiki International. Inc.
26794 Vista Terrace Drive
Lake Forest, CA 92630
1-800-242-3454

Sharp Electronics Corporation
LCD Products Division—Industrial Sales
Sharp Plaza
Mahwah, NJ 07430

Dukane Corporation
2900 Dukane Drive
St. Charles, IL 60174
708-584-2300

In Focus Systems, Inc.
7770 SW Mohawk Street
Tualatin, OR 97062
503-692-4968

nView Corporation
11835 Canon Boulevard
Newport News, VA 23606
804-873-1354

Sayett
17 Tobey Village Office Park
Pittsford, NY 14534
716-264-9250

Electrohome
1-800-265-2171

Sony Corporation
Business and Professional Group
3 Paragon Drive
Montvale, NJ 07645
201-930-1000

Other Multimedia and Presentation Resources

Multimedia Technology Laboratory
Georgia Institute of Technology
Atlanta, GA 30332
404-894-3539

The E.P.I.C. Software Group, Inc.
5 Grogan Park Drive
Suite 111
The Woodlands, TX 77380
713-363-3742

MediaNet, Inc.
305 Madison Avenue
Syite 564
New York, NY 10165
212-682-2250

Presentation Products Magazine
23410 Civic Center Way
Suite E-10
Malibu, CA 90265
310-456-2283

Redgate Communications Corporation
660 Beachland Boulevard
Vero Beach, FL 32963
407-231-6904

Association for Multi-Image (AMI)
8019 N. Himes Avenue (Suite 401)
Tampa, FL 33614
813-932-1692

International Interactive Communications Society (IICS)
2120 Steiner Street
San Francisco, CA 94115
415-922-0214

International Communications Industries Association
3150 Spring Street
Fairfax, VA 22031

American Society of Technical Communicators (ASTC)
815 15th Street
Washington, DC 20005
202-737-0035

REFERENCES

CHAPTER ONE

1. Toastmasters International, 23182 Arroyo Vista, Rancho Santa Margarita, CA 92688. (714) 858-8255.

2. National Speakers Association, 1500 South Priest Drive, Tempe, AZ 85281. (602) 968-2552.

3. Interview with Linnet Deily, Chairman of First Interstate Bank of Texas, N.A., in Houston.

4. Walter Elisha, *USA Today*, March 25, 1993, p. 2B.

5. Richard Saul Wurman, *Information Anxiety*. New York: Bantam Books, 1989.

CHAPTER TWO

1. Interview with Pat Shinn.

2. Interview with Peter Blakeney, IBM's manager, U.S. Operations Multimedia.

3. Interview with Buck Rogers, IBM marketing vice president (retired).

4. *Texaco: Our Vision and Values*, 1989.

5. *"Intel Corp. Serves as Role Model for Aerospace Companies in Transition," Aviation Week & Space Technology*, August 24, 1992, p. 60.

6. *Our Vision and Values*, 1989.

CHAPTER THREE

1. Interview with James Cornehlsen, partner Heidrick & Struggles, Inc., New York.

2. Interview with Walter Kitchel, Assistant Managing Editor *Fortune.*

3. Interview with former Houston mayor Kathy Whitmire, now a professor at Rice University, Houston.

4. Interview with Lynn Tendler Bignell, Principal/Cofounder, Gilbert Tweed Associates, Inc., New York.

5. "Executive Pay: The Part Ain't Over Yet," *Business Week*, April 26, 1993, p. 57.

6. "Executive Profile: A Decade of Change in Corporate Leadership." Korn Ferry International, New York.

7. *Business Week*, October 19, 1990, P. 39.

8. Barbara Killinger, *Workaholics: The Respectable Addicts.*

9. *CEO: Who Gets to the Top in America*, Louis E. Boone, David L. Kurtz, and C. Patrick Fleenor.

10. *Houston Chronicle,* "Tenneco Chief Reveals Brain Tumor", Jan. 21, 1991, p. 1C.

CHAPTER FOUR

1. *"Meetings That Work: Plans Bosses Can Approve" Harvard Business Review*, November-December 1988, p. 38.

2. Interview with Bryce Lensing, executive vice-president of credit at First Interstate Bank of Texas, N.A., Houston.

3. Interview with Bill Teague, CEO and president Gulf Coast Regional Blood Center, Houston.

4. Interview with Allen Brown, executive vice president of trust and private banking First Interstate Bank of Texas, N.A. Houston.

CHAPTER FIVE

1. David Wallechinsky, *The Book of Lists*. New York: William Morrow & Co., Inc., 1977.

2. Roger Ailes, *You Are the Message*. Homewood, IL: Dow Jones-Irwin, 1988.

3. Joseph Wolpe, *Our Useless Fears*.

4. Robert Fried Ph.D., *The Hyperventilation Syndrome*, Baltimore: John Hopkins University Press, 1987.

5. Larry Dossey, *Healing Words: The Power of Prayer and the Practice of Medicine*. San Francisco: Harper, 1993.

CHAPTER SIX

1. Interview with Helen Perry, corporate image consultant, Houston.

2. "Polishing Your Professional Image" by Bobbi Linkemer. New York: AMACOM, 1987, p. 7.

3. Interview with Andy Sherwood, Chairman and CEO Goodrich & Sherwood Company, in New York.

4. *Success*, "Executive Style," September 1986, p. 49.

5. Interview with John McGrath, executive speech writer, consultant and director, Management Communications, Argonne National Laboratory.

6. Interview with Buck Rogers.

7. "Reagan Style Sublime, Substance Somewhat Less" by K. Baker Ross, *Houston Chronicle*, January 17, 1989, p. 11C.

8. *The Essence of Leadership,* Edwin A. Locke and Associates. New York: Lexington Books, 1991,. pp. 32-33.

9. *Newsweek*, February 1, 1993, p. 23.

10. *Houston Chronicle*, Personality Mailbag (King Features, New York), January 9, 1994, p. 7.

11. Interview with Lynn Tendler Bignell.

12. Used with permission by Christina Ward, president of Optima Image, Houston.

13. "The Glass Ceiling: A Barrier to the Boardroom Too, Judith H. Dobrzynski, *Business Week*, November 22, 1993, p. 50.

14. Interview with Leslie Smith, associate director of National Association of Female Executives, New York.

CHAPTER SEVEN

1. Texaco's 1991 annual report, p. 3.

2. Interview with Linnet Deily, of Texas.

3. *The Sir Winston Churchill Method. The Five Secrets of Speaking the Language of Leadership.* James C. Hume's. New York: William Morrow and Company, Inc., 1991, pp. 112–113.

4. John W. Garner, *On Leadership*. New York: The Free Press, 1990, p. 1.

5. Allen Krowe, vice-chairman, Texaco, Inc.

6. Interview with Linett Deily.

7. L. P. Williams, "Parallel Lives," *Executive*, 1980, 6 (3), p. 12.

8. Writings of Warren Bennis, Burt Nanus, H. Mintzberg, R. M. Stodgdill, Daniel Isenberg, Theodore Levitt, and John Kotter among others.

9. *Leaders: The Strategies for Taking Charge,* Warren Bennis and Burn Nanus. New York: Harper & Row, 1985, p. 4.

10. Chairman Carl W. Menk. Canny, Bowen, Inc., 200 Park Avenue, New York, NY 10166.

11. Interview with Kathy Whitmire.

12. Interview with retired Buck Rogers.

13 Interview with Lynn Bignell.

14. Interview with Linnet Deily.

15. Interview with Allen Krowe.

16. Dr. Harry Andrews, senior vice president, 3M Corporation.

17. Interview with Buck Rogers.

18. Interview with Elton Yates, senior vice-president, Texaco, Inc.

19. James Cornehlsen, partner Heidrick & Struggles, Inc., New York.

20. *Tough-Minded Leadership,* Joe Batten. New York: AMACOM, 1989, p. 131.

21. "In the End, Bush Is Faulted for Lacking 'Vision Thing,'" Ana Puga, *Houston Chronicle*, January 20, 1993, p. 4A.

22. "How the Next CEO Will Be Different" Lester Korn, *Fortune*, May 22, 1989, p. 157.

23. "IBM's Quest for Visionary," Kevin Maney, *USA Today*, February 2, 1993, p. 3B.

24. *USA Today*, Leslie Cauley, February 1, 1993, p. 1B.

25. "The Vision Thing," Chris Lee, *Training*, February 1993, pp. 25–32.

26. *The Wall Street Journal,* "Visioning" Missions Becomes Its Own Mission," January 7, 1994, p. B4.

27. *USA Today*, "Bell's Brash CEO Bets Big on TV Dream," April 22, 1993, p. 1B.

28. H. C. Hickman, and M. A. Silva. 1984. *Creating Excellence: Managing Corporate Culture, Strategy, and Change in the New Age.* New York: New American Library, 1984 p. 151.

29. *Aviation Week and Space Technology*, September 28, 1992, p. 31.

30. "Texaco: Our Vision and Values," p. 1.

31. Interview with Dr. Harry Andrews.

32. Interview with Allen Krowe.

33. Interview with John McGrath.

34. Guy Kawasaki, *Selling the Dream*. New York: HarperCollins Publishers, 1991.

35. Interview with Robert P. Marcell.

36. Interview with Malcolm Kushner, author of *The Light Touch: How to Use Humor for Business Success.* New York: Simon & Schuster, 1990.

37. *Forbes*, November 2, 1987, p. 216

CHAPTER EIGHT

1. "A Study of the Effects of the Use of Overhead Transparencies on Business Meetings," September 1981, Lynn Oppenheim, Ph.D., at Wharton Applied Research Center, The Wharton School, University of Pennsylvania, Philadelphia, PA 19104.

2. "Persuasion and the Role of Visual Presentation Support," June 1986, Vogel, Dickson, Lehman, Shuart. *Management Information Systems Research Center,* School of Management, University of Minnesota. Minneapolis, MN 55455.

3. "Reagan Style Sublime, Substance Somewhat Less," Professor Ross K. Baker, *Houston Chronicle*, January 17, 1989, p. 11C.

4. Interview with Tom Mucciolo of MediaNet, Inc., New York.

5. Interview with Jack Grayson, president of the American Productivity and Quality Center in Houston, Texas.

6. Interview with consultant and author Frank Sonnenberg.

7. Interview with Dr. Harry Andrews.

8. Interview with John McGrath.

9. *The Wall Street Journal*, Feb. 23, 1993, p. B13.

10. Interview with Walter Kiechel, assistant managing editor, *Fortune.*

11. *How to Make Type Readable.*

12. Interview with Frank Sonnenberg.

13. Interview with Tom Mucciolo.

14 Interview with Tom Mucciolo.

15. Interview with Buck Rogers.

16. Interview with Peter Goldman, editor, Boardroom Reports.

CHAPTER NINE

1. "Visual Overload," *USA Today*, June 15, 1993, p. 1B.

2. "CIA Shares Secret of Languages" Reuters News Service, *Houston Chronicle*, March 12, 1993, p. 8A.

3. Interview with John Manzo, corporate manager of Advanced Technology Marketin, Digital Equipment Corporation (DEC).

4. Michael P. Schulhof, vice-chairman Sony Corporation of America entertainment, *Business Week,* September 7, 1992, p. 64.

5. Interview with Fred Dyer, codirector of the Multimedia Technology Laboratory, Georgia Institute of Technology.

6. "The Best in Boardrooms," *Presentation Products,* October 1992, pp. 14–40.

7. Interview with Dr. W. Arthur Porter.

8. Interview with and multimedia demonstration from Vic Cherubini, president of E.P.I.C. Group, The Woodlands, Texas.

9. Interview with and multimedia demonstration from Vic Cherubini, president of E.P.I.C. Group, The Woodlands, Texas.

10. Robert E., Ornstein, *The Psychology of Consciousness*. New York: Viking Penguin, 1975.

11. Carl Sagan, *The Dragons of Eden*. New York: Random House, 1977.

12. *Make the Most of Your Mind*. Tony Buzan, New York: Fireside, 1984.

14. "3M Provides New Data on Audience Response to Computer-generated Graphics *Presentations in Meeting Management News*, Volume 4, Number 3, September 1992.

CHAPTER TEN

1. Donald W. Blohowiak, *Mavericks . . . How to Lead Your Staff to Think Like Einstein, Create Like DaVinci, and Invent Like Edison*. Homewood, IL: Business One Irwin, 1992.

2. Ideafisher Systems, Inc., 2222 Martin Street, Suite 110, Irvine, CA 92715. (714) 474-8111

3. Inspiration Software,™ Inc., P.O. Box 1629, Portland, OR 97207. (503) 245- 9011.

INDEX